WITHDRAWN

Music and Literature in German Romanticism

Studies in German Literature, Linguistics, and Culture

Edited by James Hardin
(*South Carolina*)

Music and Literature in German Romanticism

Edited by
Siobhán Donovan
and Robin Elliott

CAMDEN HOUSE

First published 2004
by Camden House

Camden House is an imprint of Boydell & Brewer Inc.
668 Mt. Hope Avenue, Rochester, NY 14620, USA
www.camden-house.com
and of Boydell & Brewer Limited
PO Box 9, Woodbridge, Suffolk IP12 3DF, UK
www.boydell.co.uk

ISBN: 1–57113–258–9

Library of Congress Cataloging-in-Publication Data

Music and literature in German romanticism / edited by Siobhán Donovan
and Robin Elliott.
    p. cm. — (Studies in German literature, linguistics, and culture)
"The papers collected in this volume were presented at the interdisciplinary
conference Music and Literature in German Romanticism held in
University College Dublin from 8 to 10 December 2000."
Includes bibliographical references and index.
ISBN 1–57113–258–9 (hardcover: alk. paper)
    1. German literature — 18th century — History and criticism —
Congresses.   2. German literature — 19th century — History and
criticism — Congresses.   I. Donovan, Siobhán, 1966–   II. Elliott, Robin,
1956–   III. Title.   IV. Series: Studies in German literature, linguistics,
and culture (Unnumbered).

PT363.M8M87 2004
830.9′357—dc22

                                                            2004002993

A catalogue record for this title is available from the British Library.

This publication is printed on acid-free paper.
Printed in the United States of America.

Contents

German Romantic Music Aesthetics

Responses to Goethe

Acknowledgments

THE PAPERS COLLECTED IN THIS VOLUME were presented at the interdisciplinary conference *Music and Literature in German Romanticism* held in University College Dublin from 8 to 10 December 2000. Of the thirty-two papers delivered at the conference by delegates from Australia, Belgium, England, Germany, Holland, Ireland, Scotland, Switzerland, the United States, and Wales, thirteen were selected to be published here. We thank all those who participated at the conference and who provided us with such stimulating debate and insights, making the conference a memorable occasion.

We would particularly like to thank the three keynote speakers at the conference: Werner Keil, Steven Paul Scher, and Susan Youens. We are pleased to include Werner Keil's paper on E. T. A. Hoffmann and Lev Termen in this volume. Steven Paul Scher of the Department of German Studies at Dartmouth College gave a virtuoso performance on "Goethe's *Faust* and the composers" that, by its very nature, could only be delivered as a "live" performance and was not translatable into the medium of print. Susan Youens of the Department of Music at Notre Dame University gave a paper entitled "Of great composers, lesser poets, and music at the close: Carl Gottfried Ritter von Leitner and Schubert's 'Der Winterabend.'" An expanded version of this paper has since been published in her book on the late songs of Schubert: "Of song, sorrow, and censorship: Schubert and Carl Gottfried Ritter von Leitner," in *Schubert's Late Lieder: Beyond the Song-Cycles* (Cambridge: Cambridge UP, 2002), 202–300.

We acknowledge with gratitude the enormous support and assistance — financial and other — we have received from a number of individuals and institutions in the organizing of the conference and in the preparation of this volume. The publication of the volume has been made possible by grants from the Office of Funded Research Support Services (Academic Publications Scheme) at University College Dublin and the National University of Ireland (Grant in Aid of Publication Award), and for these we are most grateful.

Our thanks also go to the Office of Funded Research Support Services at UCD, the Goethe-Institut Dublin, and to our own departments of German and Music for financing the conference. We are grateful to our respective heads of departments, Anne Fuchs and Harry White, for their encouragement and support. We acknowledge also with gratitude the support of the German Embassy in Dublin, and particularly of the German Ambassador, Dr. Gottfried Haas.

We are very grateful to Andrew Johnstone of the School of Music, Trinity College Dublin, for his help in co-translating the papers by Werner Keil and Andrea Hübener and in the final preparation of the manuscript for publication. To James Hardin and James Walker of Camden House we record our gratitude for their professionalism and continued support of our project.

Siobhán Donovan and Robin Elliott
Dublin and Toronto, June 2003

Foreword

"THERE ARE NO TRANSLATIONS." This lapidary formula, invented by George Steiner in 1958 (in the afterword to a translation of Thomas Mann's *Felix Krull* by Denver Lindley), has long been a source of fertile amusement to one of the editors of *Music and Literature in German Romanticism*. I should add straight away that it was the writer of this foreword who introduced him to it, and I should probably explain that quite apart from my own unabashed admiration for Steiner's work in general, the phrase itself has often served as a lofty (if ironic) excuse for my own incompetence in finding satisfactory renditions in English for a multitude of German expressions, not all of them connected directly to matters musical. If Steiner is right in his assertion that each language frames the world differently ("*Pain* is not 'bread' "), how much more so is this the case between language and music. Indeed, the obvious paraphrase of Steiner's illustration in the context of this volume might be "Music is not Language." One could add, perhaps, that this paraphrase circumscribes the debate which lies at the heart of German Romanticism itself.

The publication of this volume, which marks a vital contribution to the growing body of work that has addressed the subject of music and literature in German Romanticism within the past twenty years, is a richly significant event. In the disinterested (and increasingly virtual) world of international scholarship, *Music and Literature in German Romanticism* will take its place as an interdisciplinary meditation of immense value on those enduring issues and themes that have dominated our recent reception of the German literary and musical imagination. Anyone with even a passing interest in this subject will surely welcome these freshly written and authoritative deliberations on German musical aesthetics, on Beethoven, Berlioz, Brahms, Brentano, Goethe, Hoffmann, Liszt, Novalis, Ritter, Schubert, Wagner, and Wackenroder, to say nothing of the afterlife of Romanticism in the fiction of Robert Schneider and in the sound of the theremin. As the co-editors have shown in their illuminating overview of the field to which this book now belongs, the principal tonality of such scholarship is an interdisciplinary one. It is certainly the key in which this book is written.

Music and Literature in German Romanticism is also significant for another reason. It is, quite simply, the first book on this subject to issue from an Irish conference. More specifically, it confirms the growth of musicological studies in Ireland and it confers upon them a new dimension, expressly because of that vital intersection between music and literature that this book so memorably explores. Conferences can seem naturally ephemeral, but they are perhaps less so when they are infrequent and when they are novel. In any case, the conference from which this volume is derived not only introduced Ireland to a gathering of scholars at the heart of German musical Romanticism: it also provided younger scholars (some of whom are represented here) with a truly first-class arena in which to develop their work. It is certainly no accident that at the time of writing this foreword, another stimulating conference on a closely related theme, "Goethe and Schubert in Perspective and Performance," has just taken place in Trinity College Dublin. Taking part on this occasion were several of the participants from the Dublin conference from which the present volume sprang (Jürgen Barkhoff, Lorraine Byrne, David Hill, and Susan Youens).

It would, self-evidently, be an error of decorum (and fact) to claim this densely plural and versatile collection of essays exclusively for musicology. Germanic and musical studies both profit enormously by its publication. But it would likewise be disingenuous to pass silently over its pivotal role in the advancement of international scholarship in Ireland and more specifically its origins as a fruitful collaboration between the Departments of German and Music at University College Dublin. At a time when the humanities (and notably music of the European art tradition) are under severe stress in Ireland, the appearance of this book could scarcely be more opportune. At a time, too, when the consolidation of Irish musical studies is signified by the formation of a society for musicology in Ireland, the publication of *Music and Literature in German Romanticism* speaks to the notion that Ireland has, at last, become an international venue for the pursuit of German studies not only in literature (wherein it has long since enjoyed distinction) but also in music. For that alone, and for the book itself, the editors and contributors deserve our heartfelt congratulations.

Harry White, Dublin, April 2003
Professor of Music
University College Dublin
President of the Society for Musicology in Ireland

Introduction

"MAN MUß SCHRIFTSTELLEN, WIE COMPONIREN" proclaimed Novalis, the pioneering German Romantic. His aphorism formulated, at the dawn of the nineteenth century, the Romantic belief in the transformation of the arts — here: the two auditory arts of music and literature — and the interaction between them.[1] Its ultimate implication — the superiority of music over verbal language — would be rather more forcibly expressed by his contemporary Friedrich Schlegel, who, comparing music with sculpture, hailed music as the highest art form and "eigentlich die Kunst dieses Jahrhunderts."[2]

Many representatives of literary and philosophical German Romanticism held music to be the most expressive of the arts: not bound by the limitations of conceptual thought, it was freer and more immediate. In *Die Welt als Wille und Vorstellung* (The World as Will and Idea, 1819), Schopenhauer contrasted music with the other arts. While those arts represent ideas, he declared, music is an image of the will itself and thus able to communicate the essence of things:

> Die Musik ist also keineswegs gleich den andern Künsten das Abbild der Ideen; sondern *Abbild des Willens selbst*, [. . .]: deshalb eben ist die Wirkung der Musik so sehr viel mächtiger und eindringlicher als die der andern Künste: denn diese reden nur vom Schatten, sie aber vom Wesen.[3]

E. T. A. Hoffmann, an accomplished musician, draughtsman, and man of letters, was the most multifaceted of the German Romantics. In a now famous review of Beethoven's Fifth Symphony (1810) and also in *Gedanken über den hohen Wert der Musik* (Reflections on the High Value of Music, 1814) from the *Kreisleriana* (1812–20), he elevated music to the "most Romantic of all the arts," seeing in Beethoven's music a symbol of the longing that is quintessentially Romantic.[4] These and other writers worshipped music as an expression of the absolute and the metaphysical. For Ludwig Tieck it was, quite simply, a perfect example of revealed religion.[5] Such religious fervor was, of course, susceptible to idolatry and extreme disillusionment. That this sacralization of music (and other arts) went hand in hand with an increasing secularization of music (and indeed, all aspects of life) was apparent in the cultivation of many new forms of non-liturgical music, and in the rise of instrumental music.[6]

Musico-literary relations flourished under Romanticism, and especially under German Romanticism. Music was, according to the philosopher

Hegel, the art form most closely related to poetry, as both make use of the medium of sound.[7] While Hegel viewed literature as the most ideal form of expression, with music in second place, Novalis's characteristically avant-garde linguistic skepticism revealed itself in his denunciation of the verbal medium and his plea for its musical rejuvenation: "Unsere Sprache — sie war zu Anfang viel musicalischer und hat sich nur nach gerade so prosaisirt — so *enttönt.* [. . .] Sie muß wieder *Gesang* werden."[8]

Many Romantic writers and philosophers were strongly influenced by music, and, as is demonstrated in this volume, the influence was reciprocal: literature (along with other art forms and extra-musical sources) provided an invaluable stimulus for German Romantic composers. The vitally important genres of art song or Lied, German Romantic opera, and programmatic instrumental music are inextricably bound up with literary texts: some, as in the case of the Lied, with an art form already complete in itself, others, as in the case of the opera, with a paraliterary, verbal subtext that relies on music (along with other sign systems) for its completion. In a related phenomenon, German composers turned to literary efforts as never before, Robert Schumann's work as a music critic and Richard Wagner's philosophical and aesthetic treatises being the most important such contributions.[9] On the literary side, music became a popular theme, particularly in narrative prose. The genre of the Romantic music novella was thus born, featuring the musician protagonist torn between the demands of philistine, bourgeois reality and the Romantic musical ideal.[10] In a cogent formulation, Walter Wiora refers to the "poeticization of music" and the "musicalization of poetry" during German Romanticism.[11]

Music clearly had its attractions for the Romantic writer alienated from bourgeois society and longing for a release into the unfettered and immediate world of sound. What literature and the verbal medium had to offer to music might seem less obvious at first glance. As Hans Schulte points out, composers were drawn to the mythical element in literary writing: the German *mythos.* The *Faust* myth and Wagner's project to create a new mythology in his *Ring* cycle are two obvious examples.[12] Apart from the general trend toward artistic collaboration that characterizes Romanticism, literature was subject to a host of socio-historical influences: improvements in education and schooling, and, concomitant with that, rapid developments in the printing, circulation, and general accessibility of books for private consumption among the middle classes (the phenomenon of reading-circles, salons, and lending libraries), not to mention the establishment of municipal theaters and opera houses for the educated middle-classes. The pursuit of literature was no longer the prerogative of academics and the nobility.

To claim that music and literature enjoyed a uniquely cross-fertilizing relationship in the German Romantic era would, however, be erroneous. Generally speaking, the writers of the period remained tied to the written word, while the composers were still active principally in the world of notes. None of the artists of the German Romantic era achieved the cross-disciplinary brilliance of, for example, Guillaume de Machaut, the greatest poet and musician of fourteenth-century France, or Jiang Kui, the famed poet-composer-calligrapher-scholar of the Southern Song dynasty of China (twelfth/thirteenth century A.D.). A comparable figure from the German Romantic era would combine the achievements of Goethe and Beethoven. Wagner, admittedly, might have thought that he had achieved this with his reform of the opera and creation of the *Gesamtkunstwerk,* but later critics have not thought as highly of his work as a writer as they have of his work as a composer.

Hans Schulte rightly sees this program of reintegration as a response to the "reductionist aesthetics" of the so-called "enlightened" age,[13] and there is no doubt that Romanticism reacted to and grew out of the rationalism of the Enlightenment. It must be remembered, however, that Romantic aesthetics built on enlightened ideology, and furthermore, that the interaction between the arts, and particularly between the auditory arts of music and literature — the "sister arts"[14] — started to emerge as a discrete area of research in the eighteenth century.[15] Many of the earliest treatises were by English theoreticians, but from the mid-eighteenth century onwards, German theoreticians began to contribute important works: Lessing's *Laokoon oder über die Grenzen der Malerei und Poesie* (Laocoon: An Essay on the Limits of Painting and Poetry, 1766), Herder's *Kritische Wälder* (Critical Forests, 1769), Sulzer's *Allgemeine Theorie der schönen Künste* (General Theory of the Fine Arts, 1771–74), and Forkel's *Allgemeine Geschichte der Musik* (General History of Music, 1788 and 1801) are just a few of these.

New to the nineteenth century was the heated debate between, on the one hand, the advocates of absolute (a term coined by Richard Wagner), self-referential, autonomous music repudiating all links with words or indeed extra-musical ideas or functions and, on the other hand, the advocates of programmatic, referential, heteronomous music that strives to represent extra-musical subjects and in doing so frequently relies on another medium or art form. For those Romantic writers concerned with the supremacy of music over the other arts — in their case, over the verbal medium — non-referential, textless instrumental music furnished a model of Romantic aesthetics. Tieck advocated such self-sufficient instrumental music that "sich um keinen Text, um keine untergelegte Poesie kümmert, für sich selbst dichtet, und sich selber poetisch kommentiert." Words, he contested, belong to the realm of vocal music, and should be performed without any instrumental accompaniment.[16] Of the two philosophers quoted above, Schopenhauer was a vehement supporter of purely instrumental — absolute — music, while Hegel championed the dual genre of vocal music. It became commonplace to cite Hoffmann as the advocate of absolute music par excellence, for his above-mentioned review of Beethoven's Fifth Symphony seems unconditionally to favor such music:

> Wenn von der Musik als einer selbstständigen Kunst die Rede ist, sollte immer nur die Instrumentalmusik gemeint sein, welche, jede Hülfe, jede Beimischung einer andern Kunst verschmähend, das eigentümliche, nur in ihr zu erkennende Wesen der Kunst rein ausspricht.[17]

As Werner Keil contends in his essay in this volume, however, to interpret this literally is both incorrect and naive. Hoffmann's fictional writings suggest that it is vocal music — the synthesis of music and literature, performed by female singers and having its origins in a higher realm — that truly embodies the Romantic artistic ideal.

With the rise to prominence of Liszt, Wagner, and their New German School, a steady stream of propaganda favoring programmatic music and the Wagnerian union of the arts emanated from the Liszt circle in Weimar and from Wagner himself. In Wagner's opinion, the choral finale of Beethoven's Ninth Symphony proved the necessity of the marriage of text with music and the superiority of the resulting union over any purely instrumental genres. This aesthetic viewpoint met its staunchest opposition in Eduard Hanslick, whose treatise *Vom Musikalisch-Schönen: ein Beitrag zur Revision der Ästhetik der Tonkunst* (On the Musically Beautiful: A Contribution to the Revision of Music Aesthetics) was published in Leipzig in 1854. Hanslick was the most eloquent and important representative of the formalist point of view, which held that the content of music is not feelings, emotions, or literary texts, but rather "tönend bewegte Formen." The fluidity of positions in the middle of the century is indicated by Hanslick's early championing of Wagner (or at least *Tannhäuser*), and Brahms's writing to Clara Schumann, upon becoming acquainted with Hanslick's treatise, that he wanted to read it, but "fand aber gleich beim Durchsehen so viel Dummes, daß ich's ließ."[18] The fact remains, though, that the lack of any overtly programmatic works in Brahms's *oeuvre* attests to his solidarity with the aesthetic position of Hanslick. This particular war of aesthetic viewpoints between the expressionists and the formalists was, in the end, inconclusive, as demonstrated by the fact that Stravinsky in the twentieth century felt that he had to join battle with the Wagnerian viewpoint by proclaiming that "music is, by its very nature, essentially powerless to *express* anything at all."[19]

Musico-literary or melopoetic[20] scholarship is a growing discipline that has seen many significant publications and interdisciplinary conferences in the last decade, including the founding of the International Association for Word and Music Studies in 1997 (known in brief as the Word and Music Association, or WMA). An international conference takes place every two years under the aegis of the WMA, and the proceedings are subsequently published in the Word and Music Studies series.[21] It is usual to draw on the threefold schematic approach to the field outlined by its first pioneer, Calvin Brown: the relationship between text and music in the dual genres of vocal music, the mutual influences of music on literature and literature on music, and finally, the elements shared by both art forms.[22] In his introduction to the handbook *Literatur und Musik* (1984) Steven Paul Scher revises these guidelines, providing a diagram — which has since proven to be very influential — of the typology of music and text studies.[23] He divides the field into "literature in music" (program music and all musical compositions inspired by literature), "music and literature" (all forms of texted vocal music or dual genres, including Lieder and opera), and "music in literature" (music as a theme in literary works, word music, verbal music,[24] and the application of musical forms and structures in literature). Scher's typology, although much debated, still provides a sound basis for the overall conceptualization of music and text studies.[25] A useful refinement of Scher's scheme has since been provided by Werner Wolf, who distinguishes between overt (or direct) intermediality, in which the different media could theoretically be separated out to stand alone (for example, opera, song, or film), and covert (or indirect) intermediality, in which one medium (or more) is subsumed into another dominant medium (e.g. program music).[26] As a rule, musicologists tend to concentrate more on Scher's categories of "literature in music" and "music and literature," while literary scholars are concerned in the main with "music in literature."

The present volume contains articles from literary historians, musicologists and comparative scholars, groups that correspond to Brown/Scher's categories. They are arranged under five headings: German Romantic Music Aesthetics; Responses to Goethe; Sounds of Hoffmann; Lieder; and Romantic Overtones in Contemporary German Literature. A volume of this nature is naturally unable to be comprehensive in scope. The only genre and major area of musicological research in the field of German Romanticism not represented in the present volume is opera. From Beethoven's *Fidelio* and Schubert's *Singspiele* to the operas of Spohr, Hoffmann, and Weber (*Der Freischütz*, The Marksman, 1821, is generally recognized as the first German Romantic opera), and on to the works of Marschner, Nicolai and Lortzing, German opera, which had been for the most part dormant during the eighteenth century, advanced by giant strides. The process culminated with Wagner and his creation of the music drama and *Gesamtkunstwerk*.[27] Inevitably, Wagner tends to dominate the field, both on the stage and on the page. The revitalization of Wagner research in the past thirty years has resulted in a body of scholarly work that is at the leading edge of musicology. Truly international in scope, Wagner scholarship ranges from traditional source studies and editions (the flagship enterprise here being the new complete works edition and the *Wagner-Werke-Verzeichnis*[28]) to the farthest ends of the new musicology, wherein the authors bring a variety of critical methods to bear upon the study of Wagner's life, work, and posthumous influence. It seems a safe bet that Wagner will continue to elicit deep interest and ongoing critical inquiry for as long as music scholarship will endure.

From the wealth of literature that has been published in the general field of music and text relationships in German Romanticism, it is worth mentioning here those works that particularly concern the general fields treated in this volume, before moving on to a consideration of the articles themselves.[29]

In the field of German Romantic musical aesthetics, musicologists have taken a leading role in both German- and English-language studies. Publications of Carl Dahlhaus are central to the field. In *Musikästhetik* (1967)[30] he provided a cogent overview of the entire field and discussed in succession the works of Kant, Wackenroder, Schopenhauer, Hegel, and Hanslick. A longer and more narrowly focused work is his *Klassische und romantische Musikästhetik* (1988), whose last section is devoted entirely to Wagner.[31] On one of the central philosophical issues in the field of nineteenth-century German music, the contrast between absolute and program music, Dahlhaus wrote an influential work entitled *Die Idee der absoluten Musik*.[32] Here he discussed the concept of absolute music, which entails a quasi-religious faith in the ability of pure instrumental music to reveal profound truths, and traced its origins back to German Romanticism. In support of this thesis he quoted and commented on many writers of the period, including Forkel, Hanslick, Hegel, Hoffmann, Nietzsche, Novalis, Schleiermacher, Schopenhauer, Schumann, Tieck, Wackenroder, and Wagner. Dahlhaus also co-edited a one-volume anthology of philosophical texts in the field of music aesthetics in German,[33] and a similar but more comprehensive four-volume anthology in English.[34] Edward Lippman has also edited a multi-volume music aesthetics anthology in English translation; the second volume deals with German Romanticism.[35] The musical essays from Wackenroder's *Phantasien über die Kunst* (Fantasies on the Arts, 1799) are the first items in this volume, and a discussion of them leads off the section on "Romantic Aesthetics" in Lippman's own history of music aesthetics.[36] An essay by Richard Littlejohns on these same texts opens the present volume. Much valuable work has been conducted in recent years by Germanists and comparative scholars in the field of Romantic music aesthetics and semiotics. Two monographs in particular must be mentioned here, as they examine how concepts of "musicality" are integrated in the literary discourse around 1800: *Musikalisches Ideen-Instrument* by Barbara Naumann (1990), and *Mythos Musik* by Christine Lubkoll (1995).[37]

At least seven books by German scholars entitled *Goethe und die Musik* have appeared over the last century, including three written for the celebrations of the bicentenary of Goethe's birth and one for the 250th anniversary of his death.[38] *Goethe e la musica* is the title of the proceedings in French and Italian of a conference held in Martina Franca, Italy in 1999.[39] The volume closes with an essay by Bertrand Vacher on musical settings of *Faust,* which was also the subject of the keynote address by Scher at our Dublin conference.[40] Other recent books dealing in a general way with the subject of Goethe and music are those by Willy Tappolet, Ernst-Jürgen Dreyer, Robert Spaethling, and Udo Quak, and an anthology edited by Hedwig Walwei-Wiegelmann.[41]

Further studies, including the three essays in the present volume by Byrne, Hill, and Larkin, are devoted to exploring in more detail the relationship between Goethe and individual composers. There have been at least a dozen short books on Beethoven and Goethe, and their relationship was also the subject of the *Internationales Beethovenfest* held in Bonn in 1999. The Bonn event resulted in the collection *Beethoven, Goethe und Europa.* Though this includes contributions from thirteen musicologists, none, curiously enough, deals with the relationship between Beethoven and Goethe.[42] Aside from the incidental music to *Egmont* (the subject of David Hill's paper in the present volume) Beethoven unfortunately did not find occasion to set a Goethe text to music in a major composition. His plan to compose a musical setting of Goethe's *Faust* remains, along with Verdi's intended opera on *King Lear,* one of the most significant works of musical theater never composed.[43]

Though Schubert, unlike Beethoven, never met Goethe, he wrote some of his greatest Lieder to Goethe's poetry. Two recent books in English are devoted to a study of Schubert and Goethe, one by Kenneth S. Whitton and the other by Lorraine Byrne (who has also contributed an article to the present volume).[44] Schubert's songs lie at the heart of the large musicological literature dealing with Lieder. Susan Youens, a keynote speaker at our Dublin conference, has to date written five books on the subject. The first is a detailed examination of *Winterreise.*[45] *Die schöne Müllerin* (The Fair Maid of the Mill, 1823), Schubert's earlier song cycle to poems by Wilhelm Müller, is the subject of two books by Youens: a shorter handbook on the cycle itself, and a much longer book that looks also at poetic and musical treatments of the same or similar themes before and after Schubert's time.[46] In the preface to her *Schubert's Poets and the Making of Lieder* (1996) Youens notes that "musicians seem curiously uninspired to delve into literary waters, to discover the when, where, how, what, and why of the verbal text."[47] She begins her study (as, of course, did Schubert) with the poems rather than the music, examining in detail four poets whose texts Schubert set at progressively later stages of his brief life.[48] Youens's most recent book is concerned with the Lieder composed during the last six years of his life.[49] In *Franz Schubert: Sexuality, Subjectivity, Song,*[50] Lawrence Kramer applies theories of gender and sexuality to the Lieder of Schubert, whose sexuality has been the focus of much heated debate since a famous article by Maynard Solomon examined the coded sexual subtexts of Schubert and his circle of friends.[51] This engagement with recent ideas from literary and cultural theory, colonialism/postcolonialism, gender and sexuality studies, and other areas of non-musical scholarship falls under the heading of "new musicology."[52]

Turning to more general studies of the Lied, the anthology *German Lieder in the Nineteenth Century* (1996), edited by Rufus Hallmark, contains a variety of authors and approaches, but the overall framework is that of a historical survey.[53] *Poetry into Song* (1996), in contrast, is organized by analytical topic (poetry, performance, and music) rather than by composer; the book is intended as a primer for advanced Lieder recitalists.[54] The inclusion of full texts and translations, scores, a glossary, and a selected bibliography enhances the usefulness of this book well beyond its intended readership of singers and pianists. A more straightforward historical survey is presented in *The Nineteenth-Century German Lied* by Lorraine Gorrell, which begins with general chapters and continues with a survey of the major Lieder composers from Beethoven to Strauss.[55] Luise Reichardt, Josefine Lang, and Clara Schumann are treated together in a chapter on "Women Musicians in Nineteenth-Century Society," but Fanny Mendelssohn Hensel is discussed in a chapter of her own, reflecting her recent rise to prominence, partly as a result of the increased sensitivity to gender issues in recent musicological scholarship.[56] Finally, the second section of *The Cambridge Companion to the Lied,* edited by James Parsons (whose essay on Schubert's "Der Wanderer" is included in the present volume), contains essays on the nineteenth-century Lied.[57]

E. T. A. Hoffmann is one figure around whom both music scholars and German literary specialists often join hands. Today he is, of course, remembered mainly for his literary writings — both literary fiction and critical writings on music — but during his life he was extremely active as a composer and Kapellmeister.[58] Three of the eight papers on Hoffmann presented at the Dublin conference are published here (by Jeanne Riou, Andrea Hübener, and Werner Keil). Hoffmann studies in English, German, and French are flourishing, but a substantial proportion of the huge literature in German on Hoffmann is still not well-known to English-language writers.[59] Werner Keil, one of the keynote speakers at the Dublin conference, has made a number of contributions to Hoffmann research in recent years.[60] He also led a project at the Musicological Seminar in Detmold that edited and organized premières of previously unheard or reconstructed Hoffmann compositions for the stage.[61] The most recent publication on the interrelationship between Hoffmann's musical and literary *oeuvre* is a doctoral dissertation by Anja Pohsner.[62]

The papers collected in the present volume not only cover the Romantic nineteenth century, but also look ahead to the reception of Romanticism in the modern and postmodern age. Familiar and not so familiar faces and sounds are discussed, new readings are put forward, traditionally held

assumptions and myths are challenged, differing approaches and interpretative methodologies are applied, new links between philosophy and music
are established, and new models of aesthetics are advanced.

The volume opens with a section on German Romantic Music
Aesthetics. In the first essay Richard Littlejohns looks at the influential early
Romantic collaborative work, *Phantasien über die Kunst,* a collection of
essays on the arts by Wilhelm Heinrich Wackenroder and Ludwig Tieck. The
second half of the *Phantasien* consists of nine musical essays attributed —
in true Romantic style — to the fictional composer Joseph Berglinger,
a literary creation from Wackenroder's earlier work *Herzensergießungen
eines kunstliebenden Klosterbruders* (Effusions of an Art-loving Friar,
1796), and the protagonist of the final and only musical essay in the
collection, *Das merkwürdige musikalische Leben des Tonkünstlers Joseph
Berglinger* (The Strange Musical Life of the Composer Joseph Berglinger).
This was the first Romantic music novella. Littlejohns argues that, in contrast to the generally positive view of artistic experience depicted in the
Herzensergießungen, it is the ambiguous side of music that predominates
in the *Phantasien.* Through the mouthpiece of Berglinger, Wackenroder
and Tieck expose the Janus-face, or paradoxical nature, of music: its divine
and demonic potential, its capacity to redeem and to condemn. Thus the
dangers of such religious worship — "art religion" — are exposed, and as
Littlejohns points out, this notion of daemonic possession by music,
expressed here for the first time, becomes a central concern for later German
Romantics.

James Hodkinson's paper explores how Novalis's musical aesthetics
inform his theories of language and practice of writing (*Poësie*), thus producing what Hodkinson terms his "polyphonic and intersubjective model
of discourse." The paper first considers the impact on Novalis of Jacob
Böhme's ideas on universal music, also looking at his critical response to
Fichtean egocentrism, and then goes on to offer new readings of the prose
texts *Die Lehrlinge zu Saïs* (The Novices at Saïs, 1800) and *Heinrich von
Ofterdingen* (1802). Hodkinson argues that the ideal of universal musical
polyphony — in Böhmian terms, the "cosmic symphony" — is only
sketched in the narrative structure of the *Lehrlinge,* and is realized fully in
Ofterdingen.

A contemporary of Novalis (and greatly admired by him and other
Romantic poets) is Johann Wilhelm Ritter (1776–1810), an established
figure in the field of Romantic science (*Naturphilosophie*). The focus in
Thomas Strässle's paper is on Ritter's lesser-known original contributions
to Romantic music aesthetics and his reflections on the relationship between
music and language in the appendix to his main work, the *Fragmente aus
dem Nachlasse eines jungen Physikers* (Fragments from the Literary Estate
of a Young Physicist, 1810). Strässle, however, points out that Ritter had
a considerable influence on Walter Benjamin's philosophy of language,

a fact duly acknowledged by Benjamin. The paper discusses Ritter's synesthetic metaphor of light (*Lichtfigur* in analogy to Oersted's and Chladni's *Klangfigur*) in the context of his deliberations on the inner representation of tone and his belief that the whole of creation can be represented in music.

The final paper in the section, by Jeanne Riou, on music and non-verbal reason in Hoffmann, is primarily concerned with the acoustic character of imagination in Hoffmann. In a further step, the utopian quality of Hoffmann's treatment of music is discussed in relation to the critique of Romanticism in Hegel and Adorno. For Hoffmann, music has a utopian dimension that challenges bourgeois subjectivity: unlike either Adorno or Hegel, whose work is characterized by a dialectical approach, Hoffmann and the Romantics do not shy away from the expectation that aesthetic experience — especially music — can transform reality.

The second section of the volume brings together papers on the Romantic reception (musical and literary) of Johann Wolfgang von Goethe. While Goethe's literary writings have been an especially rich source of inspiration for Romantic musicians, Goethe's own musical appreciation and ability have been harshly criticized. It has been customary to see Goethe as an "Augenmensch," for whom the visual had much greater relevance than the aural. The first paper, by Lorraine Byrne, criticizes this long-held assumption with particular reference to Goethe's opinion of Schubert. Her paper assesses the reasons behind Goethe's initial silence towards Schubert and his settings, taking relevant pragmatic, social, personal, and political issues into consideration, and pointing to Goethe's (admittedly belated) acknowledgment of Schubert in later years. Byrne debunks the traditional myth that places the two artists in opposition to each other, showing Goethe to be more musical than hitherto assumed, and concluding that their ideas on the nineteenth-century Lied are quite similar.

In any discussion of German writers and their inspiration for Romantic composition, it is fair to say that one towers above the rest — Goethe. The papers by David Hill and David Larkin address programmatic musical compositions inspired by and evoking two of Goethe's dramas: his freedom drama, *Egmont* (1787), and *Faust* (1808, 1832). Hill's paper focuses on the Victory Symphony that concludes both the incidental music to the play *Egmont* and its overture, both of which Beethoven composed during the Napoleonic occupation of Vienna some twenty years after Goethe had completed his play. Research has tended to take a cynical view of the nature of Egmont's victory at the end of the play, branding him as a failure. The energetic heroism of the music thus seems incongruous. Hill offers a reading that seeks to reconcile this tension between the two *Egmonts*, taking into account the aesthetic and ideological differences between the two works and interpreting Beethoven's music as a response to the latent Romantic traits in Goethe's drama.

Goethe's *Faust* tragedy was — and still is — the stimulus for countless artists in all media, but particularly for composers of opera and program music. David Larkin's paper concentrates on the musical responses of Franz Liszt and Richard Wagner. Their resulting instrumental works: Liszt's *Faust* Symphony (1854, revised 1857) and Wagner's *Faust* Overture (1840, revised 1855) owe their existence to the literary source, but also to the mutual influence between the two composers during their genesis. A detailed study of both works and the conditions surrounding their composition shows the striking extent of this fruitful collaboration.

Another of Goethe's works that influenced and sparked off the imagination of subsequent generations of artists was his Bildungsroman *Wilhelm Meisters Lehrjahre* (Wilhelm Meister's Apprenticeship Years, 1796). Of particular attraction to the Romantic sensibility were the characters of Mignon and the harpist; their songs "Kennst du das Land, wo die Zitronen blühn" (Knowest thou the land where the lemon blossom grows) and "Nur wer die Sehnsucht kennt" (Only one who knows longing) have been set to music countless times. Stefanie Bach examines the Romantic reappropriation of Mignon, a musical gypsy, in the two characters Mitidika and Michaly in Clemens Brentano's novella *Die mehreren Wehmüller und ungarische Nationalgesichter* (The Multiple Wehmüllers and Hungarian National Faces, 1817), reading Brentano's novella as the Romantic counterargument to Goethe's classical aesthetic discourse. Where Mignon's self-expression through the intuitive, non-verbal medium of music is doomed, Mitidika and Michaly's musicality is celebrated. Thus, for Brentano, music is a transcendent aesthetic force.

Like the papers of Hill and Larkin, Andrea Hübener's paper in the section on E. T. A. Hoffmann is concerned with literature as inspiration for the composer, in this case with the literary antecedents for Berlioz's *Huit scènes de Faust* (Eight *Faust* scenes, 1828), the forerunner to *La Damnation de Faust* (1845/46) and *Lélio, ou le retour à la vie* (Lélio, or the Return to Life, 1855). She discusses the interplay between literature and music in these works, interpreting them as a series of musico-dramatic answers to the questions of music and language raised by Hoffmann in his literary writings, and comparing this structure to Hoffmann's narrative framework in his tales.

The first part of the book focuses on early Romanticism; the papers by Werner Keil in this section and by Jürgen Barkhoff in the final section bring Romanticism into the twentieth century. Keil explores Hoffmann's "poetics of artificiality" and the uncanny, artificial world of musical automata and mechanical instruments (the latter played as a rule by male performers) in Hoffmann's tales, juxtaposing this with another type of music: the otherworldly pure sound emanating from the female singing voice. But the pure sound — tonal perfection — cannot transcend the earthly dualism, and so Antonie (in *Rat Krespel*, Councillor Krespel, 1819) and her counterparts in the other tales must die. This Romantic ideal of sound, however, finds its realization in the sine tones produced by the early twentieth-century electronic instrument, the theremin (or aetherophone).

The two papers on art song in the section on Lieder offer critical readings of single Lieder using different methodological approaches. James Parsons's article considers Schubert's setting of Friedrich Schlegel's "Der Wanderer" (The Wayfarer, 1819) from the vantage-point of Schlegel's theoretical discussion on Romantic poetry and Romantic irony, and shows how the formal design of the poem and its place within a larger framework (the poem-cycle *Abendröte*, Sunset, 1802) influence the musical setting. By contrast, Natasha Loges takes an interpretative approach to a Brahms love-song, which has implications for performance. Using Edward Cone's psychology of personae, she undertakes a threefold analysis (poetic, poetic-melodic, and vocal-instrumental) of Brahms's "Bitteres zu sagen denkst du" (You mean to say something bitter, 1864), and demonstrates how Brahms's musical interpretation transforms, questions, and, in keeping with Brahms's aesthetic demands, completes this rather minor poem by Georg Friedrich Daumer.

In the final section on Romantic undercurrents in contemporary literature, Jürgen Barkhoff asks whether *Schlafes Bruder* (Brother of Sleep, 1992), the cult first novel of the Austrian writer Robert Schneider, can be read as a neo-Romantic work, a sequel to Romantic musician novellas, and furthermore, whether this might account for its success. His analysis draws on the features of Romantic literary discourse on music with particular reference to Novalis and Hoffmann, and demonstrates that, while the novel is indebted to the Romantic tradition in its themes, intertextuality, and concepts of music, it also plays with or even trivializes the Romantic myth of the musical genius, thus revealing its unmistakable postmodern imprint.

Novalis's aphorism expressing disillusionment with verbal language (quoted above on page xii) opens with the words "Über die allg[emeine]n *Sprache* der Musik" — thus proceeding from the premise that music is a kind of language, but one which is for Novalis and many fellow German Romantics superior to verbal language.[63] In the essay, "Fragment über Musik und Sprache" almost two hundred years later, Theodor Adorno admits that music is indeed similar to language ("sprachähnlich"), but concludes that this similarity reaches fulfillment precisely in its deviation from language.[64] The relationship between music and language, music and literature is often for the German Romantics a dialectical one, but always a symbiotic one — and one that bore much fruit: musical, literary, and philosophical. It is hoped that the essays in this volume will take another step in drawing attention to the musico-literary relations that flourished during German Romanticism.

Notes

[1] "Fragmente und Studien 1799–1800," in Novalis, *Schriften: Die Werke Friedrich von Hardenbergs,* ed. Paul Kluckhohn and Richard Samuel (Darmstadt: Wissenschaftliche Buchgesellschaft, 1968), 3:563.

[2] "Bildung und Erfindung ist das Wesen der bildenden Kunst, und Schönheit (Harmonie) ist das Wesen der Musik, der höchsten unter allen Künsten." Friedrich Schlegel, *Literary Notebooks 1797–1801,* ed. Hans Eichner (London: U of London Athlone P, 1957), 147 (no. 1417) and 162 (no. 1606). John Daverio draws specific attention to the early writings of Friedrich Schlegel as a motivating force for German Romantic music. See Daverio, *Nineteenth-Century Music and the German Romantic Ideology* (New York: Schirmer Books, 1993), 3–17.

[3] Arthur Schopenhauer, *Sämtliche Werke,* ed. Wolfgang Freiherr von Löhneysen, 2nd ed. (Darmstadt: Wissenschaftliche Buchgesellschaft, 1968), 1:359.

[4] E. T. A. Hoffmann, *Schriften zur Musik: Nachlese,* ed. Friedrich Schnapp (Darmstadt: Wissenschaftliche Buchgesellschaft, 1971), 34, 36; and E. T. A. Hoffmann, *Fantasie- und Nachtstücke,* ed. Walter Müller-Seidel (Munich: Winkler, 1960), 39. As is well known, Hoffmann reworked the Beethoven-review (where the reference is to instrumental music) for the *Kreisleriana.*

[5] "Denn die Tonkunst ist gewiß das letzte Geheimnis des Glaubens, die Mystik, die durchaus geoffenbarte Religion," "IX: Symphonien," *Phantasien über die Kunst,* Wilhelm Heinrich Wackenroder, *Sämtliche Werke und Briefe: Historisch-kritische Ausgabe,* ed. Silvio Vietta and Richard Littlejohns (Heidelberg: Winter, 1991), 1:241. See also the conclusion of Hoffmann's narrator, Cyprian, in the essay *Alte und neue Kirchenmusik,* which extols music's inherent spirituality and religiosity: "Keine Kunst, glaube ich, geht so ganz und gar aus der inneren Vergeistigung des Menschen hervor, keine Kunst bedarf nur einzig rein geistiger ätherischer Mittel, als die Musik. Die Ahnung des Höchsten und Heiligsten, der geistigen Macht, die den Lebensfunken in der ganzen Natur entzündet, spricht sich hörbar aus im Ton. [. . .] Ihrem innern eigentümlichen Wesen nach ist daher die Musik religiöser Kultus und ihr Ursprung einzig und allein in der Religion, in der Kirche zu suchen und zu finden." E. T. A. Hoffmann, *Die Serapionsbrüder: Gesammelte Erzählungen und Märchen* (Darmstadt: Wissenschaftliche Buchgesellschaft, 1971), 409.

[6] On music as art religion see Carl Dahlhaus, "Instrumentalmusik und Kunstreligion" in *Die Idee der absoluten Musik* (Kassel: Bärenreiter; Munich: dtv, 1978), 91–104. On Wagner's influence in this regard see Charlotte Farrow Liddell, "Music as Religion: An Inquiry into Wagner's Concept of the Function of Art" (Ph.D. diss.: University of Michigan, 1964).

[7] *Vorlesungen über die Ästhetik III* (1835), vol. 15 of Georg Wilhelm Friedrich Hegel, *Werke,* ed. Eva Moldenhauer and Karl Markus Michel (Frankfurt a. M.: Suhrkamp, 1970), 144. See also Calvin Brown's categorization of the arts according to the senses in his important work *Music and Literature: A Comparison of the Arts* (Athens, GA: U of Georgia P, 1948).

[8] "Das allgemeine Brouillon — Materialien zur Enzyklopädistik 1798/99," in Novalis, *Schriften,* 3:283–84.

[9] The most important study of Schumann's work as a writer remains Leon Plantinga, *Schumann as Critic* (New Haven: Yale UP, 1967). A recent useful guide to the extensive literature on Wagner is Michael Saffle, *Richard Wagner: A Guide to Research* (New York: Routledge, 2002).

[10] Wilhelm Heinse's pre-Romantic novel *Hildegard von Hohenthal* (1795/96) was influential in this regard. See the annotated edition prepared by Werner Keil: Wilhelm Heinse, *Hildegard von Hohenthal: Musikalische Dialogen,* ed. Werner Keil (Hildesheim: Olms, 2002). The secondary literature on the literary treatment of music in narrative prose is vast. For a brief but comprehensive overview on music as a motif in narrative prose see Thomas Horst, "Musik als Motiv in der neueren Erzählliteratur," in Franz Grillparzer, *"Der arme Spielmann": Erläuterungen und Dokumente,* ed. Helmut Bachmaier (Stuttgart: Reclam, 1986), 104–13. Another useful shorter publication dealing with the Romantic music novella is the article by Karl Prümm, "Berglinger und seine Schüler: Musikernovellen von Wackenroder bis Richard Wagner," *Zeitschrift für deutsche Philologie* 105 (1986): 186–212.

[11] Walter Wiora, "Die Musik im Weltbild der deutschen Romantik," in *Beiträge zur Geschichte der Musikanschauung im 19. Jahrhundert,* ed. Walter Salmen (Regensburg: Gustave Bosse Verlag, 1965), 11–50 (here, 21).

[12] Hans Schulte, "A Re-union of the Arts, and a Critical Dilemma," in *The Romantic Tradition: German Literature and Music in the Nineteenth Century,* ed. Gerald Chapple, Frederick Hall, and Hans Schulte, vol. 4 of The McMasters Colloquium on German Studies (Lanham: UP of America, 1992), 515–21 (here, 519).

[13] Ibid., 516.

[14] The title of a seminal work by Hildebrande Jacob: *Of the Sister Arts* (London: William Lewis, 1734).

[15] See Calvin Brown's overview in his article "The Relations between Music and Literature as a Field of Study," *Comparative Literature* 22/2 (1970): 97–107.

[16] Wackenroder, *Sämtliche Werke,* 1:302–3. Earlier (245–46), Tieck goes so far as to claim that Reichardt's overture to Shakespeare's *Macbeth* is superior to the drama itself!

[17] Hoffmann, *Schriften zur Musik,* 34.

[18] Brahms to Clara Schumann, letter of 15 January 1856 in *Clara Schumann, Johannes Brahms: Briefe aus den Jahren 1853–1896: Im Auftrage von Marie Schumann,* ed. Berthold Litzmann (Leipzig: Breitkopf & Härtel, 1927), 1 (1853–1871):168.

[19] Igor Stravinsky, *An Autobiography* (New York: Simon and Schuster, 1936), 54.

[20] The term, coined by Lawrence Kramer in 1989 ("Dangerous Liaisons: The Literary Text in Musical Criticism," *19th-Century Music* 13 [1989]: 159–67), is, while widely used, not always universally accepted. See Steven Paul Scher's article: "Melopoetics Revisited: Reflections on Theorizing Word and Music Studies," in *Word and Music Studies: Defining the Field,* ed. Walter Bernhart, Steven Paul Scher, and Werner Wolf, vol. 1 of Word and Music Studies series (Amsterdam and Atlanta, GA: Rodopi, 1999), 9–24 (here, 9, n. 1).

[21] Proceedings of the 1999 conference in Ann Arbor: *Word and Music Studies: Essays on the Song Cycle and on Defining the Field,* ed. Walter Bernhart, Werner Wolf, and David Mosley, vol. 3 of Word and Music Studies (Amsterdam and Atlanta, GA: Rodopi, 2001). Proceedings of the 2001 conference in Sydney: *Word and Music Studies: Essays in Honor of Steven Paul Scher and on Cultural Identity and the Musical Stage,* ed. Suzanne M. Lodato, Suzanne Aspden, and Walter Bernhart, vol. 4 of Word and Music Studies (Amsterdam and New York: Rodopi, 2002). Vol. 2 in the series was intended as a Festschrift to mark the eightieth birthday of the pioneer of modern music and text studies, Calvin S. Brown, but Brown died before the book reached press and it was issued as a memorial tribute: *Word and Music Studies: Musico-Poetics in Perspective: Calvin S. Brown in Memoriam,* ed. Jean-Louis Cupers and Ulrich Weisstein, vol. 2 of Word and Music Studies (Amsterdam and Atlanta, GA: Rodopi, 2000).

[22] Calvin Brown, "The Relations between Music and Literature as a Field of Study," *Comparative Literature* 22/2 (1970): 97–107 (here, 102–4).

[23] *Literatur und Musik: Ein Handbuch zur Theorie und Praxis eines komparatistischen Grenzgebietes,* ed. Steven Paul Scher (Berlin: Erich Schmidt Verlag, 1984), 14.

[24] See Steven Paul Scher, *Verbal Music in German Literature,* vol. 2 of Yale German Studies (New Haven: Yale UP, 1968).

[25] In "Melopoetics Revisited: Reflections on Theorizing Word and Music Studies," in *Word and Music Studies,* ed. Walter Bernhart et al., Scher responds to some criticisms of his typology (18–19).

[26] Werner Wolf, "Musicalized Fiction and Intermediality: Theoretical Aspects of Word and Music Studies," ibid., 37–58. On p. 52 Wolf translates Scher's typology diagram from *Literatur und Musik* into English and provides his own expanded version of it. Wolf prefers the term "intermediality" over "interart" as the former is broader and not confined to or linked with the traditional high arts. Wolf's ideas are further developed in part one ("Theory") of his book *The Musicalization of Fiction: A Study in the Theory and History of Intermediality,* vol. 35 of Internationale Forschungen zur Allgemeinen und Vergleichenden Literaturwissenschaft (Amsterdam and Atlanta, GA: Rodopi, 1999).

[27] For a comprehensive overview of the development of German opera, see John Warrack, *German Opera: From the Beginnings to Wagner* (Cambridge: Cambridge UP, 2001).

[28] *Richard Wagner: Sämtliche Werke,* ed. Carl Dahlhaus, Egon Voss, et al. (Mainz and New York: Schott, 1970–); *Wagner-Werke-Verzeichnis: Verzeichnis der musikalischen Werke Richard Wagners und ihrer Quellen, erarbeitet im Rahmen der Richard Wagner-Gesamtausgabe,* ed. John Deathridge, Egon Voss, and Martin Geck (Mainz and New York: Schott, 1986).

[29] The year 1992 should perhaps be singled out, as this was something of a watershed year. No fewer than three conference volumes appeared during that year: *The Romantic Tradition: German Literature and Music in the Nineteenth Century,* ed. Gerald Chapple et al. (as n. 12); *Music and German Literature: Their Relationship since the Middle Ages,* ed. James M. McGlathery, vol. 66 of Studies in German Literature, Linguistics, and Culture (Columbia, SC: Camden House, 1992); *Music*

and Text: Critical Inquiries, ed. Steven Paul Scher (Cambridge: Cambridge UP, 1992).

[30] Carl Dahlhaus, *Musikästhetik* (Cologne: Hans Gerig, 1967); trans. William W. Austin, *Esthetics of Music* (Cambridge: Cambridge UP, 1982).

[31] Carl Dahlhaus, *Klassische und romantische Musikästhetik* (Laaber: Laaber, 1988). Other German Romantic writers treated in detail include Hoffmann, Kant, Kleist, A. B. Marx, and Schiller (in addition to those covered in the earlier volume).

[32] Carl Dahlhaus, *Die Idee der absoluten Musik* (Kassel: Bärenreiter; Munich: dtv, 1978); trans. Roger Lustig, *The Idea of Absolute Music* (Chicago: U of Chicago P, 1989).

[33] *Musik — zur Sprache gebracht: Musikästhetische Texte aus drei Jahrhunderten,* ed. Carl Dahlhaus and Michael Zimmermann (Kassel: Bärenreiter; Munich: dtv, 1984).

[34] *Contemplating Music: Source Readings in the Aesthetics of Music,* ed. Carl Dahlhaus and Ruth Katz, 4 vols. (Stuyvesant, NY: Pendragon Press, 1987–93). The volumes are divided by subject matter rather than by time period. See also the anthology of German excerpts in translation: *German Essays on Music,* ed. Jost Hermand and Michael Gilbert, vol. 43 of The German Library (New York: Continuum, 1994).

[35] Edward A. Lippman, *Musical Aesthetics: A Historical Reader,* vol. 2: *The Nineteenth Century,* vol. 2 (no. 4) of Aesthetics in Music (Stuyvesant, NY: Pendragon Press, 1988).

[36] Edward Lippman, "Romantic Aesthetics," in Lippman, *A History of Western Musical Aesthetics* (Lincoln and London: U of Nebraska P, 1992), 203–38.

[37] Barbara Naumann, *Musikalisches Ideen-Instrument: Das Musikalische in Poetik und Sprachtheorie der Frühromantik* (Stuttgart: Metzler, 1990); and Christine Lubkoll, *Mythos Musik: Poetische Entwürfe des Musikalischen in der Literatur um 1800* (Freiburg im Br.: Rombach, 1995). Other works that have appeared in recent years are Ulrich Tadday, *Das schöne Unendliche: Ästhetik, Kritik, Geschichte der romantischen Musikanschauung* (Stuttgart: Metzler, 1999); Pia-Elisabeth Leuschner, *Orphic Song with Daedal Harmony: Die "Musik" in Texten der englischen und deutschen Romantik* (Würzburg: Königshausen & Neumann, 2000), and: Christoph Vratz, *Die Partitur als Wortgefüge: Sprachliches Musizieren in literarischen Texten zwischen Romantik und Gegenwart* (Würzburg: Königshausen & Neumann, 2002).

[38] In chronological order the books are: Hermann Abert, *Goethe und die Musik* (Stuttgart: J. Engelhorns, 1922); Hans John, *Goethe und die Musik* (Langensalza: Beyer, 1928); Friedrich Blume, *Goethe und die Musik* (Kassel: Bärenreiter, 1948); Samuel Fisch, *Goethe und die Musik, mit Liedbeispielen* (Frauenfeld: Huber, 1949); Hans Joachim Moser, *Goethe und die Musik* (Leipzig: C. F. Peters, 1949); Hans Joachim Schaefer, *Goethe und die Musik: Variationen über ein unterschätztes Thema* (Kassel: Verlag Jenior & Preßler, 1993); and Claus Canisius, *Goethe und die Musik* (Munich: Piper Verlag, 1998).

[39] *Goethe e la musica: atti del convegno internazionale, Martina Franca, 29 luglio 1999,* ed. Giovanni Dotoli (Fasano: Schena editore, 2000).

[40] Bertrand Vacher, "*Faust* en musique," in ibid., 145–75. The title of Steven Scher's Dublin paper was "Goethe's *Faust* and the composers."

[41] Willy Tappolet, *Begegnungen mit der Musik in Goethes Leben und Werk* (Bern: Benteli Verlag, 1975); Ernst-Jürgen Dreyer, *Goethes Ton-Wissenschaft: Vom Ursprung der Musik, Die Tonmonade, Vom Tod der Musik* (Frankfurt a. M.: Ullstein Materialien, 1985); Robert Spaethling, *Music and Mozart in the Life of Goethe*, vol. 27 of Studies in German Literature, Linguistics, and Culture (Columbia, SC: Camden House, 1987); Udo Quak, *Trost der Töne: Musik und Musiker im Leben Goethes* (Berlin: Aufbau-Verlag, 2001); *Goethes Gedanken über Musik: Eine Sammlung aus seinen Werken, Briefen, Gesprächen und Tagebüchern*, ed. Hedwig Walwei-Wiegelmann (Frankfurt a. M.: Insel Verlag, 1985). When talking about Goethe and music, mention must be made of Frederick William Sternfeld's pioneering publication from 1954: *Goethe and Music: A List of Parodies, and Goethe's Relationship to Music: A List of References* (New York: New York Public Library, 1954).

[42] *Beethoven, Goethe und Europa: Almanach zum Internationalen Beethovenfest Bonn 1999*, ed. Thomas Daniel Schlee (Laaber: Laaber, 1999). This book includes essays by Dieter Borchmeyer on "Goethe und die Musik" (41–61) and by Detlef Altenburg and Matthias Schäfer on Liszt's *Faust* Symphony (171–93).

[43] The only published setting by Beethoven of a text from *Faust* is Mephistopheles's satirical *Flohlied:* "Es war einmal ein König," which appeared in 1809 as op. 75, no. 3.

[44] Kenneth S. Whitton, *Goethe and Schubert: The Unseen Bond* (Portland, OR: Amadeus Press, 1999); Lorraine Byrne, *Schubert's Goethe Settings* (Aldershot and Burlington, VT: Ashgate, 2003).

[45] Susan Youens, *Retracing a Winter's Journey: Schubert's Winterreise* (Ithaca and London: Cornell UP, 1991). Youens also provided an introduction for the facsimile edition of the autograph score (New York: Dover Publications, 1989).

[46] Susan Youens, *Schubert: Die schöne Müllerin*, Cambridge Music Handbooks series (Cambridge: Cambridge UP, 1992); Youens, *Schubert, Müller, and Die schöne Müllerin* (Cambridge: Cambridge UP, 1997).

[47] Susan Youens, *Schubert's Poets and the Making of Lieder* (Cambridge: Cambridge UP, 1996), ix.

[48] Gabriele von Baumberg, Theodor Körner, Johann Mayrhofer, and Ernst Schulze.

[49] Susan Youens, *Schubert's Late Lieder: Beyond the Song-Cycles* (Cambridge: Cambridge UP, 2002). This book includes an expanded version of the keynote address that Young delivered at the Dublin conference in December 2000: "Of song, sorrow, and censorship: Schubert and Carl Gottfried Ritter von Leitner" (202–300).

[50] Lawrence Kramer, *Franz Schubert: Sexuality, Subjectivity, Song* (Cambridge: Cambridge UP, 1998).

[51] Maynard Solomon, "Franz Schubert and the Peacocks of Benvenuto Cellini," *19th-Century Music* 12 (1989): 193–206. Lawrence Kramer edited an entire issue of *19th-Century Music* 17:1 (summer 1993) entitled *Schubert: Music, Sexuality, Culture,* which is devoted to a debate about Solomon's article. Schubert is also the subject of two chapters in Kramer's *Musical Meaning: Toward a Critical History* (Berkeley, Los Angeles, London: U of California P, 2002). A CD accompanying

the book features a computer realization of Kramer's composition *Revenants: 32 Variations in C minor.* This composition cleverly presents in musical terms some of the same ideas on cultural memory, originality, and intertextuality that Kramer explores in the book.

[52] See Nicholas Cook, *Music: A Very Short Introduction* (Oxford: Oxford UP, 1998), 117.

[53] *German Lieder in the Nineteenth Century,* ed. Rufus Hallmark (New York: Schirmer Books, 1996).

[54] Deborah Stein and Robert Spillman, *Poetry into Song: Performance and Analysis of Lieder* (New York and Oxford: Oxford UP, 1996).

[55] Lorraine Gorrell, *The Nineteenth-Century German Lied* (Portland, OR: Amadeus Press, 1993).

[56] Ibid., 169–89 and 191–207. For a recent survey of this topic see Suzanne G. Cusick, "Gender, Musicology, and Feminism," in *Rethinking Music,* ed. Nicholas Cook and Mark Everist (Oxford, New York: Oxford UP, 1999), 471–98. Specifically on the Lied see Marcia J. Citron, "Women and the Lied, 1775–1850," in *Women Making Music: The Western Art Tradition, 1150–1950,* ed. Jane Bowers and Judith Tick (Urbana and Chicago: U of Illinois P, 1986), 224–48.

[57] *The Cambridge Companion to the Lied,* ed. James Parsons (Cambridge: Cambridge UP, [forthcoming]).

[58] See Patrick Thewald, *Die Leiden der Kapellmeister: zur Umwertung von Musik und Künstlertum bei W. H. Wackenroder und E. T. A. Hoffmann* (Frankfurt a. M.: Lang, 1990). On Hoffmann's writings see the useful earlier work by R. Murray Schafer, *E. T. A. Hoffmann and Music* (Toronto: U of Toronto P, 1975) and *E. T. A. Hoffmann's Musical Writings: Kreisleriana, The Poet and the Composer, Music Criticism,* ed. David Charlton, trans. Martyn Clarke (Cambridge: Cambridge UP, 1989). Schafer provides translations into English of a selection of diverse musical writings by Hoffmann (including examples of both verbal music and music criticism) and intersperses them with reflective articles of his own about Hoffmann's life and work. Charlton provides a lengthy introductory essay and extensive prefatory remarks on each of Hoffmann's essays.

[59] The monograph by Klaus-Dieter Dobat remains a central work in German Hoffmann musico-literary studies: *Musik als romantische Illusion: Eine Untersuchung zur Bedeutung der Musikvorstellung E. T. A. Hoffmanns für sein literarisches Werk* (Tübingen: Niemeyer, 1984). Dobat argues that Hoffmann's concept of music is a differentiated and essentially modern portrayal of reality. The conference volume *E. T. A. Hoffmann et la musique. Actes du colloque international de Clermont-Ferrand,* ed. Alain Montandon (Bern: Lang, 1987), contains many articles in French and German.

[60] For example Werner Keil, *E. T. A. Hoffmann als Komponist: Studien zur Kompositionstechnik an ausgewählten Werken* (Wiesbaden: Breitkopf & Härtl, 1986); Werner Keil, *"Seelenaccente"* — *"Ohrenphysiognomik": Zur Musikanschauung E. T. A. Hoffmanns, Heinses, Wackenroders,* ed. Werner Keil and Charis Goer, vol. 8 of Diskordanzen (Hildesheim: Olms, 2000).

[61] Many of Hoffmann's compositions are no longer extant today and only a few of his compositions for the stage were performed during his own lifetime. See the CD

recordings: E. T. A. Hoffmann, *Arlequin Ballet, Overtures: Music for the Stage,* Deutsche Kammerakademie Neuss / Johannes Goritzki, notes by Werner Keil (cpo / Westdeutscher Rundfunk Cologne, 1999), and E. T. A. Hoffmann, *Dirna,* Kammerchor "Cantemus," Deutsche Kammerakademie Neuss / Johannes Goritzki, notes by Werner Keil (cpo / Westdeutscher Rundfunk Cologne, 2001). In this context see Judith Rohr, *E. T. A. Hoffmanns Theorie des musikalischen Dramas,* vol. 71 of Sammlung musikwissenschaftlicher Abhandlungen (Baden-Baden: Koerner, 1985).

[62] Anja Pohsner, " 'Wenn ich von mir selbst abhinge, würd' ich Componist . . .': Die Umwege des Musikers E. T. A. Hoffmann: Wechselwirkungen innerhalb seines musikalischen und literarischen Werkes" (Ph.D. diss. [online]: University of Heidelberg, 2002) URL: http://www.ub.uni-heidelberg.de/archiv/2218

[63] Novalis, *Schriften,* 3:283.

[64] "Ihre Sprachähnlichkeit erfüllt sich, indem sie von der Sprache sich entfernt." Theodor Adorno, "Fragment über Musik und Sprache," in *Literatur und Musik: Ein Handbuch,* ed. Steven Paul Scher, 141.

German Romantic Music Aesthetics

Iniquitous Innocence: The Ambiguity of Music in the *Phantasien über die Kunst* (1799)

Richard Littlejohns

IN THE HETEROGENEOUS COLLECTION of essays, reflections, anecdotes, and fictional letters on the visual arts, architecture, and music published in 1799 under the title *Phantasien über die Kunst, für Freunde der Kunst* (Fantasies on the Arts, for Lovers of the Arts) there is one hymnic section in praise of music: "Die Wunder der Tonkunst" (The Wonders of Music). It opens with two similes followed by two metaphors — a "herrliche Fülle der Bilder,"[1] as they are termed in the euphoric style of the whole section — in which the speaker attempts to convey the mysterious and poignant appeal of music. First he suggests that music resembles the phoenix, a bird that rises up "zu eigener Freude [. . .] zu eignem Behagen." Then he compares music to a dead child transported to heaven, its liberated soul experiencing "goldne Tropfen der Ewigkeit." Finally, after drawing a relatively mundane parallel between the limited duration of a performance of music and the transience of human existence, he likens music to a tiny island in a vast ocean, green and blessed "mit Sonnenschein, mit Sang und Klang" (*W*1:205).

A mythical creature that eludes death in constant self-regeneration, an innocent infant carried off by premature death but transfigured in immortality, an Arcadian isle remote from civilization and undisturbed in its sensual bliss: Romantic images indeed, clichés even, and not without a touch of sentimentality. Yet these images betray significant assumptions about music. All of them imply that music has some kind of autonomous existence independent of those human beings who participate in its individual manifestations. Music is not merely a human activity engaged in by composers, performers, and their audience; it exists as a force or phenomenon in its own right. Romantic writers do not normally present the other arts in this way. Novalis or Shelley, for example, talk about "Poetry" or "Poesy" in general terms, as a spirit or attitude that they would like to see informing all aspects of human or even cosmic existence. However, they do not suggest that it has an objective reality, a being, which could be characterized figuratively in animal or topographical terms. Equally striking about the three images of music in the *Phantasien* is the fact that each of them implies in a different way that this force has supernatural, magical, or mythical features or capabilities that defy mortal limitations and reflect its transcendent origins. Human beings can, therefore, only encounter the "Wunder der Tonkunst" passively, as a rationally inexplicable experience that they undergo. Even the remote island, fairy-tale-like, represents a pre-societal idyll that cannot be replicated in the empirical human community.

Yet there is an even more significant feature of these images. The superhuman force of music is, so to speak, ethically neutral. We do not know whether the "Wunder der Tonkunst" are by provenance and intent benevolent or malevolent. The phoenix impresses the onlooker, but is its indestructibility divine or uncanny? The disembodied soul of the child experiences eternal bliss, but the heaven it inhabits is conspicuously not identified with a state of explicitly Christian redemption. The sensual delights of the island are at best amoral, and at worst, orgiastic. Music is, then, a morally indeterminate power beyond rational control: it may astonish or delight the human recipient, but it is ultimately incomprehensible and ambiguous. The speaker in the *Phantasien* is quite explicit: music regenerates the human spirit precisely *not* by answering our metaphysical questions, but by exposing us to still greater mysteries, to "Wundern, die noch *weit unbegreiflicher* und erhabener sind" (*W1*:206; emphasis in the original text). Nowhere does this speaker say expressly that the miracles of music derive from the Christian god or, indeed, from any sort of benevolent godhead, however defined. There is a clear contrast with the *Herzensergießungen eines kunstliebenden Klosterbruders* (Effusions of an Art-loving Friar, 1796), the text by the same authors that preceded the *Phantasien* by a couple of years. There they had declared that painting was the medium through which divine mysteries were revealed, the miraculous act of inspiration being unequivocally the result of divine intervention ("unmittelbaren göttlichen Beystand": *W1*:58).

At this point it is necessary to clarify the not uncomplicated question of the authorship and genesis of these texts. Tieck and Wackenroder's *Herzensergießungen,* dated 1797 but published in 1796 and written some time after the summer of 1794, appeared anonymously; indeed, one contemporary reviewer ascribed them to Goethe. In Tieck's subsequent reports they are presented as a collaborative enterprise, what recent scholars have called a "Gemeinschaftswerk";[2] but the available evidence suggests that the bulk of the ideas emanated from Wackenroder, whilst Tieck did no more than add a few — not entirely compatible — sections of his own, before editing the text as a whole. The *Phantasien über die Kunst* of 1799 are not quite the sequel that they appear to be. Published after Wackenroder's death and with an editor's preface by Tieck, making no secret of their authorship, they are divided into two equal parts that are differentiated thematically: the first half contains ten sections on painting and the visual arts and closely resembles the *Herzensergießungen* in style and approach, while the second half consists of nine sections on music under the general heading "musikalische Aufsätze von Joseph Berglinger." Of these nine musical sections three are undoubtedly by Tieck, despite the fictional attribution to Joseph Berglinger, who is in part an autobiographical *alter ego* of Wackenroder; and five are definitely by Wackenroder. The authorship of one musical section, "Ein Brief Joseph Berglingers" (A Letter from Joseph Berglinger), is unclear; but since an important article by Richard Alewyn in 1944[3] the majority of scholars have been inclined to attribute it to Wackenroder.[4] In the case of the *Phantasien*, the term "Gemeinschaftswerk" is still less appropriate, as arguably even is the concept of co-authorship, for the posthumous sections by Wackenroder were published in a final form over which he had no control and in which Tieck was free to exercise even more of a skewing influence than he had done — as has become clear — in the *Herzensergießungen*.[5]

Here I intend to focus on the nine "musikalische Aufsätze" in the *Phantasien* (in the original version), irrespective of whether they are by Tieck or by Wackenroder. Common to all of them is, of course, the narrative situation: they are filtered through the personality of the fictional composer and *Kapellmeister* Joseph Berglinger, a figure whose view of music is prejudiced (as the reader may recall from the *Herzensergießungen*) both by his own inability to compose and perform music without inner turmoil, and by his alienation from a philistine public.[6] A "Vorerinnerung" (preface) to these nine contributions makes this point but gives it an interpretative spin, remarking that they contain a harmony tragically lacking in the general course of his existence (*W*1:199). I shall argue here, however, that this alleged harmony at best exists in some of the contributions and certainly does not prevail in this half of the *Phantasien* as a whole.

Since the publication of the critical edition of Wackenroder's works in 1991[7] and the publications of Silvio Vietta[8] and of Dirk Kemper,[9] an undistorted understanding of the aesthetic doctrines of the *Herzensergießungen* has been established. It is now recognized that this text does not, as was supposed for at least 150 years, advocate an art based exclusively on Christian, let alone narrowly Catholic faith. It is appreciated instead that the *Herzensergießungen*, particularly in the sections "Einige Worte über Allgemeinheit, Toleranz und Menschenliebe in der Kunst" (A Few Words about Universality, Tolerance, and Philanthropy in Art) and "Von zwey wunderbaren Sprachen" (Of Two Miraculous Languages), plead for a historical relativism in the reception of art, in which, for example, both classical Greek temples and medieval Gothic churches are equally valid expressions of the human creative impulse.[10] This theme reflects Wackenroder's roots in the German Enlightenment.

The other major theme in the *Herzensergießungen*, however, is new and decidedly Romantic: that art, all the arts, are irrational in origin, dependent on unpredictable inspiration, and in this metaphorical sense divine. Metaphorical because — despite the narrative voice of the fictional *Klosterbruder* — there is no evidence to suggest that the authors of the text themselves suppose that artistic inspiration derives directly from a numinous being. Gerhard Sauder points out that the *Klosterbruder* is a stock figure in the literature of *Empfindsamkeit* (sensibility) and, as such, without specifically religious significance.[11] The point made in the *Herzensergießungen* is simply that through the medium of art — this "Hieroglyphenschrift" (hieroglyphic script, *W*1:98) — humanity is vouchsafed intimations of spiritual truth inaccessible to rationality and thus worthy of a veneration comparable to religious devotion. Even the *Klosterbruder* himself makes this distinction: "Ich *vergleiche* den Genuß der edleren Kunstwerke dem *Gebet*" (*W*1:106; my emphasis on "vergleiche"). The concept of a religious vision has been secularized. What remains beyond doubt, however, is the edifying and inspiring nature of the experience of art: it reveals our inner lives and shows us the divine and invisible ("alles was edel, groß und göttlich ist") in human form (*W*1:99). The Renaissance painters who recognized this uplifting function of art, Dürer and Raphael above all, reflect its beneficial results in their contented and purposeful lives, hence their hagiographic portrayal in the *Herzensergießungen*. Only in the case of artists who are congenitally unstable or neurotic, such as Piero di Cosimo — or possibly Joseph Berglinger — does divine inspiration operate destructively.

Critics have sometimes yielded to the temptation to assume that the same positive view of artistic experience prevails in the *Phantasien*. Yet, as has already been indicated in outline, the effect of music on the individual is here presented with some ambiguity. The section "Die Wunder der Tonkunst" certainly describes music as wholly therapeutic in its influence on the hearer: faced with the pressures and frictions of human existence we withdraw into music "wo alle unsre Zweifel und unsre Leiden sich in ein tönendes Meer verlieren" (*W*1:206). There is even an echo here of the notion that such experience may to some extent be religious in character: "ich möchte glauben, daß die unsichtbare Harfe Gottes zu unsern Tönen mitklingt, und dem menschlichen Zahlengewebe die himmlische Kraft verleiht" (*W*1:207). In the allegory of the section "Ein wunderbares morgenländisches Mährchen von einem nackten Heiligen" (A Wondrous Oriental Fairy-tale about a Naked Saint), music achieves a fully redemptive status. The hermit, driven by the delusion that he must rotate the wheel of time in perpetuity, is released from his obsession by the ethereal music and song generated by passing lovers, and his soul ascends to heaven. The very first note of this harmonious music ended the nightmare of the wheel of time (*W*1:203–4). Moreover, the hermit in his torment appears to represent a society oppressed by utilitarian values, an interpretation supported by a remark about human creativity in "Ein Brief Joseph Berglingers": "was von keinem gemeinen *Zweck* und *Nutzen* verschlungen wird" is equated with "was von keinem Rade des großen Räderwerks getrieben wird, und keines wieder treibt" (*W*1:224; emphases in the original text). Thus the tale of the hermit seems to suggest symbolically that music releases not only an individual but also a whole community from distress, as does the song of the young man in the "Atlantis" tale in Novalis's *Heinrich von Ofterdingen* (1802). At the same time, however, it is a practicing musician, Joseph Berglinger, the ostensible author of these essays in praise of the curative benefits of music, who imagines the suffering of the hermit and thus appears all too aware of the nightmare of futile, repetitive, but also psychotic and even homicidal activity.

Tieck's three contributions to this group of "musikalische Aufsätze" are predominantly positive in their view of music. In the section "Unmusikalische Toleranz" (Unmusical Tolerance) the speaker reflects that the unpredictable vicissitudes of human existence may tempt us into an existential indifference that is frequently passed off as sublime composure. But such indifference is, in fact, living death. The arts, and music in particular, release us from this condition. Music awakens in us a feeling of bliss that puts the banal privations of societal life in the correct perspective: "Wer vermöchte da noch auf die Dürftigkeiten des Lebens einen Rückblick zu werfen?" (*W*1:230). At the same time, so the argument continues in this section, there is a danger that in our elation at the impact of music we may enter into a state of presumptuous egocentricity, in which our hearts hear only "den Triumphgesang der eignen Vergötterung" (*W*1:230), and in such moments of voluptuousness it is our duty to exercise self-denial in order not to disdain the trivial but legitimate needs of others. There are no such misgivings in Tieck's section "Symphonien." It recapitulates all the themes of the *Herzensergießungen* — tolerance of divergent types of culture, opposition to analytical and judicial criticism, skepticism about the value of verbalization, the "Sprache der Worte" — and in this context dramatically exaggerates Wackenroder's assertion of the mystical nature of music: "die Tonkunst ist gewiß das letzte Geheimniß des Glaubens, die Mystik, die durchaus geoffenbarte Religion" (*W*1:241).

Such radically positive remarks about music in the sections indubitably written by Tieck tend to confirm that the one disputed section, "Ein Brief Joseph Berglingers," must have been written by Wackenroder. For here the point that absorption in music may lead to voluptuous egocentricity is taken up and driven home with bitter emphasis. Music is presented by the despairing Berglinger as a false god, as an idol worshipped by fools, as delusion and superstition: "täuschender, trüglicher Aberglaube,"[12] as a temptation into which we may be lured by the voices of sirens, and as an addiction to which the devotee may fall prey. Art — and music in particular — is a forbidden fruit that, once tasted, becomes irresistible and undermines the addict's life in the community, ultimately destroying his or her mental equilibrium. It alienates its victims from society, leaving them in a

state of solipsistic hermitage and indifferent to the sufferings and disasters
that befall their fellow human beings — worse, it induces an arrogant con-
tempt for others. Abandonment of the self to music is an act of hubris, a form
of self-indulgence ("selbsteignen Genuß") that impairs social responsibility
and engenders a callousness in which human suffering appears only as an
object for aesthetic gratification. The allusion to the Garden of Eden myth
in the metaphor of enjoying forbidden fruit is not isolated, for in this letter there is a whole series of phrases that suggest that total surrender to
music is akin to the biblical Fall, a lapse into sin: music is a "wollüstige[r]
Scherz" which produces "lüsterne Kunstfreuden," its exponents are daring
and arrogant, and both music itself and those who indulge in it are "frevel-
haft," iniquitous — so Berglinger remarks three times in a dozen lines of
text. Those musicians like him who gain this insight cannot but feel intense
guilt and seek some form of masochistic punishment to atone for it.[13] The
result of this indulgence is total loss of self-identity and sense of purpose:
"Was bin ich? Was soll ich, was thu' ich auf der Welt?" Music is a poison
that has entered his system, Berglinger says twice, and now his soul is sick.
Figuratively at least, music induces disease.

An equally important section in the *Phantasien* — and one which
definitely stems from Wackenroder — is "Das eigenthümliche innere Wesen
der Tonkunst, und die Seelenlehre der heutigen Instrumentalmusik"
(The Peculiar Inner Essence of Music, and the Psychology of Modern
Instrumental Music). Here music is portrayed in a predominantly positive
fashion. It is a means by which human feelings can be articulated and
reproduced with a profundity, subtlety, and complexity that could never be
achieved through reason and speech. It possesses deep spiritual or religious
significance, and in this respect is superior to all other art forms:
"Demnach hat keine andre Kunst einen Grundstoff, der schon an sich mit
so himmlischem Geiste geschwängert wäre, als die Musik" (*W*1:217). The
flow of music is the only suitable medium in which to convey the constant
flux of human emotions. Yet the emotions that Berglinger at this point lists
for reproduction in music are conventional and relatively one-dimensional:
happiness, contentment, joy, longing, pain, whimsy ("Laune").

It is when he moves on to discuss "Symphoniestücke" that his view of
music becomes innovative. Symphonies — by which he seems to mean
mainly the classical form of symphony recently introduced by Haydn and
Mozart, that is the "*heutige* Instrumentalmusik" (my emphasis)[14] — are
capable of presenting not just a single tableau of sentiment, but the whole
gamut of human emotions in a complex, sustained, and evolving form:
"nicht eine einzelne Empfindung [. . .], sondern eine ganze Welt, ein
ganzes Drama menschlichen Affekten" [*sic*] (*W*1:221–22). He imagines or
anticipates the course of one such drama. In a protracted vision (which has
been analyzed in detail by Steven Paul Scher[15]) he personifies the symphony
as "die tönende Seele" (the sonorous soul: *W*1:222) and charts the

emotions it undergoes during its metaphorical life. It moves from the spontaneous joy of childhood to the audacity of youth, plunges into reckless abandon and thence into depression and suffering, struggles in vain against misfortune and despair, and finally recalls its early innocence nostalgically before disintegrating into oblivion. What is striking in this vision of the emotions embodied in symphonic music is their violence and their sheer intensity. The soul of the symphony fearlessly exposes itself to danger, it "wagt sich plötzlich mitten in die schäumenden Fluthen zu stürzen," "dringt verwegen in wildere Labyrinthe"; it seeks out melancholy and pain, "die Schrecken des Trübsinns, die bitteren Quaalen des Schmerzes"; and it is assailed by misfortune, by "die Kriegsschaaren des Unglücks" that "wälzen sich in verzerrten Gestalten fürchterlich, schauerlich wie ein lebendig gewordenes Gebirge über einander" (*W*1:222). Here the emotions are unleashed in a cataclysm that earlier in this section Berglinger had termed "Herzenswuth" (*W*1:219), frenzied passion. From conventional portrayals of bland sentiment, music has moved up a gear to an intense and overwhelming melodrama of extreme and often terrifying sensations that is new, disturbing — in a word, Romantic.

Near the beginning of this section there is a reference to "Das Dunkle und Unbeschreibliche" to be found in music and no other art (*W*1:216). If music is uniquely mysterious and irrational, if its effect defies description and definition, then it may possess not only redemptive power, but equally, as in the imaginary symphony evoked in this section, disquieting and ultimately traumatic potential. It is this realization of the dangerous ambiguity of music that concerns Berglinger towards the end of his rhapsodic essay (*W*1:222–23). The music of a symphony, he reflects, may bear us away from the fatuous pretensions of the physical world and raise us up "mit edlem Stolz zum Himmel"; but equally we may be impelled towards a purely profane and amoral delight, which insolently spurns the divine. To describe this "orakelmäßig-zweydeutige Dunkelheit" he finds a remarkable oxymoron: "frevelhafte Unschuld." Music may be innocent but simultaneously iniquitous, impious, monstrous.

It is apparent that the view of music in the *Phantasien* differs sharply from the view of painting in the *Herzensergießungen*. In the earlier text, painting is regarded in an unequivocally positive light, as the repository of spiritual truth and the vehicle for inspired human creativity. In the *Phantasien* music appears as an ambiguous force that may have either a beneficial or a destructive impact on its recipient. That is not to say that the position of the author or authors changed between 1796 and 1799. As pointed out in the lucidly argued but neglected dissertation by Rose Kahnt,[16] it is rather that in particular Wackenroder had throughout a concept of painting that differed from his view of music. This interpretation is confirmed when we note the treatment of music in the Berglinger section of the *Herzensergießungen*, for here too we see both an ambiguous view of music and an incipiently Romantic awareness of its capacity to overwhelm the participant. The *Klosterbruder* records Berglinger's alienation from society, his seduction by music into the "dämmernden Irrgängen der poetischen Empfindung," the labyrinth of poetic feeling (*W*1:132), and his ultimate self-destruction in a frenzy of composition. In this terminal state his soul is said to resemble someone who is ill and who "in einem wunderbaren Paroxismus größere Stärke als ein Gesunder zeigt" (*W*1:144). The problematic treatment of music in both texts may reflect psychological crises in Wackenroder's own experience, for he played the piano well enough to perform in public during his period in Erlangen, he had studied music under Karl Friedrich Fasch in Berlin, and he made repeated attempts at composition.[17] Painting, however, was not an art that he himself practiced, but rather a study — however passionate — that he only took up after visiting the art gallery in Pommersfelden and under the influence of the art historian Johann Dominicus Fiorillo in Göttingen.

The interpretation of music in the two texts remains consistent. Wackenroder and through him Tieck were still indebted to the eighteenth-century *Affektenlehre,* the doctrine that music exists to reflect and portray specific human feelings. Wackenroder had learned this in particular from Johann Nikolaus Forkel, whose *Allgemeine Geschichte der Musik* (General History of Music, 1788) he borrowed from the library in Göttingen in 1794 and whose lectures he probably attended. However, this doctrine is supplemented and overlaid by the notion of immersion in the emotions stimulated by music, a view which Wackenroder may have found prefigured in the musical writings of Johann Friedrich Reichardt, to whose personal influence he had been exposed since the late 1780s. What is new and typically Romantic in the *Herzensergießungen* and the *Phantasien* is the idea of possession by music, complete loss of independence. In the Berglinger narrative in the *Herzensergießungen* the young musician laments in a poem that in his attraction to music he has become the prey of unknown powers (*W*1:138). The basis of this idea, as suggested at the outset in the analysis of the images in "Die Wunder der Tonkunst," is that music is an unfathomable, autonomous, and superhuman force. It is "eine abgesonderte Welt für sich," Tieck has Berglinger remark in "Die Töne" (Sounds, *W*1:236). To abandon oneself to this ambiguous force is to surrender self-direction and risk possession by an alien power offering aesthetic blandishments that are beyond ethical restraint and ultimately destabilizing. In short, and in true Romantic fashion, music is daemonic:[18] "den Engeln nicht näher als den Dämonen" as Gerhard Fricke puts it.[19] For Elmar Hertrich, the Berglinger sections in the two texts together are representations of an isolated individual under the spell of music, entranced and hexed by it.[20] In "Ein Brief Joseph Berlingers" we learn that those who eat the forbidden fruit of music are irretrievably lost to the active world (*W*1:225).

This notion of possession by music, and by artistic inspiration and experience in general, was to become central in late Romanticism. Consider, for example, the torments suffered by E. T. A. Hoffmann's Johannes Kreisler. In the section of the *Kreisleriana*[21] entitled "Kreislers musikalisch-poetischer Klubb" (Kreisler's Musical-Poetic Club, ca. 1810) we see Kreisler improvising on the piano, carried away by his musical visions to the point where he reaches a level of distraction that threatens his sanity. To his horror he himself recognizes the daemonic potential of his enthrallment to music: "Kreisler — Kreisler!" he cries out, "raffe dich auf! — Siehst du es lauern, das bleiche Gespenst mit den rot funkelnden Augen — die krallichten Kochenfäuste aus dem zerrissenen Mantel nach dir ausstreckend? [. . .] Es ist der Wahnsinn."[22] The danger to the musician lies not only — perhaps not even mainly — in his subjection to an unsympathetic society, but in his or her personal exposure to music itself. The Kreisler of Hoffmann's *Kater Murr* (Tomcat Murr, 1819–21) a decade later, still finds himself driven by musical inspiration into an alarming cycle of elation and despair that, so the ingenious structure of this novel indicates, must inexorably be repeated *ad infinitum*. More generally this sense of the destructive potential of artistic experience — once the human victim succumbs to its seduction — is expressed in the work of Joseph von Eichendorff, in poems such as "Der stille Grund" (The Silent Valley, 1837), "Die zwei Gesellen" (The Two Companions, 1818), and "Schlimme Wahl" (Dilemma, 1839). In the metaphor of the first two poems, all artists, poetic and musical, sail the boat of their psyche into uncharted and turbulent waters, and the danger of shipwreck is inevitable. In fact, as the third poem suggests, the artist who does not run the risk of possession by daemonic inspiration is not a true artist at all. Enervation in one's social activity and traumatization of the psyche — or at least the risk of these — are the inescapable concomitants of art. From here it is only a short step to Thomas Mann's Buddenbrooks family and Adrian Leverkühn.

In the *Phantasien,* the section "Ein Brief Joseph Berglingers" ends with another revealing image. Berglinger compares his soul to an Aeolian harp. This eighteenth-century instrument, which also plays a part in Hoffmann's *Kater Murr,* consisted of a set of wires of different thickness stretched over a basin in the open air, producing haunting, mysterious, and eerie melodies as the wind played through the strings. Berglinger imagines that in his soul too "ein fremder, unbekannter Hauch weht, und wechselnde Lüfte nach Gefallen herumwühlen" (*W*1:227). The image offers a perfect characterization of the new Romantic conception of the experience of music: subjection to the afflatus (literally), being played upon by a strange and incomprehensible power that at its own whim agitates the soul of its victim, causing it to vibrate with exquisite poignancy, but at the same time perturbing it to the point of trauma.

Notes

[1] Wilhelm Heinrich Wackenroder, *Werke,* ed. Silvio Vietta, vol. 1 of *Sämtliche Werke und Briefe: Historisch-kritische Ausgabe,* ed. Silvio Vietta and Richard Littlejohns (Heidelberg: Winter, 1991), 205. Further references to this volume are cited in the text as "*W1*" with the page number.

[2] See Martin Bollacher, *Wackenroder und die Kunstauffassung der frühen Romantik* (Darmstadt: Wissenschaftliche Buchgesellschaft, 1983), 19.

[3] Richard Alewyn, "Wackenroders Anteil," *Germanic Review* 19 (1944): 48–58.

[4] See Bollacher, *Wackenroder und die Kunstauffassung der frühen Romantik,* 11–16; also *W1*:368–71.

[5] The text entitled *Phantasien über die Kunst, von einem kunstliebenden Klosterbruder,* published in 1814, is, for the record, irrelevant here: it is not a "new and revised edition," as alleged on the title page, but simply a reprint exclusively of Wackenroder's contributions to both the *Herzensergießungen* and the original *Phantasien,* re-shuffled into sections on painting and music. The full title is misleading too: it is an arbitrary conflation of the titles of the two original texts. The 1814 compilation offers no new texts or significant amendments to the previous texts and might be regarded as in reality the first attempt at an edition of Wackenroder's collected works.

[6] The Berglinger narrative in the *Herzensergießungen* and the musical sections ascribed to him in the *Phantasien* are considered together in the important monograph by Elmar Hertrich: *Joseph Berglinger: Eine Studie zu Wackenroders Musiker-Dichtung* (Berlin: de Gruyter, 1969).

[7] See note 1.

[8] See especially Silvio Vietta, "Raffael-Rezeption in der literarischen Frühromantik: Wilhelm Heinrich Wackenroder und sein akademischer Lehrer Johann Dominicus Fiorillo," in *Geschichte und Aktualität: Studien zur deutschen Literatur seit der Romantik,* ed. Klaus-Detlef Müller, Gerhard Pasternack, Wulf Segebrecht, and Ludwig Stockinger (Tübingen: Niemeyer, 1988), 221–41; also Vietta, "Vom Renaissance-Ideal zur deutschen Ideologie: Wilhelm Heinrich Wackenroder und seine Rezeptionsgeschichte," in *Romantik und Renaissance: Die Rezeption der italienischen Renaissance in der deutschen Romantik,* ed. Silvio Vietta (Stuttgart: Metzler, 1994), 140–62.

[9] Dirk Kemper, *Sprache der Dichtung: Wilhelm Heinrich Wackenroder im Kontext der Spätaufklärung* (Stuttgart: Metzler, 1993).

[10] See Richard Littlejohns, "Humanistische Ästhetik? Kultureller Relativismus in Wackenroders *Herzensergießungen eines kunstliebenden Klosterbruders,*" *Athenäum* 6 (1996): 109–24.

[11] Gerhard Sauder, "Empfindsamkeit und Frühromantik," in *Die literarische Frühromantik,* ed. Silvio Vietta (Göttingen: Vandenhoeck & Ruprecht, 1983), 85–111 (here, 97).

[12] This and all quotations in the analysis of this section are taken from *W1*:224–26.

[13] On the theme of martyrdom and masochism generally in Wackenroder's works and correspondence, see Richard Littlejohns, *Wackenroder-Studien* (Frankfurt a. M.: Peter Lang, 1987), 38–39, 100–102.

[14] See the editor's note on "Symphoniestücke" in *W*1:394.

[15] Steven Paul Scher, *Verbal Music in German Literature* (New Haven and London: Yale UP, 1968), 13–25.

[16] Rose Kahnt, *Die Bedeutung der bildenden Kunst und der Musik bei W. H. Wackenroder* (Marburg: Elwert, 1969), esp. 121.

[17] See the editor's note under "Komposition" in *Briefwechsel,* vol. 2 of Wackenroder's *Sämtliche Werke,* 460.

[18] I use the term "daemonic" to translate the German "dämonisch" in the sense initiated by Goethe. It refers to potentially dangerous elemental forces ("Dämonen") — whether supernatural or subconscious — which human beings may be tempted to invoke but which cannot then be controlled. It should be clearly differentiated from "demonic" in the sense of "diabolical." Goethe sought to illustrate the concept in his ballad "Der Zauberlehrling" (The Sorcerer's Apprentice): the apprentice recites an incantation to summon magical help in fetching water, but cannot halt the process and prevent an inundation.

[19] Gerhard Fricke, "Bemerkungen zu W. H. Wackenroders Religion der Kunst," in *Festschrift für Paul Kluckhohn und Hermann Schneider* (Tübingen: Mohr, 1948), 345–71 (here, 366). Fricke's perceptive essay was, fortunately, reprinted in his *Studien und Interpretationen* (Frankfurt a. M.: Menck, 1956), 186–213. Michael Neumann also argues that for Wackenroder art may be simultaneously both divine and daemonic: *Unterwegs zu den Inseln des Scheins: Kunstbegriff und literarische Form in der Romantik von Novalis bis Nietzsche* (Frankfurt a. M.: Klostermann, 1991), 143–205.

[20] Hertrich, *Joseph Berglinger,* 221.

[21] Miscellaneous pieces about Kreisler, first published in collected form in the *Fantasiestücke in Callots Manier* (Fantasies in the Manner of Jacques Callot, 1814–15).

[22] E. T. A. Hoffmann, *Fantasie- und Nachtstücke,* ed. Walter Müller-Seidel (Munich: Winkler, 1960), 295.

The Cosmic-Symphonic: Novalis, Music, and Universal Discourse

James Hodkinson

IT WAS AMONGST THE DYING WISHES of Friedrich von Hardenberg (Novalis) in March 1801 to hear his brother play a piece by Mozart on the harpsichord.[1] Mention of any great knowledge or appreciation of music, of specific composers and musical works, and evidence of any practical musical skill are, nevertheless, absent from the corpus of his writing. It is of no slight significance, however, that the conference from which this volume grew should have heralded itself with reference to Novalis's formulation "Unsere Sprache [. . .] muß wieder *Gesang* werden" (*SN*3:284:245), which is typical of the many abstract references to song and music strewn throughout his theoretical and literary writings.

This paper will explore Novalis's complex theoretical understanding of music within the context of his own philosophical-aesthetic system, examining its role in co-determining his theories of language and poetic writing, *Poësie*. In calling for language to become song again, Novalis appears to offer us a prescription for transforming the way in which we as individuals speak and write. In this discussion, however, I will move on to look at other theoretical models of music that had a bearing on Novalis, suggesting that music also plays a vital role in defining a conception of intersubjective discourse. Specifically, the marriage of a Romantic re-reading of the seventeenth-century theosophist Jacob Böhme and his ideas of universal music on the one hand, with Novalis's philosophical dissatisfaction with the egocentrism of Fichtean idealism on the other, allowed the poet to produce a polyphonic model of discourse that is inclusively intersubjective. Having traced the development of these ideas, I shall re-examine the prose fragments *Die Lehrlinge zu Saïs* (The Novices at Saïs, 1802) and *Heinrich von Ofterdingen* (1802), and highlight the way in which the musical model of discourse makes provision for the meaningful return of those "other" voices traditionally excluded from patriarchal canonical literature.

To begin with, I shall offer a brief sketch of the fundamentals of Novalis's writing practice and its relationship to theories of music. That Novalis's thought and writing flow primarily from his engagement with Fichte's idealist philosophy is now the standard view amongst scholars of

Romanticism and requires no further justification here.[2] Novalis's post-Fichtean system of aesthetic cognition forms the context for his definition of music and its relationship to language and discourse in general. Novalis read Fichte's *Wissenschaftslehre* (Theory of Knowledge, 1794) intensively between 1795 and 1796, producing in parallel his *Fichte-Studien* (Fichte-Studies), which contain a subtle but fundamental advancement on Fichte's position.

The very first sentence of the *Studien* critically re-reads Fichte's proposition that the *Ich* determines its identity through its own productive activity. The very fact that the subject must self-define was, for Novalis, proof of its inability to define or capture the essence of itself. An act of definition occurring within the finite structure of reflection cannot enclose or fix the absolute nature of identity, but merely figure its possibility. Importantly for Novalis, the figuration is not identical with the essence of that being figured, but at most a statement of equivalence: "Das Wesen der Identität läßt sich nur in einem *Scheinsatz* aufstellen. Wir verlassen das *Identische,* um es darzustellen" (*SN*2:104).[3] In Novalis, the subject has access only to *fictions* of being and knowing. Our only real contact with the absolute is through a non-theoretical feeling ("Gefühl") of what is, a sense beyond understanding of the essence of ourselves and of the objects beyond ourselves.

Fictions can be rewritten, however, and this forms the basis of what Novalis called *Poësie,* his own writing practice. This is defined in the *Logologische Fragmente* (Logological Fragments, 1797). Here, the logical structure of language, the "Grammatik des höheren Denkens oder Sprechens" (*SN*2:526:16) is the focus. The logical system relating words or thoughts is in itself a form of language, but remains inherent in the relationships between signs. The order of logic does not always prevail. Novalis reflects on two opposing tendencies within language: first, the action of logic, which would seek, as William O'Brien puts it, to "abolish randomness and diversity" within signification — the use of language —, and second, language's own tendency to promote such change.[4] Novalis personifies these two tendencies as two figures, the "Scholastiker" and the "Dichter": the former seeking to preserve the fixed relationships between sign and signified, with the latter seeking to disrupt these (*SN*2:524:13). Ultimately, neither the scholastic nor the poet can ever entirely succeed in their respective tasks of fixing language absolutely, or rendering it entirely arbitrary. Therefore, whilst the practice of *Poësie* will promote the arbitrariness implied by the (figurative) poet, it will not and cannot become entirely a matter of chaotic disruption. Thus the poet proper engages in the proposition of structures of meaning and identity, but also, ironically, in the attempt to excite change experimentally within them.[5]

Scholars have looked in varying detail and in varying contexts at Novalis's conception of music and its relationship to this definition of

Poësie. Carl Dahlhaus's paradigm-making work, *Die Idee der absoluten Musik* (The Idea of Absolute Music, 1978) made first mention of Novalis's comparison between wordless, instrumental music and the poetic quality to Novalis's understanding of mathematics, as both represent a medium for speculating the shifting relationships between things in an internally self-referential manner, without having to refer to empirical reality.[6] For Dahlhaus, Novalis's music thus becomes an isolated world, a metaphor for the universe.[7]

In the relevant chapter of his *Aesthetics and Subjectivity,* Andrew Bowie extends the discussion to look at Novalis's theories of how music is processed by the listener.[8] Novalis conceives of music as escaping the "reflexivity" of language, and the resultant, apparently absolute, properties bring a feeling of wholeness to the listener: such an expressive structure cannot be understood theoretically, but rather on the level of non-reflexive feeling. Thus music becomes an "antidote" for the lack of the absolute within the finite structures of identity, to which the conscious mind is otherwise bound.[9] However, music also represents the ideal system for speculating on the relationships between things. Within music, it is rhythm that allows for the points of transition between differing melodic and harmonic structures and which thus constitutes the speculative dimension of the medium. Bowie shows Novalis also to have conceived of an allegorical sense of rhythm operating within language and other semantically bound systems of knowledge, where it also constitutes transition between forms of articulation and between differing interpretative possibilities, and informs the speculative and dynamic property of Novalis's *Poësie.*[10]

Barbara Naumann also focuses on how music serves as a blueprint for speculative poetics, with rhythm again playing a vital role.[11] The disparate characteristics of the phenomenal world represented in reflection can be connected, disconnected, repeated, and varied in "musical" fashion, as an *ars combinatoria.*[12] The strength of Naumann's work is its breadth and detail, its analyses of the musical elements inherent to the theoretical foundations of Novalis's poetic project, but also its meticulous readings of his fragments, natural-scientific writings, and literary works. She argues, for instance, that notions of musicality can be shown to inform Novalis's semiotic epistemology, as contemporary scholars have understood it.[13] For all its range, however, Naumann's study disregards the models of *Naturmusik* Novalis inherited from the holistic cosmologies of Christian theosophy and mysticism.[14] Instead, she presents the Novalissian *Ich* or ego as an active, constructing agent that is not passive or subordinate to any cosmological context and has rather to build its own vision of the universe. To an extent, of course, this is true, though Naumann seems to dispute the idea that Novalis's subjects exist in any form of transsubjective context and, consequently, loses the opportunity to envision their participation in a holistic model of discourse.[15]

Naumann is right, of course, to say that Novalis does not reduce the *Ich* to a passive instrument of some mystical whole, but her alternative precludes the use of such holistic models *per se,* losing the opportunity to think of self as autonomous and yet, simultaneously, bound within an intersubjective discursive context.

In his masterly reception history of Novalis scholarship, Herbert Uerlings reminds us that understanding Novalis's work involves tracing the poet's combination of mystical-theosophical models of the universe with his own post-Fichtean subjectivism.[16] Carl Pascheck's doctoral dissertation of 1967 attempted just this, and was the first to explore the impact of Jacob Böhme's writings upon Novalis.[17] Böhme's writings can be seen as a series of variations upon a central motif, in which the physical universe is por-trayed as an emanation from God. In *De Signatura rerum* (The Signature of All Things, 1622) this emanation is portrayed as a system of signs. Here, Böhme contends that all objects of the physical universe contain within them a unique and communicable essence or *Signatur* which is self-revelatory: "Ein iedes Ding hat seinen Mund zur Offenbarung. Und das ist die Natur-Sprache, daraus iedes Dings aus seiner Eigenschaft redet, und sich immer selber offenbaret und darstellet [. . .]."[18] All things in creation appear to be communicating entities in their own right. Critics have noted, however, that the *Signaturen* buried deep within their objects could never be accessed and disclosed in full and had, moreover, to be coaxed forth, to be "read" actively or intuited by sensually perceptive individuals; all things must be *made* to speak.[19] Significantly, the individual's speculation of the objects of nature has been seen as a "musical" process and physical phenomena as musical instruments that can be blown upon, strummed, plucked or beaten in order that they give voice to themselves.[20] Despite such emphasis on the role of the subject, it is precisely within this extended musical allegory that Jacob Böhme reveals the ultimately theocentric character of his ideas. It is God who orchestrates the divine ensemble of the cosmos:

> 13. [. . .] Ich soll sein Instrument und Saitenspiel seines ausgesprochenen Wortes und Halles seyn; und nicht alleine ich, sondern alle meine Mit-Glieder in dem herrlichen zugerichteten Instrument Gottes; wir sind alle Saiten in seinem Freudenspiel; der Geist seines Mundes ists, der unsere Saiten seiner Stimme schlaeget.[21]

This ultimately undermines the autonomous nature of human undertaking, be it individual or collective; God gives us the need and the capability to speculate nature: an endeavor, which ultimately expresses our dependence upon Him. Indeed, God is seen in this extract as a universally composite instrument, of which individuals are merely the strings or subordinate parts.

In Novalis, however, things are different. Pascheck has shown evi-dence of Novalis's familiarity with the tradition of holistic Christian cos-mology in general, especially with Böhme's work and with *De signatura rerum* in particular.[22] Concurring with the received view, Pascheck does point out that Novalis's full and mature reading of Böhme occurred early in 1799, after Ludwig Tieck introduced his fellow poet to the theosophist's work. Formulations by Novalis, such as the following of 1798: "Der Mensch spricht nicht allein — auch das Universum *spricht* — alles spricht — unendliche Sprachen. Lehre von den Signaturen" (*SN*3:267–68:143), which describes the plurality of voices in the universe, are, therefore, more likely traceable to the works of the Reformation doctor and amateur theosophist Paracelsus, whose holistic models were not supported by allegories of the musical. Nevertheless, Novalis's above formulation is already starting to move beyond both Paracelsus and, by way of anticipation, beyond Böhme through its treatment of discursive agency: in Novalis, all things appear able to speak for themselves. This appears to generate a tension. For Novalis, there is some form of universal whole governing the discursive activity of the individuals comprising it, yet *also* allowing for the free discursive agency of those individuals. An entry in the *Fichte-Studien* prefigures this apparent contradiction within a quite different thematic context. There, the physical body is shown to be both unique to the individual, but *also* inseparably part of the universal cycle of matter; it is determined by the individual and the whole *simultaneously:*

> Ich finde meinen Körper durch sich und die Weltseele zugleich bestimmt und wirksam. Mein Körper ist ein kleines Ganzes, und hat also auch eine besondere Seele; denn ich nenne Seele, wodurch Alles zu einem Ganzen wird, das individuelle Princip. — — Was die Belebung des besonderen Gliedes betrifft, so finde ich mich in dieser Hinsicht bloß durch mich selbst, und zwar mittelbar durch die allgemeine Belebung bestimmt. Die Belebung selbst aber betreffend, so ist sie nichts anderes, als eine Zueignung, eine Identification. (*SN*2:550:118)

This dialectic of autonomy and limitation, of self-determination and pre-determination from without is also precisely what makes Novalis's model of polyphony work. On the one hand, this provides for the individual's rights of (apparently unfettered) utterance. On the other hand, the tension prevents the polyphony from degenerating into cacophony. Wholly free individuals will speak over and across each other, trampling each other's discursive rights; within such anarchy, exercising the right to discourse cannot be expressive of an egalitarian ideal founded in mutual recognition and respect. If the inclusion of all voices is to grow from such recognition and respect, then polyphony must be dependent on some degree of external determination of the individual by the whole, on a loss of his or her absolute freedom.

Novalis's polyphony, though, is not just a matter of the individual's subordination to a democracy imposed from without, but of the poetic individual's conscious and willing participation. Now, certain of Novalis's writings appear to collapse the poet's voice entirely, whilst others inflate its importance: on occasions the poet is conceived of in apparently Böhmian terms as the harp: "der Mensch ist die Harfe, soll die Harfe seyn" (*SN3:434:855*), on others shown to be the voice of the cosmos (*SN3:679:705*), thus giving voice to otherwise mute nature. Ultimately, though, Novalis strikes a balance. The poet must develop and articulate his own voice; in *Das allgemeine Brouillon* (General Notebook, 1798/99) Novalis writes: "Um die Stimme auszubilden, muß man sich mehrere Stimmen anbilden" (*SN3:290:282*), implying that the poet's singular voice is dialogical (to use Bakhtin's term), composed of many strands, which he has inherited — or here, taken — from others. And whilst, furthermore, "[. . .] um seine Individualität auszubilden muß er immer mehrere Individualitäten anzunehmen," the poet must also learn to assimilate himself (*SN3:290:282*). So, the poet's voice must not replace the voices it echoes, but integrate itself into a manifold, which preserves the integrity and position of those other voices.

That Novalis's theories involve the subject both recognizing and acting to uphold that position by sacrificing its own sovereignty is clearest in his plans for an encyclopaedia, *Das allgemeine Brouillon:*

> Wir erblicken uns im System, als Glied — mithin in auf und absteigender Linie, vom Unendlich kleinen bis zum Unendlich Großen — *Menschen* von unendlichen Variationen. [. . .]
>
> Selbstheit ist der Grund aller Erkenntniß — als der Grund der Beharrlichkeit im Veränderlichen — auch das Prinzip der höchsten *Mannichfaltigkeit* — (Du) (Statt N[icht] I[ch] — Du.). (*SN3:429–30:820*)

Whilst maintaining that selfhood is the mode by which individuals intuit all things, including the notion that there are other selves beyond the individual, this extract also demands that subjectivity recognize itself within a multitude of other equivalent selves, which Novalis calls "Du." This remarkable gesture recognizes those others as valid centers of experiences, each potentially with their own discursive rights. The ideal of "utmost diversity" would appear to imply that *Poësie* involves the cultivation of a polyphony inclusive of many distinct voices. It is this combination of this philosophy of intersubjectivity and musical allegorical models of the self within a multitude of other voices that makes for a sense of genuinely egalitarian polyphony in Novalis. It now remains to see how these ideas — both music as a poetic way of discoursing and the "musical" discursive context in which this occurs — translate into literature.

Novalis's prose fragment *Die Lehrlinge zu Saïs* has long been thought of as documenting the early Romantic poetic construction of nature. The text opens with a single narrative voice describing the multiple paths men follow in speculating upon nature. This journey reveals to the poet of nature myriad signs and symbols, making nature a "Chiffernschrift," an encoded text to be read and interpreted by him (SN1:79). This act of "reading" is not a matter of unlocking objective truths, however. The poet of nature feels as if an "Alcahest," a solution in the tradition of alchemy thought to dissolve of existing forms of matter, had been poured metaphorically over his senses. Thus, in approaching the truths implied by the signs of nature, the poet finds that these dissolve before his eyes at the crucial moment (SN1:79). As a result, one of the other voices to emerge as the text develops is able to claim: "Man verstehe die Sprache nicht, weil sich die Sprache selber nicht verstehe, nicht verstehen wolle [. . .]" (SN1:79), that is: the language of nature, like spoken language, does not understand itself and cannot, therefore, enclose or disclose truths that inform our understanding. Thus the language of nature is like music, because it is internally self-referential. As poets engage with this language, the "meanings" they construe from the aesthetic patterns of nature are relative, artificial, and ephemeral, all of which allows them to be speculated upon in "rhythmical" fashion.

In the second half of the extract, the journey undertaken by the novice's teacher earlier in his life is recounted. Whilst traveling, he recognizes that natural phenomena hitherto unknown to him are, in fact, merely combinations of familiar phenomena. This insight allows him to begin his own speculations: his contemplation of nature is presented through an explicitly musical metaphor that is both *harmonic,* combining experimentally disparate elements of nature, and *rhythmical,* marking transitions between experimental attempts: "[. . .] er [. . .] griff so selbst in den Saiten nach Tönen und Gängen umher" (SN1:79–80). However, the passage does not only focus on the individual's aesthetic production, but also on the *context* of production. The image of nature speculation as the striking of chords is reminiscent of the passage above — chords are drawn from the whole of the cosmic symphony. This model of the cosmic symphony, although not inherited directly from Böhme at this stage in Novalis's career, shows that the poet was thinking along similar though not identical lines to the theosophist: the whole is dependent on the contributions of a plurality of voices or players, each choosing freely to play, but each recognizing the importance of the whole and its other individuals, and surrendering a degree of absolute autonomy.

The text goes on to realize this polyphony formally: the central narrative voice, apparently omnipresent and omniscient, is, in fact, neither and is slowly decentered by the emergence of the other voices.[23] In the second part of the *Lehrlinge,* the voices of the novices gathering at Saïs are drawn into an increasingly discordant argument. The novices argue about individual interpretations of natural phenomena, as well as the methodologies by which these can be reached. It is at this point that the teacher takes the initiative and tells the tale of Hyacinth and Rosenblüthe. Herbert Uerlings has shown this to be, amongst other things, a tale about initiation into the poetic cognition of nature.[24] At the end of the tale the veiled Goddess of

Isis, the object of Hyacinth's quest, is unveiled, but his original lover, Rosenblüthe, falls into his arms. In contrast to existing interpretations, the two women are *not* identical; Rosenblüthe's re-appearance is an interruption of an eternal ideal by a finite reality, of the metaphysical by the physical — not some combination of the two.[25] If the feminine is taken to represent nature here, then this narrative is the teacher's instruction to his pupils that no one absolute construction of nature is accessible to the individual. The individual must be prepared to revise his conception of the world and seek insight from sources beyond himself. Having heard this tale, the novices embrace each other and the nature of the polyphony becomes more harmonious:

> Die Lehrlinge umarmten sich und gingen fort. Die weiten hallenden Säle standen leer und hell da, und das wunderbare Gespräch in zahlosen Sprachen unter den tausendfaltigen Naturen, die in diesen Sälen zusammengebracht und in mannichfaltigen Ordnungen aufgestellt waren, dauerte fort. (*SN1:95*)

This is not monotone, but rather harmonious polyphony. This arises from the fact that each speaker relinquishes the notion that he can speak one truth which invalidates all others, with each speaker retaining the right to speak, whilst recognizing the rights of others and no longer speaking over them.[26] The tale is not, however, successful in realizing its ideal. The opening of the *Lehrlinge*, "Mannigfache Wege gehen die Menschen," is exclusive of women in that it is only men within this text who travel the speculative paths of nature, who find a voice within the polyphony. As Rosenblüthe or Isis, woman — as an aesthetic construction of nature — remains a passive object, more speculated upon than speculating. The text is successful in realizing the idea of music as ideal discourse, but not wholly successful in realizing music as a polyphonic discursive system. The cosmic symphony thus remains unfinished.

The case is different, however, for the unfinished novel *Heinrich von Ofterdingen*. The main torso of the text was composed between the end of November 1799 and September 1800. Although the *Lehrlinge* had made steps towards realizing a model of polyphony, *Ofterdingen* profited from Novalis's in-depth acquaintance with the musical model of polyphony in evidence in Böhme. We might, then, expect a more fully developed and inclusive treatment of the issue in this later work. This text has already been shown to be inclusive of female voices and discourses, though not in the context of musical polyphony.[27] As I have shown elsewhere, the novel departs from the traditional model of the Bildungsroman, in which the personal development of a single, usually male character is focused upon, with his experiences on a linear path through time and space defining the dynamic of the plot. Whilst Heinrich does go on a journey, the purely linear and subject-centered dynamic is finally halted. In the notes for the completion of the novel that Novalis left behind him on his death, Heinrich enters a transcendental and ideal mode of existence, called the "Geistige Gegenwart" (*SN*2:461:109). Here linear time and physical space are meaningless, and the various figures left behind with the novel's episodes return to take part in a polyphonic discursive exchange.[28]

The progress of the novel can also be read as Heinrich's gradual and conscious assimilation into this ideal (and musically inspired) polyphony. The opening of the novel, the famous dream of the blue flower, marks the beginnings of this process. Within the dream, Heinrich emerges from having bathed in the springs of the cavern, only to encounter the blue flower. Through a process of self-transformation, the flower reveals itself — and, in the process, all of nature — as a sentient being that demands a discursive space for self-representation.[29] This sets the discursive structure for the rest of the novel: Heinrich awakens and goes out into a world in which he encounters many voices. As well as developing his own poetic voice, part of his education is about being silent, learning to listen and to assimilate himself into this multitude of songs.

Heinrich hears a number of tales on his journey. The *Atlantis Märchen* (Atlantis Fairy-Tale) of the third chapter, for instance, depicts a royal court in which a king lives with his daughter and his chorus of poets. The chorus represents a musical multitude of voices, but it is exclusively patriarchal. Woman, in the shape of the princess, is again marginalized. Initially she is the silent muse who, by appearing as "die sichtbare Seele jener herrlichen Kunst," that is: the "visible soul" or manifestation of art, remains the inspiration for art, rather than an artistic subject; she only ever listens "mit tiefstem Lauschen" to the poet's songs, instead of singing her own (*SN*1:214). But things do not remain thus. When she strays from the palace, we witness her birth as a subject in her own right. The point of narrative focalization shifts to her perspective and we are given insight into her thoughts and feelings. Upon meeting her young lover in the forest, himself a fledgling poet, she is allowed to unfold her own creative talents. His poetic receptivity to the song of others opens out a discursive space into which she sings with an "überirdische [. . .] Stimme," an otherworldly voice (*SN*1:220) and makes her plea: "wie Geistergesang tönende Bitte" (*SN*1:216).

Whilst her apparently spiritual utterance again raises suspicions that Novalis intended her as an otherworldly muse, one can equally contend she is merely demonstrating that musicality evokes a sense of transcendent wholeness. More significant is her emergence from silence into song, whereby she fulfils the promise of universal polyphony, making the transition from muse to musician. When the couple return to the palace a year later with their newborn child, however, it is the young poet rather than the poetess who sings his songs in the presence of the court. When the court poets sing their final song of thanks, she appears to have taken on the Romantic, neo-Rousseauian role of the demure and silent mother.

The tale is, admittedly, related second-hand to Heinrich by the merchants with whom he travels, who concede they are themselves no poets. It represents an imperfect attempt at depicting a model of perfection.

In the notoriously complex text *Klingsohrs Märchen* (Klingsohr's Fairy-Tale), one figure in particular attempts to marginalize the voices of women again. While the court scribe constantly attempts to record the various goings-on in the tale's allegorical household as reflexive, written language, the female figures of the novel practice musical discourse. Both the child Fabel and the priestess figure Sophie achieve this. Sophie's manipulation of signs in language is reminiscent of the rhythmical method of speculation. When she splashes water from her bowl onto the children's cradle, the droplets dissolve "in einen blauen Dunst [. . .], der tausend seltsame Bilder zeigte, und beständig um sie herzog und sich veränderte" (*SN*1:294). Strange pictures emerge from the vapor. When the pages of the scribe's log are washed in the fluids of Sophie's bowl, Fabel's own attempts to use language remain, whereas the scribe's are erased (*SN*1:295–96). Fabel also appears to produce language which, in Bowie's words, "escapes the trap of reflexivity"[30] by accepting that the true use of language cannot be used to fix truths, but rather to speculate their possibilities through the method of "rhythmic" variation. The scribe's subsequent attempt to dominate the royal household, to fix meaning and thus silence the music of language, is his undoing (*SN*1:308). Fabel refuses to be silenced and returns from her journey, spinning a golden thread from her body, which is simultaneously a kind of wordless music (*SN*1:314), the scribe is vanquished, and a new order inclusive of Fabel's voice is established.[31]

Heinrich exhibits his growing ability and willingness to function within the polyphony of *Poësie* through his interaction with "real" women outside the inset narratives. In the fourth chapter Heinrich encounters the Christian crusaders, who also sing their own songs. However, the words of their song sung in the banquet hall depict the Muslims occupying Jerusalem as wild heathens defiling Christ's grave (*SN*1:231). Their songs appear to allow no space for the voices of other religions or ethnic groups.[32] One real example of this discursive exclusion of others is the fact that they hold a female Muslim slave captive outside the castle. Heinrich withdraws from their company to meet this slave, Zulima. Like the young poet in the previous chapter, Heinrich is very receptive and opens a space into which she can sing her song, the words of which tell of her homeland and abduction from it by the knights. But Zulima's song is not merely the missing link to complete some token ethno-religious polyphony; she practices the "music" of natural speculation, as the novices in Saïs do. She teaches Heinrich how to speculate "musically" on the natural world and on written texts, using as an example her "rhythmical" method for deriving a range of meanings from the hieroglyphics on the ancient temples of her homeland. Significantly, though, she explains that in speculating on the natural world, nature speaks back to her with its *own* voice, returning images of its own that constitute a dualistic or doubled vision of reality. "Die Natur scheint dort menschlicher und verständlicher geworden, eine dunkle Erinnerung unter der durchsichtigen Gegenwart wirft die Bilder der Welt mit scharfen Umrissen zurück, und so genießt man eine doppelte Welt" (*SN*1:237). Thus, Zulima also teaches Heinrich about polyphonic poetics, about allowing others to sing alongside him. This lesson he learns well, as ultimately he refuses to silence her songs. In parting, Heinrich will not accept her lute as a gift, insisting that she keep the means by which she accompanies her song.

In Augsburg Heinrich meets his future lover, Mathilde. From the outset she says little. She shies away from Heinrich's attempts to coerce her to teach him the guitar (*SN*1:276). Of course, Heinrich's love for Mathilde is a source of inspiration for his songs. In his room at night Heinrich exclaims: "O! Sie ist der sichtbare Geist des Gesangs. Eine würdige Tochter ihres Vaters. Sie wird mich in Musik auflösen" (*SN*1:277). Here Mathilde is in danger, like the princess in Atlantis, of becoming muse rather than musician. That night, however, Heinrich dreams of Mathilde and in this dream she comes to him and speaks a "wunderbares geheimes Wort in seinen Mund" (*SN*1:279). Whilst this could be seen again as a conventional image of the muse breathing the breath of inspiration into the poet, this section can equally be read as a prefiguration of Mathilde's own forthcoming participation in poetic discourse, as a result of which Heinrich wholly relinquishes his exclusive right to speak as poet.

When, sometime between the novel's first and second parts Mathilde dies, the danger arises that the already tenuous polyphony will collapse. It is precisely then, towards the end of Novalis's notes for the continuation of the novel that the aforementioned state of the "Geistige Gegenwart" is sketched out. Here, music in both senses is realized. On the one hand, the figures of the text re-figure their own identities through strange metamorphoses, applying the method of speculative rhythm to their own identities. On the other hand, Mathilde returns to take command of the process by which Heinrich reinvents himself. After Heinrich's identity is dissolved in a metaphorical sacrifice, Mathilde "macht ihn durch seine eigenen Lieder" (*SN*1:348). Mathilde re-constitutes Heinrich's identity here again through an allegory of music. Although she works with pre-existing fragments of songs, the act of re-combining them is her own; she re-designs him. Her act demonstrates that she is a musician and her inclusion in this ideal discursive system represents the final realization of the universal musical polyphony. The final sentence of Novalis's plans for the novel run, appropriately: "Während dieser Verwandlungen hat er allerlei wunderbare Gespräche," telling of the many wondrous conversations Heinrich has during these transformations (*SN*1:348).

Novalis appears to have experimented with (often musical) models of polyphony from 1798 onwards. Whilst the narrative structure of the

Lehrlinge might appear to realize more visibly the ideal of polyphony, however, it was the later work *Ofterdingen,* with its more universal and post-Böhme treatment of the model that offered a more genuine and inclusive polyphony through its inclusion of the traditionally marginalized voices of non-Christians and women. I hope to have shown from this discussion that Novalis was not only concerned with the fact that music offered the aesthetic blueprint for a new approach to poetic language, which alone might appear somewhat esoteric, but that he was also keen to adapt the polyphonic formulation of music as he found it in Jacob Böhme, taking this as the blueprint for a discursive system that is genuinely universal, upholding the rights of all to speak, sing, and play.

Notes

[1] *Schriften Novalis: Die Werke Friedrich von Hardenbergs,* ed. Paul Kluckhohn et al., 6 vols., 3rd ed. (Stuttgart: Kohlhammer, 1977ff.), 4:531. All subsequent quotations from Novalis are expressed in brackets in the text by the abbreviation *"SN,"* volume number, page number, and, where applicable, fragment number.

[2] See Herbert Uerlings, *Friedrich von Hardenberg, genannt Novalis: Werk und Forschung* (Stuttgart: Metzler, 1991), 105–19. In fact, Novalis criticized Fichte in explicitly musical terms: "Es wäre wohl möglich, daß Fichte Erfinder einer ganz neuen Art zu denken wäre — für die die Sprache noch keinen Namen hat. Der Erfinder ist vielleicht nicht der fertigste und sinnreichste Künstler auf seinem Instrument" (*SN*2:524:11).

[3] This notion of identity lacking within reflection has been a central concern of all good Novalis scholars since Manfred Frank. See Frank, "Die Philosophie des sogenannten 'magischen Idealismus,'" *Euphorion* 63 (1969): 88–116.

[4] See William Arctander O'Brien, *Novalis: Signs of Revolution* (Durham and London: Duke UP, 1995), esp. 133.

[5] See Uerlings's understanding of *Poësie* as an aesthetic form of ironic absolutism: *Friedrich von Hardenberg,* 229–32.

[6] Carl Dahlhaus, *Die Idee der absoluten Musik* (Kasel: Bärenreiter-Verlag, 1978), 58, 73, and esp. 143–44. For a good English translation see *The Idea of Absolute Music,* trans. Roger Lustig (Chicago: U of Chicago P, 1989).

[7] Ibid., 143.

[8] Andrew Bowie, *Aesthetics and Subjectivity: from Kant to Nietzsche* (Manchester: Manchester UP, 1990). My discussion of these facts was also informed by the even more lucid discussion written by Bowie for the second edition of this work (Manchester UP, 2003). I am indebted to him for access to the pre-publication manuscript.

[9] Ibid., 79.

[10] Bowie continued the discussion of the rhythm of language in his later monograph *From Romanticism to Critical Theory* (London: Routledge, 1997), focusing there

on its treatment in Novalis's *Monolog* (1798). Novalis believed that all sciences or systems of formal study and discourse ought to be practiced rhythmically. Bowie points to *Das allgemeine Brouillon:* "Alle Methode ist *Rhythmus*" (*SN3*:309).

[11] See Barbara Naumann: *Musikalisches Ideen-Instrument: Das Musikalische in Poetik und Sprachtheorie der Frühromantik* (Stuttgart: Metzler, 1990). Naumann reconstructs in far greater detail the development of rhythm in Novalis's theory, from a purely acoustical phenomenon to an intrinsic dynamic of all representational systems, and finally, to a tool for the poetic speculator.

[12] Ibid., 178–81.

[13] In all self-consciousness there is a "dissonant seed" or "germ": "Jeder Keim ist eine Dissonanz — ein Mißverhältnis, was sich nach gerade ausgleichen soll" (*SN2*:581:242), which Naumann reads as "eine Entzweiung, eine Spaltung im Identischen ("dem Keim"); mithin als Mittel, um etwas in sich Entzweites zu denken, das die Motivation zu einer Bewegung hin auf Vereinigung, auf Kon-Sonanz, auf Harmonie abgeben kann, und dennoch als in sich Geeintes, Zusammengehörendes, vorgestellt werden muß" (Naumann, *Musikalisches Ideen-Instrument*, 162–65). Thus Novalis's model of self-consciousness is itself "musical" from the outset, in that it is constituted by a unified but internally mobile (or dissonant) dialectic of theoretical reflection and feeling. The transreflexive "feeling" of absolute selfhood undermines reflexive constructions of self and necessitates a perpetual search for self — the resolution to which is conceived as being "harmonious" (ibid., 177–78).

[14] Ibid., 158.

[15] Ibid., 159.

[16] See Uerlings, *Friedrich von Hardenberg*, 113.

[17] Carl Pascheck, "Der Einfluß Jacob Böhmes auf das Werk Friedrich von Hardenbergs (Novalis)" (Ph.D. diss., Bonn, 1967).

[18] See Jacob Böhme, *Sämtliche Schriften*, ed. W. E. Peuckert, 11 vols. (1730; facsimile reprint, Stuttgart: Frommanns Verlag, 1957), vol. 6, book 14, ch. 1, 16–17.

[19] See Gernot Böhme's essay "Jacob Böhme," in *Klassiker der Naturphilosophie: Von den Vorsokratikern bis zur Kopenhagener Schule,* ed. Gernot Böhme (Munich: Beck, 1989), 158–71.

[20] Ibid., 167–68.

[21] Jacob Böhme, *Sämtliche Schriften*, vol. 6, book 14, ch. 12.

[22] Pascheck, "Der Einfluß Jacob Böhmes," 77.

[23] Building on Jurij Striedter's *Die Fragmente des Novalis als Präfiguration seiner Dichtung* (Munich: Fink, 1985), Naumann shows awareness that Novalis's theories of music inform the structural composition of his prose work. However, neither critic examines fully the impact of Böhme's universal music on the structure of these texts.

[24] Herbert Uerlings, "Novalis und die Weimarer Klassik," *Aurora: Jahrbuch der Eichendorff Gesellschaft* 50 (1990): 27–46.

[25] See, for example, Katherine Mary Padilla, "The Embodiment of the Absolute: Theories of the Feminine in the Works of Schleiermacher, Schlegel and

Novalis" (Ph.D. diss.: Princeton, 1988), 147–227. Padilla believes the male subject conflates his fantasy of woman with his earthly love.

[26] Cf. Novalis's distinction between monotony, discordant polyphonies, and harmonious polyphonies: "Der Übergang von der Monotonie zur Harmonie wird freilich durch Disharmonie gehen und nur am Ende wird eine Harmonie entstehen" (*SN2*:546:111).

[27] Alice Kuzniar has shown women's voices to be present and influential in the text. She begins by likening woman's voice to the French feminist conception of women's writing as an *écriture féminine,* a mode of writing founded in woman's sexual difference and expressing an eroticized, body-centered mode of discursive production. The women of the novel create their texts in a similar manner, and Heinrich must attempt to emulate this: "Hearing Women's Voices in *Heinrich von Ofterdingen,*" *PMLA* 107:5 (1992): 1196–1208. Elsewhere I have attempted to move beyond this standpoint, showing that women need not merely serve as a template for male development. I show that the novel allegorizes genius as a process of quasi-mystical transformation and, given that the male subject is displaced from the center position and relinquishes its monopoly over discourse, women can partake in this allegory and themselves become poetic subjects and geniuses. See James Hodkinson, "Genius beyond Gender: Novalis, Women and the Art of Shapeshifting," *MLR* 96:1 (2001): 103–15. It can be noted here that the model of genius is also explicitly musical: "*Rythmischer* Sinn ist Genie" (*SN3*:310:382).

[28] See ibid., 113–14.

[29] For a full discussion of the discursive dynamics of the dream see ibid., 108–9.

[30] Bowie, *Aesthetics and Subjectivity,* 79.

[31] The final tableau of figures excludes only those figures that have attempted to suppress the voices of others; Fabel and her song are present. This does not, of course, explain the problematic fate of the mother who is burned alive by the scribe, yet kept alive symbolically through a rite of Romantic Holy Communion. By being reduced to a symbol, the mother's voice is rendered silent.

[32] For a more in-depth discussion of the Crusaders' perceptions of the ethno-religious other, see again Hodkinson, "Genius beyond Gender," 111.

"Das Hören ist ein Sehen von und durch innen": Johann Wilhelm Ritter and the Aesthetics of Music

Thomas Strässle

L IKE VIRTUALLY NO OTHER FIGURE, Johann Wilhelm Ritter (1776–1810) epitomizes the relationship between Romanticism and the sciences. He is considered the prototype of the Romantic natural scientist who was in revolt against the omnipotent Newtonian system of physics.[1] In turn, Romantic natural sciences, which were substantially indebted to Schelling's *Naturphilosophie*[2] (though not in an uncritical way[3]) and thus adopted the *organism* as the principle metaphor for nature, were subjected to constant and harsh criticism throughout the nineteenth century by the traditional, mechanical natural sciences.[4]

When scientists concern themselves with Ritter, the mistrust that tends to characterize their attitudes towards Romantic Science in general becomes all the more acute, thanks to his tendency to gesture beyond empirical grounds towards speculation. In her eminent volume from the close of the nineteenth century, *Die Romantik: Ausbreitung, Blütezeit und Verfall* (The Spread, Blossoming, and Decline of Romanticism, 1899–1902), Ricarda Huch attempted to give a psychological explanation for this underestimation of Ritter's scientific genius, attributing it to his own inability to make the most of his discoveries.[5] Nevertheless, despite Ritter's undeniably speculative approach, his scientific achievements have since been widely acknowledged by scholars, not least because many of his conclusions have been verified by researchers in non-Romantic natural sciences.[6] As early as 1894, Wilhelm Ostwald attempted in an address to the *Deutsche Elektrochemische Gesellschaft* to do justice to Ritter, a thinker who has always been regarded as one of the most enigmatic figures among those who formed the core group of early Romanticism in Jena.[7] Today a considerable number of publications, mostly written by scientists or historians of science, recognize Ritter as a leading figure of Romantic Science. He is considered not only to have founded electrochemistry, but also to have made crucial contributions to research into the phenomenon of *galvanism,* which was very popular at the time, and to have proved the existence of the ultraviolet spectrum by means of a bold speculation upon the polarity of light following the discovery of the corresponding infrared radiation.[8]

While Ritter has attracted a remarkable amount of attention among historians of science, scholars in the humanities have shown surprisingly little interest in him. Yet the natural sciences formed an integral part of early German Romanticism, as Friedrich Schlegel intimates when he takes the "jetzige Philophysik" to be the only sign of the times.[9] Rudolf Haym's verdict on Ritter seems to have had a lasting effect. In his famous book on the *Romantische Schule,* written in 1870, Haym maintains that Ritter's mind was confused, and that he seldom attempted to express concepts clearly.[10] Haym has no doubt as to the reason for Ritter's purportedly confused method: he puts it down to lack of education and knowledge.[11] Even today, only a very sparse number of publications in the fields of literary studies, philosophy or musicology have undertaken a reassessment of Haym's verdict. Ritter tends to be mentioned, if at all, only in a biographical context, as he was on friendly terms not only with Romantic poets such as Novalis, the Schlegels, and Achim von Arnim, but also with Goethe[12] and Herder.[13] Scholars of literature like to quote a celebrated passage from Novalis's letter to Caroline Schlegel of 20 January 1799, in which he extols his friend, punning on his surname (which means "knight"): "Ritter ist Ritter und wir sind nur Knappen." — By comparison, Novalis sees himself and his contemporaries as mere squires.[14] Similarly, Novalis describes Ritter in a letter from 31 January 1800 to Dietrich von Miltitz, requesting financial assistance, as "von Geist und Herz der herrlichste Mensch von der Welt," maintaining he is one of the noblest people, someone whose work holds endless promise (*WTBH*1:729:15–20). Not least, Ritter was held in high esteem by Goethe, who once called him an amazing apparition, a veritable giant of knowledge.[15] Despite these various endorsements, which come both from Goethe and from some of the most painstakingly researched Romantic figures, Ritter's name either does not appear or is mentioned only in passing in most of the recent comprehensive publications on early German Romanticism; moreover, it is conspicuously absent from those that focus on the aesthetics of music around 1800.[16]

This neglect of Ritter in the humanities seems to be due to various factors. The rather abstruse and scientific style of much of Ritter's work has hitherto prevented scholars from accessing his speculative philosophy, and particularly from recognizing his highly original contributions to questions of musical aesthetics.[17] Accordingly, Ritter's common epithet among critics is "dark" — an implicit reference both to Goethe[18] and to Novalis: "der philosophische, dunkle Ritter" (*WTBH*1:731:1). Simultaneously, however, the continuing disregard for Ritter in the humanities may well be due to the fact that Ritter's reflections on aesthetic matters are widely scattered over his *Fragmente aus dem Nachlasse eines jungen Physikers* (Fragments taken from the Literary Estate of a Young Physicist, 1810), a collection of disparate fragments put together by Ritter himself and published in the year of his death. The apparently fragmentary character of Ritter's thought has caused critics with an uncritical preference for systematic philosophy to look askance on his *Fragmente,* which, it is argued, undoubtedly point to an ambitious, pandynamic worldview, but sadly, owing to their fragmentary nature and the inadequacy of their over-ambitious author, fail to make up a system.[19] In the interest of a rehabilitation of Ritter's unsystematic work, it should be pointed out that the same could be said of Novalis, who paradigmatically stated and was faithful to his reservations concerning systematization, and, indeed, that early German Romanticism is largely characterized by its inability and unwillingness to systematize.

Yet the fact remains that Ritter's aesthetic reflections are developed in short notes, aphorisms, and fragmentary thoughts, which, as Wetzels puts it, run "the gamut from sheer nonsense, platitudes, playfully suggestive analogies, to scientific speculations,"[20] and, more important, in the extensive and relatively coherent, but at first glance almost frivolously mystical appendix to his *Fragmente.* Questions relating to the aesthetics of music are not of primary concern to Ritter in this work, and, as with Novalis, there is no biographical evidence for any kind of musical activity, nor does Ritter undertake any examination of a specific composer or composition. Ritter's elusive ideas concerning aesthetic questions nonetheless merit an analysis in the context of early German Romanticism, particularly as they reflect on the subject of language and incorporate certain quintessentially early Romantic concerns such as the natural sciences.

In contrast to the general neglect of his work in the humanities, Ritter received a distinguished endorsement from Walter Benjamin in the tradition of literary criticism. In a letter to Gershom Scholem dated 5 March 1924, Benjamin outlines his plans for a treatise on the origin of the German mourning play. After giving a brief account of the expected structure of his study, Benjamin mentions Ritter's name so prominently that it seems fair to assume that some of the latter's ideas lie at the core of his *Ursprung des deutschen Trauerspiels* (The Origin of the German Mourning Play, 1928), at least at this preliminary stage of its conception. Furthermore, Benjamin's commentary focuses on the relationship between music and language, and can therefore serve as a point of departure for us:

> Das letzte Kapitel [of the treatise on the German Mourning Play] führt reißend in die Sprachphilosophie hinein, indem es sich dabei um das Verhältnis von Schriftbild zu Sinnbestand handelt. Die Bestimmung der Arbeit ebenso wie ihr Entstehungsrhythmus erlaubt mir natürlich nicht, eine durchaus selbständige Entfaltung von Gedanken zu dieser Frage zu geben, die Jahre der Besinnung und des Studiums erfordern würde. Aber historische Theorien darüber gedenke ich in einer Anordnung vorzulegen, mit welcher ich die eigne Überlegung vorbereiten und andeuten

kann. Ganz erstaunlich ist in dieser Hinsicht Johann Wilhelm Ritter, der Romantiker, in dessen "Fragmenten eines jungen Physikers" Du im Anhange Erörterungen über die Sprache findest, deren Tendenz ist, das Schriftzeichen als ebenso natürliches oder offenbarungshaftes Element (dies beides im Gegensatz zu: konventionellem Element) zu statuieren[,] wie von jeher für die Sprachmystiker das Wort es ist[,] und zwar geht seine Deduktion nicht etwa vom bildhaften, hieroglyphischen der Schrift im gewöhnlichen Sinne dabei aus, sondern von dem Satze[,] daß das Schriftbild Bild des *Tones* ist und nicht etwa unmittelbar der bezeichneten Dinge.[21]

Several other remarks in Benjamin's letters[22] could be quoted in order to illustrate further the extraordinarily high esteem in which Benjamin held Ritter. For the most part, Benjamin is concerned here with the preface to Ritter's collection of fragments, a supplement that Ritter — in a typically Romantic manner — attributes to a fictional editor. According to Benjamin, Ritter's inimitable tone makes this much neglected preface the most significant piece of confessional prose ("Bekenntnisprosa") in German Romanticism.[23]

In the passage from the letter to Scholem cited above, however, Benjamin is exclusively concerned with Ritter's appendix to the *Fragmente,* in which he departs to some extent from the natural sciences. Benjamin attempts to interpret Ritter's text in terms of the philosophy of language. For him it is the problem of signification, the relationship between "Schriftbild" (signifier) and "Sinnbestand" (signified) that is at stake here. Benjamin implicitly recalls Haym's assessment of Ritter as the "Böhme des achtzehnten Jahrhunderts"(Böhme of the eighteenth century)[24] (although without Haym's pejorative emphasis), when he ascribes to Ritter the traditional mystical concept of linguistic representation that stresses *revelation* ("offenbarungshaftes Element") rather than *convention*. In Ritter's thought, Benjamin claims, language as such — the original and natural script — does not merely depict what it refers to in a hieroglyphic, pictorially reproductive way, but somehow corresponds to *tone*. In his correspondence with Scholem, however, Benjamin goes no further than to paraphrase what he takes to be Ritter's axiom regarding language: that linguistic representation does not directly correspond to so-called things, but is related to tone. Benjamin implies that a natural relationship between music and language must therefore lie at the heart of Ritter's aesthetic theory, in which the signified tends to withdraw behind its tone, or rather, to manifest itself only as an acoustic phenomenon. In other words, objects of representation are, in a manner of speaking, set in a state of oscillation. Hence the relationship between music and language appears to be to a great extent intrinsic rather than merely complementary. From Ritter's perspective, they have a common origin, and yet the question of the exact nature of their interaction remains to be answered.

The problems raised by this peculiar relation highlight a major difficulty in our understanding of Ritter's aesthetic deliberations. The referential relationship between music and language can only be understood against the background of Romantic Science (*Naturphilosophie*), whose most characteristic element is perhaps the presupposition of the original identity of *Natur* and *Geist*.[25] It follows from this tenet that the laws pertaining to each of these concepts are congruent and can be reciprocally translated or transposed. Chladni and Oersted had experimented with so-called *Klangfiguren* (sound-figures), attempting to make intelligible the silent, inner processes of nature,[26] above all with respect to electricity. As a physicist, Ritter had, of course, a natural interest in such experiments, and he was in close contact with Oersted, who studied with him for a while.[27]

Nevertheless, Ritter's claim went beyond such investigations, as is clear from the following remark taken from the appendix to his *Fragmente*: "— Schön wäre es, wie, was hier *äußerlich* klar würde, genau auch wäre, was *uns* die Klangfigur *innerlich* ist: — *Licht*figur, *Feuerschrift*" (R2:227). Here Ritter is obviously, albeit very tentatively and vaguely, trying to penetrate beyond mere externality. In general, the emphasis on introspection can be taken as characteristic of Ritter's attitude towards scientific experimentation: "Experimentation as an investigation of the self was the key technique of Ritter's strategy."[28] This peculiarity was appreciated by Novalis, who writes in his fragments:

647. Ein gutes physicalisches Experiment kann zum Muster eines innern Experiments dienen und ist *selbst ein* gutes *innres* subj[ectives] Experiment mit. (vid. Ritters Experimente) (*WTBH2*:625:16–18)[29]

In a more detailed comment, he focuses specifically on Ritter, maintaining that all external processes are to be seen symbolically as internal processes:

368. Ritter sucht durchaus die eigentliche Weltseele der Natur auf. Er will die sichtbaren und ponderablen Lettern lesen lernen, und das *Setzen* der höhern geistigen Kräfte erklären. Alle äußre Processe sollen als Symbole und lezte Wirkungen innerer Processe begreiflich werden. (*WTBH2*: 816:13–17)

In fact, the search for the *anima mundi* — the *Weltseele*, as Novalis terms it, in allusion to its prominent use by Schelling — involves an approach to nature, which, thanks to the supposed identity of *Natur* and *Geist*, unavoidably veers towards an investigation of the self. Chladni's and Oersted's *Klangfiguren* were no more than external visualizations of acoustic phenomena. Ritter's aim, however, is rather different in that he is attempting to theorize the inner representation of tone. It is in this context that he introduces the term *Lichtfigur*, an introspective analog to *Klangfigur*.

Against this background, the way that natural philosophy coalesces with the investigation of the self can be observed in Ritter's use of *light* as not only the central metaphor in his aesthetics of music, but also as the foundation for the inner unity of the organic universe in his physics, thus representing the medium of galvanism: "Licht ist jene Thätigkeit, die durch die Tiefen des Weltalls reicht, und zurück zum Atom, das Band, was alles und jegliches bindet" (R1:160 [244]). Furthermore, in this fundamental respect *light* is comparable only to *tone*. Ritter recalls to an extent the classical notion of *musica mundana* when he describes the cosmos and rotation of the planets in terms of music, maintaining that all objects are oscillating and that our music is allegorical with respect to the cosmological music:

> Die Umdrehung der Erde um ihre Axe z. B. mag einen bedeutenden Ton machen, d. i., die Schwingung ihrer inneren Verhältnisse, die dadurch veranlaßt ist; der Umgang um die Sonne einen Zweyten, der Umlauf des Mondes um die Erde einen dritten, u.s.w. Hier bekommt man die Idee von einer kolossalen Musik, von der unsere kleine gewiß nur eine sehr bedeutende Allegorie ist. Wir selbst, Thier, Pflanze, *alles* Leben, mag in diesen Tönen begriffen seyn. Ton und Leben werden hier Eins. [. . .] Diese Musik kann, als Harmonie, wohl nur in der Sonne gehört werden. Der Sonne ist das ganze Planetensystem Ein musikalisches Instrument. (R1:225–26 [360])

This cosmological view has a long tradition and is invoked frequently by Ritter's contemporaries;[30] only the speculative identification of the sun as the convergence point of this harmony can be considered Ritter's innovation. In any case, the fragment on the *musica mundana* certainly should not, as Salmen argues, be considered the focal point in Ritter's scattered observations on music.[31] Indeed, Benjamin does not even consider it worth mentioning in his commentary.

As music performs an internal function within nature, natural objects can be grasped most effectively through the medium of the tones they emit: "Jeder tönende Körper, oder vielmehr sein Ton, ist gleichsam der gefärbte Schatten seiner innern Qualität. —" (R1:162 [250]). By analogy to light, which is the tie linking all things — "das Band, was alles und jegliches bindet" —, Ritter conceives of *tone* as originally lying at the core of every natural being. In this respect his views are similar to many other Romantic figures, from Novalis[32] to Eichendorff[33] — even to a certain extent to Hölderlin.[34] Moreover, nature itself and its organic correlate, tone, are endowed with consciousness only insofar as they resonate musically:

> — Wie das Licht, so ist auch der *Ton Bewußtseyn*[.] Jeder Ton ist ein *Leben* des tönenden Körpers und in ihm, was so lange anhält, als der Ton, mit ihm aber erlischt. Ein ganzer Organismus von Oscillation und Figur, Gestalt, ist jeder Ton, wie jedes Organisch-Lebendige auch. Er spricht sein

Daseyn aus. Es ist gleichsam Frage an die Somnambüle, wenn ich den zu tönenden Körper mechanisch afficire. Er erwacht vom tiefen, gleichsam Ewigkeits-Schlafe; er antwortet; und im Antworten ist er nicht sowohl sich seiner, sondern, das Leben, der Organismus, der oder das *in* ihm hervorgerufen wird, ist sich seiner bewußt. (*R2:232*)

In view of these functional correspondences between *tone* and *light* in living nature on the one hand and human perception on the other, it is not surprising that the two elements are eventually made to coincide: "Also: *Ton und Licht stören sich nicht*! — Wie aber im Grunde auch *könnten* sie es, da sie ja *Eins* sind?" (*R2:268–69*).

The meditations on the internal representation of tone, therefore, coalesce to form a speculative view of nature that approximates it to a musical instrument. Hence, music is the medium that allows nature to be apprehended from the inside. Although Ritter describes nature as illuminated from within,[35] he considers sight to be inferior to hearing as an intuitive capacity:

> Das Gehör ist ein so äußerst reichhaltiger Sinn. Es fehlt noch an irgend einer Anleitung, ihm näher zu kommen. [. . .] In jedem Körper ist Alles, so auch das Unsichtbare, enthalten. Bey der Oscillation, Vibration, u.s.w., schwingt Alles. Alles wirkt nach Einem Schema sammt und sonders zugleich. Darum kommt's auf diesem Wege *ganz* in den Menschen. [. . .] Das Hören ist ein Sehen von innen, das innerstinnerste Bewußtseyn. Darum läßt sich auch mit dem Gehör tausendmal mehr ausrichten, als mit irgend einem andern Sinn. Der Gehörsinn ist unter allen Sinnen des Universums der höchste, größte, umfassendste, ja es ist der *einzige* allgemeine, der universelle Sinn. Es gilt keine Ansicht des Universums ganz und unbedingt, als die akustische —. (*R1:223–24 [358]*)

As music is inherent in nature and tone is the expression of inner quality, hearing enables the most intimate knowledge of nature. It is therefore seen as the most immanent and inward mode of perception.[36]

In accordance with this preference for hearing, music represents the medium most adequate to the task of reproducing nature at all levels. This is also due to the essential structure of musical phenomena as Ritter conceives of them. Thinking in terms of models of polarity lay at the methodological core of *Naturphilosophie,* which took its cue from Schelling's *Urpolarität,* the dualism fundamental to all nature. In his physics experiments, particularly those involving *light,* Ritter "had found polarities at work wherever he had looked."[37] This dualistic structure also underlies music (to be understood here for once in the stricter sense of the word) which, in its consummate form, encompasses the whole of nature:

> Der Begriff, Discant : Baß = — : + zeigt: daß alle rechte Musik nichts seyn könne, als eine Potenzirung beyder Gegensätze. Die vollständigste Musik ist die, welche vom Eisen bis zum Menschen geht. Es mag welche

geben, die nur bis Quecksilber, bis zum Salz, zum Wasser, zur Luft geht, die höchste aber geht bis zum Licht, d. i. zum Menschen —. (*R1*:223 [357])

Akin to this musically structured *ordo naturae*[38] that culminates in man[39] (or via *light* in some places even in God),[40] the internal dynamics of human society itself can be represented in terms of music:

> Töne sind Wesen, die einander verstehen, so wie wir den Ton. Jeder Accord schon mag ein Tonverständniß unter einander seyn, und als bereits gebildete Einheit zu uns kommen. Accord wird Bild von Geistergemeinschaft, Liebe, Freundschaft, u.s.w. Harmonie Bild und Ideal der Gesellschaft. Es muß schlechterdings kein menschliches Verhältniß, keine menschliche Geschichte geben, die sich nicht durch Musik ausdrücken ließe. Ganze Völkergeschichten, ja die gesammte Menschengeschichte, muß sich musikalisch aufführen lassen; und vollkommen identisch. Denn der hier sprechende Geist ist derselbe, wie der unsere, und seine Verhältnisse zu seinen Geschwistern sind dieselben, wie die unsrigen zu unsern Geschwistern. (*R2*:233)

In this sense, musical structures acquire an allegorical status with respect to humanity: a chord, for example, stands for intellectual affinity, love, and friendship.

Tone, therefore, inheres in all nature as a basic and ubiquitous principle, and the whole of creation is exposed as an organism that oscillates within itself[41] and can thus be represented in music: "Alles Leben ist Musik, und alle Musik als Leben selbst — zum wenigsten sein *Bild*" (*R2*:235). Once we have clarified this premise, we can finally turn our attention to Ritter's conception of the fundamental relationship between music and language. Thanks to the influence of tone on nature, natural things transpose their oscillations directly into *Klangfiguren,* thus revealing their true essence. Furthermore, as an external visible form — a *Klangfigur* — tone naturally corresponds to and, indeed, even produces *Buchstaben* (letters): "Aller Buchstabe ist Klangfigur" (*R2*:243). As tone evolves from oscillation, words emerge beside tone: "Alle Oscillation aber giebt Ton, und damit Wort" (*R2*:229). Hence, the most ancient alphabet — the original and natural script that Ritter hoped to reconstruct by distilling its elements from *Klangfiguren*[42] — consists of letters that are formed by analogy to manifestations of oscillation: "Jeder Ton hat somit seinen Buchstaben immediate bey sich; und es ist die Frage, ob wir nicht überhaupt nur *Schrift* hören, — *lesen,* wenn wir hören, — Schrift *sehen!*" (*R2*:227–28). Thanks to this correspondence between script and tone via the *Klangfigur,* the senses of hearing and seeing (or, alternatively, reading) are so closely related as to be practically synonymous: "— Und ist nicht jedes Sehen mit dem *innern* Auge *Hören,* und Hören ein Sehen von und durch *innen?*" (*R2*:228). Such synesthetic statements cast further light on Ritter's conception of the *Lichtfigur* as an introspective analog to the *Klangfigur.*

In Ritter's aesthetics of music, all acoustic phenomena and faculties are grounded in the premise of the intrinsic correlation of light and tone. Thus, hearing is conceived as an inward seeing directed towards the *Lichtfigur*. Ritter's disruption of the relationship between light and vision in the metaphorical substructure of his aesthetics of music can perhaps even be related to his insistence on the possibility of "invisible light" in his physics.[43]

An important implication of this in the field of natural philosophy is that the representational value of language is related to the status of tone in nature. According to Ritter, referentiality has two preconditions: that the signified world expresses itself in terms of music and that the act of signification absorbs oscillation. Language is considered a direct transformation of the inner condition of nature, and the letter — the basic component of script — is oscillating, as oscillation is script. Consequently, and thanks to its reliance on the *Klangfigur*, language as such is seen as an oscillating phenomenon: "Das Wort schreibt, der Buchstabe tönt" (*R2:242*). This seemingly paradoxical statement reveals Ritter's fundamental ideas on the matter of representation: that tone is script and, conversely, that script is tone. These two aspects cannot be separated from one another; similarly: "Wort und Schrift sind gleich an ihrem Ursprunge eins, und keines ohne das andere möglich" (*R2:229*). Script, therefore, necessarily impacts upon tone, as it can be apprehended "nur am und durch den *Ton*" (*R2:242*). Effectively, thanks to its congruity with *light*, which forms "das Band, was alles und jegliches bindet," tone guarantees that an object can be represented at all: "Der Ton selbst aber ist *Licht*, das ohnehin einem anderen Sinne, als dem *Auge*, gehören mußte, weil das Auge das Licht *nicht* sieht, sondern nur *vermittelst* des Lichts = Tons" (*R2:242*).

Finally, let us return to Walter Benjamin. His letter to Scholem of 1924 quoted above anticipates a more extensive examination of Ritter in the 1925 investigation of the *Ursprung des deutschen Trauerspiels*.[44] In view of the complexity of Ritter's argument, it is no longer surprising, then, that Benjamin comments so tentatively on Ritter's *Fragmente*, "in welche[n] dem Forscher aus einem Briefe über die Chladnyschen Klangfiguren unterm Schreiben vielleicht fast absichtslos die vieles kräftig oder tastender umgreifenden Gedanken sich entspinnen." The genesis of Ritter's complex thoughts is linked with Chladni's *Klangfiguren*.[45] In the course of his reflections on the status of music in the context of the allegorical drama, Benjamin quotes a long excerpt from Ritter's appendix, much of which has already been discussed above. Benjamin's comments on these excerpts are somewhat vague:

> Mit dieser Ausführung schließt die virtuelle romantische Theorie der Allegorie gleichsam fragend ab. Und jede Antwort hätte diese Rittersche Divination unter die ihr gemäßen Begriffe zu bringen; Laut- und Schriftsprache, wie auch immer einander zu nähern, so doch nicht anders als

dialektisch, als Thesis und Synthesis, zu identifizieren, jenem antitheti-
schen Mittelgliede der *Musik, der letzten Sprache aller Menschen nach
dem Turmbau,* die ihr gebührende zentrale Stelle der Antithesis zu
sichern und wie aus ihr, nicht aber aus dem Sprachlaut unmittelbar, die
Schrift erwächst, zu erforschen. Aufgaben, die weit über das [*sic*] Bereich
romantischer Intuitionen wie auch untheologischen Philosophierens
hinausliegen.[46]

The present article is, of course, far from being able to deal with the questions Benjamin raises in this quotation, especially as they must be considered
in the context of his reflections on the subject of allegory. In the quotation
Benjamin tries above all to relate thesis, synthesis, and antithesis to spoken
and written language, and music. However, the intrinsic correlation between
music and language in Ritter's aesthetics of music, intimated by Benjamin
in his exposition of his dialectical method, and the grounding of this relationship in natural philosophy ought to have been elucidated in the course
of this discussion.

The broader influence of Ritter's thought on Benjamin's — and possibly
even on Scholem's[47] — philosophy of language has yet to be investigated,
and the marking of music as the "letzte Sprache aller Menschen nach dem
Turmbau" (the last universal language after Babel), as well as Benjamin's
implicit claim for the support of theology, give a hint in this respect. There
is no biographical evidence that Benjamin examined Ritter before 1924.
Nevertheless, it is likely that Benjamin first became acquainted with Ritter
in the course of writing his dissertation on the *Begriff der Kunstkritik in
der deutschen Romantik* (The Concept of Art Criticism in German
Romanticism) in 1918/19. As early as 1916, Benjamin produced one of
his major essays on the philosophy of language, entitled "Über Sprache
überhaupt und über die Sprache des Menschen" (On Language as Such
and on the Language of Man), in which he introduced the idea of a pure
and perfect language ("reine Sprache") that originates in the word of God,
but which has been lost in its original condition through man's sinfulness.
God's word still resonates throughout the whole of creation and may be
traced by means of translation.[48] In 1921 Benjamin wrote his famous essay
Die Aufgabe des Übersetzers (The Task of the Translator). Although this
essay precedes the first explicit reference to Ritter in the letter to Scholem,
it is clear that Benjamin's interest in Ritter can be related to his reflections
on "reine Sprache," when he quotes Rudolf Pannwitz: "er [the translator]
muß, zumal wenn er aus einer sehr fernen sprache überträgt, auf die letzten elemente der sprache selbst, wo wort, bild, ton in eins geht, zurück-
dringen [. . .]."[49] Ritter's search for an original and natural script that feeds
from his physics into his philosophy of language therefore seems to fore-
shadow Benjamin's Messianic conception of a history of language that will
culminate in the recurrence of the "reine Sprache." However, here we are
entering the realm of speculation, as Ritter's influence on Benjamin is given

only brief and rare mention in the secondary literature,[50] and this article has been able to point out only one aspect of their relationship. Ritter's relevance to Benjamin's philosophy of language clearly deserves more scholarly attention.

Notes

[1] See, for instance, Walter D. Wetzels, "Johann Wilhelm Ritter: Romantic Physics in Germany," in *Romanticism and the Sciences,* ed. Andrew Cunningham and Nicholas Jardine (Cambridge: Cambridge UP, 1990), 199–212 (here, 199–200).

[2] For possible translations of the German term *Naturphilosophie* (*natural philosophy* or *Romantic Science*) see Noel Deeney, "The Romantic Science of J. W. Ritter," *The Maynooth Review* 8 (1983): 43–59 (here, 43).

[3] See Dietrich von Engelhardt, "Romantik — im Spannungsfeld von Naturgefühl, Naturwissenschaft und Naturphilosophie: Einführendes Referat," in *Romantik in Deutschland: Ein interdisziplinäres Symposion,* special vol. of *Deutsche Vierteljahresschrift für Literaturwissenschaft und Geistesgeschichte,* ed. Richard Brinkmann (Stuttgart: Metzler, 1978), 167–74 (here, 169).

[4] Ibid., 169–70.

[5] "Die Genialität von Ritters naturwissenschaftlichen Leistungen wurde in der Folgezeit unterschätzt; niemals wußte er seine Entdeckungen zur Geltung zu bringen." Ricarda Huch, *Die Romantik: Ausbreitung, Blütezeit und Verfall* (Tübingen: Rainer Wunderlich, 1951), 218.

[6] See also Deeney's article, "Romantic Science," 57, in which it is argued that "science and Romanticism should not be seen as any embarrassment to each other, for they are two remarkably similar forms of thought."

[7] See Wilhelm Ostwald, "Johann Wilhelm Ritter," in Johann Wilhelm Ritter, *Fragmente aus dem Nachlasse eines jungen Physikers: Ein Taschenbuch für Freunde der Natur,* ed. Steffen and Birgit Dietzsch (Hanau/Main: Müller & Kiepenheuer, 1984), 321–43.

[8] On this see Wetzels, "Ritter: Romantic Physics," and for a brief survey of Ritter-reception see Wetzels, *Johann Wilhelm Ritter: Physik im Wirkungsfeld der deutschen Romantik* (Berlin & New York: Walter de Gruyter, 1973), vii–ix. See also Dorothee Hüffmeier-von-Hagen, "J. W. Ritter und die Anfänge der Elektrophysiologie," in *Von Boerhaave bis Berger,* ed. K. E. Rothschuh (Stuttgart: G. Fischer, 1964), 48–61; Jean-Paul Guiot, "Zur Entdeckung der ultravioletten Strahlen durch Johann Wilhelm Ritter," *Archives internationales d'histoire des sciences* 35 (1985): 346–56; Hans-Georg Bartel, "Johann Wilhelm Ritters Gedanken zur Selbstorganisation," *Jahrbuch für Komplexität in den Natur-, Sozial- und Geisteswissenschaften* 3 (1992): 113–28; and M. Tausch, M. Woock, and A. Grolmuss, "Vom Lichtquanz zum Sehreiz," *Praxis der Naturwissenschaften. Physik* 47:5 (1998): 26–30. On Ritter in the explicit context of *Naturphilosophie* see Wolfgang Hartwig, "Physik als Kunst: Über die naturphilosophischen Gedanken Johann Wilhelm Ritters" (Ph.D. diss.: Freiburg i. Br., 1955); also Renato Musto, "Speculazione filosofica e sperimentazione

fisica nella Naturphilosophie," *Annali: Sezione Germanica: Istituto universitario orientale di Napoli* 3:1–3 (1993): 45–69; and Musto, "Fisica Romantica," *Intersezioni* 9:1 (1989): 87–114. See also the explanatory notes in Johann Wilhelm Ritter, *Die Begründung der Elektrochemie und die Entdeckung der ultravioletten Strahlen,* ed. Armin Hermann (Frankfurt a. M.: Akademische Verlagsgesellschaft, 1968); also Johann Wilhelm Ritter, *Entdeckungen zur Elektrochemie, Bioelektrochemie und Photochemie,* ed. Hermann Berg and Klaus Richter (Leipzig: Geest & Portig, 1986).

⁹ See Schlegel's letter to Schleiermacher in *Aus Schleiermachers Leben: In Briefen,* ed. L. Jonas and W. Dilthey (Berlin: G. Reimer, 1858–63), 3:154.

¹⁰ "[. . .] krankhafte Verworrenheit des Ritter'schen Geistes" and "Am seltensten begegnet der Versuch, irgend einen Begriff durch schärferes Denken zur Klarheit zu bringen." Rudolf Haym, *Die romantische Schule: Ein Beitrag zur Geschichte des deutschen Geistes* (Berlin: Rudolph Gaertner, 1870), 616, 617. Similarly, Ricarda Huch speaks of a "trüben, verworrenen Kopfe," concluding: "Und Ritters Neigung zur Mystik scheint auch in einer gewissen Unklarheit seines Denkens begründet gewesen zu sein." Huch, *Die Romantik,* 218.

¹¹ "[. . .] eine der Hauptursachen dieser krankhaft wuchernden, wilden Geistreichigkeit [ist] die Unbildung und die Unwissenheit des Verfassers." Haym, *Die romantische Schule,* 618.

¹² See Carl Graf von Klinckowstroem, "Goethe und Ritter," *Jahrbuch der Goethe-Gesellschaft* 8 (1921): 135–51.

¹³ See Ritter's own preface to his *Fragmente,* where he pays tribute to his fatherly friend and mentor: *Fragmente aus dem Nachlasse eines jungen Physikers: Ein Taschenbuch für Freunde der* Natur, ed. Arthur Henkel with an afterword by Heinrich Schipperges, 2 vols. in one (1810: facsimile reprint, Heidelberg: Lambert Schneider, 1969), xxxi. Subsequent references to this work are cited in the text using the abbreviation *"R"* and giving the relevant volume and page numbers [with the square brackets referring to the fragment number]. Further details available in Klaus Richter, "Der Physiker Ritter und Johann Gottfried Herder," *Impulse: Aufsätze, Quellen, Berichte zur deutschen Klassik und Romantik* 3 (1981): 109–19. For general information on Ritter's biography see Schipperges's afterword to the aforementioned edition, [1]-[37], and Steffen and Birgit Dietzsch's postscript to the Müller & Kiepenheuer edition of *Fragmente* referred to in note 7, 344–64.

¹⁴ *Werke, Tagebücher und Briefe Friedrich von Hardenbergs,* ed. Hans-Joachim Mähl and Richard Samuel (Munich: Hanser, 1978–87), 1:686, line 1. Subsequent references to this work are cited in the text using the abbreviation *"WTBH,"* and giving the relevant volume, page, and line numbers.

¹⁵ "Wissenshimmel auf Erden." Letter from Goethe to Schiller of 28 September 1800, in Johann Wolfgang Goethe, *Mit Schiller: Briefe, Tagebücher und Gespräche vom 24. Juni 1794 bis zum 9. Mai 1805,* ed. Volker C. Dörr and Norbert Oellers, series II/vol. 5 [= vol. 32] of Goethe, *Sämtliche Werke,* ed. Karl Eibl (Frankfurt a. M.: Deutscher Klassiker Verlag, 1999), 77. For the esteem in which Ritter was held by Romantic contemporaries such as the Schlegels, Achim von Arnim, Oersted, etc., see also Schipperges's and Dietzsch's afterwords to the *Fragmente,* or Walter

Salmen, "Fragmente zur romantischen Musikanschauung von J. W. Ritter," *Saarbrücker Studien zur Musikwissenschaft* 1 (1966): 235–41 (here, 236–37).

[16] See, for instance, Walter Salmen, ed., *Beiträge zur Geschichte der Musikanschauung im 19. Jahrhundert* (Regensburg: Bosse, 1965); Peter le Huray and James Day, eds., *Music and Aesthetics in the Eighteenth and Early-Nineteenth Centuries* (Cambridge: Cambridge UP, 1988); Barbara Naumann, *"Musikalisches Ideen-Instrument": Das Musikalische in Poetik und Sprachtheorie der Frühromantik* (Stuttgart: Metzler, 1990); and Gerhart Hoffmeister, *Deutsche und europäische Romantik* (Stuttgart: Metzler, 1990).

[17] An exception is Salmen's short article: "Fragmente." Salmen deals exclusively with fragments from the main section of Ritter's *Fragmente aus dem Nachlasse eines jungen Physikers;* however, he ignores the appendix, which is actually most relevant to these questions as it is concerned with language.

[18] See vol. II/4 [=31] of Goethe, *Sämtliche Werke,* 580: "Ritters Vortrag ist freilich dunkel und für den[,] der sich von der Sache unterrichten will[,] nicht angenehm."

[19] "[. . .] zwar allesamt auf ein groß angelegtes pandynamisches Weltbild hinweisen, sich aber *tragischerweise* wegen der inneren *Brüchigkeit* und wegen des dazu *unzureichenden Vermögens* des früh sich am Erkenntnisstreben *verzehrenden* Autors nicht zu einem System zusammenfügen ließen." Salmen, "Fragmente," 241 (my italics for emphasis).

[20] See Wetzels, "Ritter: Romantic Physics," 210. Salmen comes to similar conclusions in "Fragmente," 237.

[21] Walter Benjamin, *Gesammelte Briefe,* ed. Theodor-W.-Adorno-Archiv, 3 vols. (Frankfurt a. M.: Suhrkamp, 1996–97), vol. 2 (1919–24), ed. Christoph Gödde and Henri Lonitz, 437.

[22] For example, in the continuation of the passage just quoted, Benjamin maintains that Ritter's preface is a perfect example of Romantic esotericism: "Das Buch von Ritter ist ferner unvergleichlich durch seine Vorrede, die mir ein Licht darüber aufgesteckt hat, was eigentlich romantische Esoterik wirklich ist. Dagegen ist Novalis ein Volksredner" (ibid.). Again, Ritter's inaccessibility seems to be his prime characteristic. Less than a year later Benjamin again draws Scholem's attention to Ritter, and again to his preface to the *Fragmente:* "Kennst Du Johann Wilhelm Ritter? Machte ich Dich auf die 'Fragmente aus dem Nachlaß eines jungen Physikers' nicht schon aufmerksam. Ihre Einleitung ist die extremste Romantik, die mir — im Moralischen — je vorgekommen ist und unendlich fesselnd" (vol. 3 of *Gesammelte Briefe* [1925–30], 17). See there too Benjamin's letter to Alfred Cohn of 1928 (p. 376).

[23] Walter Benjamin, *Gesammelte Schriften,* ed. Rolf Tiedemann and Hermann Schweppenhäuser (Frankfurt a. M.: Suhrkamp, 1972), vol. 4/1, ed. Tillman Rexroth, 176–77. This quotation is taken from a compilation of letters entitled *Deutsche Menschen,* in which Benjamin included a letter by Johann Wilhelm Ritter to Franz von Baader and prefaced it with a brief portrait of the former.

[24] See Haym, *Die romantische Schule,* 618.

[25] See, for instance, Dietrich von Engelhardt, "Die Naturwissenschaft der Aufklärung und die romantisch-idealistische Naturphilosophie," in *Idealismus und Aufklärung: Kontinuität und Kritik der Aufklärung in Philosophie und Poesie um 1800,* ed.

Christoph Jamme and Gerhard Kurz (Stuttgart: Klett-Cotta, 1988), 80–96 (here, 90).

[26] See Naumann, *"Musikalisches Ideen-Instrument,"* 46–47. See also Bettine Menke, "Adressiert in der Abwesenheit: Zur romantischen Poetik und Akustik der Töne," in *Die Adresse des Mediums,* ed. Stefan Andriopoulos, Gabriele Schabacher, and Eckhard Schumacher, vol. 2 of Mediologie (Cologne: DuMont, 2001), 100–20.

[27] On this see Dan Ch. Christensen, "The Oersted-Ritter Partnership and the Birth of Romantic Natural Philosophy," *Annals of Science* 52 (1995): 153–85.

[28] Simon Schaffer, "Genius in Romantic Natural Philosophy," in *Romanticism and the Sciences,* ed. Cunningham and Jardine (as note 1), 82–98 (here, 91).

[29] On experimentation and subjectivity see also Fergus Henderson, "Novalis, Ritter and 'Experiment': A Tradition of 'Active Empiricism,'" in *The Third Culture: Literature and Science,* ed. Elinor S. Shaffer (Berlin and New York: Walter de Gruyter, 1998), 153–69, and Shaffer, "Romantische Naturphilosophie: Zum Begriff des 'Experiments' bei Novalis, Ritter und Schelling," in *Novalis und die Wissenschaften,* ed. Herbert Uerlings (Tübingen: Niemeyer, 1997), 121–42 (here, 129–31).

[30] For *musica mundana* or *musica coelestis* in the eyes of Ritter's contemporaries see, for instance, Salmen, "Fragmente," 238–40. In the history of thought it is argued that Kepler passed on the classical idea of a musically structured cosmos to subsequent generations.

[31] "[. . .] das Kernstück der verstreuten Niederschriften Ritters zur Musikan schauung." Ibid., 239.

[32] For the relevance of music in Novalis see, for instance, Naumann, *"Musikalisches Ideen-Instrument,"* 158–240. See especially the tale of the merchants in *Heinrich von Ofterdingen,* which describes how "die mannichfaltigen Töne und die sonderbaren Sympathien und Ordnungen in die Natur gekommen seyn, indem vorher alles wild, unordentlich und feindselig gewesen ist" (*WTBH*1:257:15–18; the entire narrative: *WTBH*1:256–59). See also *Die Lehrlinge zu Saïs* for declarations similar to the following: "O! daß der Mensch, sagten sie, die innre Musik der Natur verstände, und einen Sinn für äußere Harmonie hätte" (*WTBH*1:218:28–30).

[33] See, for instance, Eichendorff's famous poem "Wünschelrute" (Wishing Rod, 1835) in Joseph von Eichendorff, *Werke,* ed. Jost Perfahl (Düsseldorf/Zurich: Artemis & Winkler, 1996), 1:132.

[34] See Pierre Bertaux, *Friedrich Hölderlin* (Frankfurt a. M.: Suhrkamp, 1978), 322–24. Bertaux quotes extensively, but does not analyze Ritter's relationship to Hölderlin and music (the chapter is entitled "Die Welt der Töne"). On Hölderlin's conception of music and its cosmological import see particularly Hans Joachim Kreutzer, "Tönende Ordnung der Welt: Über die Musik in Hölderlins Lyrik," in Kreutzer, *Obertöne: Literatur und Musik: Neun Abhandlungen über das Zusammenspiel der Künste* (Würzburg: Königshausen & Neumann, 1994), 67–102 (here, 84–93).

[35] See also fragment 459: *"Alles Leben* scheint in *Leuchten* ausbrechen zu wollen" (*R*2:64).

³⁶ In contrast to this see Salmen's comment: "Im Hören öffnet sich der mitgestaltende Mensch einer jenseitig unendlichen Welt. Er wird der Transzendenz inne, der er mit der Kraft der Sehnsucht aus der Befangenheit im Diesseits für Augenblicke entlassen entgegenstrebt." Salmen, "Fragmente," 238.

³⁷ Wetzels, "Ritter: Romantic Physics," 207.

³⁸ See also *R*2:237–39. For a discussion of the role of "Naturkreis" and "Stufenleiter" in Ritter, see Steffen Dietzsch, "Naturforschung und Historizität: Zu Johann Wilhelm Ritters geschichtlichem Naturbegriff," *Wissenschaftliche Zeitschrift der Friedrich-Schiller-Universität Jena: Gesellschaftswissenschaftliche Reihe* 34:3 (1985): 337–41 (here, 339).

³⁹ See also Peter Kapitza, *Die frühromantische Theorie der Mischung: Über den Zusammenhang von romantischer Dichtungstheorie und zeitgenössischer Chemie* (Munich: Fink, 1968), 87.

⁴⁰ See fragment 618, which seems to be inspired by biblical speech rather than by natural philosophy: "Licht = Gott. Sehen = Gottesanschauung. Auge = Gottessinn. Licht das Gute, der gute Gott, die Güte. Finsterniß das Böse, Gottesabwesenheit, Sünde" (*R*2:198).

⁴¹ *Galvanism* subsumes these phenomena, since "jede Klangfigur [ist] eine electrische, und jede electrische eine Klangfigur [. . .]" (*R*2:229–30).

⁴² "[. . .] ich wollte hierauf also die *Ur*- oder *Natur*schrift auf electrischem Wege wiederfinden oder doch suchen [. . .]" (*R*2:230).

⁴³ See Guiot, "Entdeckung der ultravioletten Strahlen," 352–53.

⁴⁴ See also Michael Rumpf, *Spekulative Literaturtheorie: Zu Walter Benjamins Trauerspielbuch* (Königstein/Ts.: Forum Academicum, 1980), 105–6.

⁴⁵ Walter Benjamin, *Ursprung des deutschen Trauerspiels* (Frankfurt a. M.: Suhrkamp, 1963), 241.

⁴⁶ Ibid., 242 (my italics for emphasis).

⁴⁷ For Scholem see, for example, Sigrid Weigel, "Gershom Scholems Sprachtheorie zwischen Kabbala und Klagelied," in *Homo medietas: Aufsätze zu Religiosität, Literatur und Denkformen des Menschen vom Mittelalter bis in die Neuzeit*, ed. Claudia Brinker-von der Heyde and Niklaus Largier (Bern: Peter Lang, 1999), 521–32.

⁴⁸ Walter Benjamin, "Über Sprache überhaupt und über die Sprache des Menschen," in Benjamin, *Angelus Novus: Ausgewählte Schriften* (Frankfurt a. M.: Suhrkamp, 1966), 2:9–26.

⁴⁹ Walter Benjamin, "Die Aufgabe des Übersetzers," in Benjamin, *Illuminationen: Ausgewählte Schriften*, ed. Siegfried Unseld (Frankfurt a. M.: Suhrkamp, 1961), 56–69 (here, 68).

⁵⁰ See, for instance, Winfried Menninghaus, *Walter Benjamins Theorie der Sprachmagie* (Frankfurt a. M.: Suhrkamp, 1995), and also Jean-Pierre Schobinger, *Variationen zu Walter Benjamins Sprachmeditationen* (Basel/Stuttgart: Schwabe, 1979), 94. I am much indebted to the author of this study for drawing my attention to Benjamin's philosophy of language in the context of Johann Wilhelm Ritter.

Music and Non-Verbal Reason in
E. T. A. Hoffmann

Jeanne Riou

IN THE FOLLOWING, attention will be focused on issues of Romantic musical aesthetics in E. T. A. Hoffmann. Music is a libidinally driven and dangerous experience in Hoffmann, holding the promise of transcendence in the Romantic sense, which is partially a protest against the rationalizations of modern life. Hoffmann's outsider-protagonists, through their pursuit of artistic transcendence, often sacrifice their ability to function as rational beings. While the disruption of rational identity is a feature of almost all Romantic writing, it is intensified in Hoffmann and takes on a psychological character that is absent in, for instance, Novalis. The radicalized form of transcendence — the violent and self-destructive nature of madness in Hoffmann-protagonists such as Medardus, Ettlinger, or Nathanael — leaves no doubt that in Hoffmann's works the Romantic tendency to undermine identity as a transitional phase in coming to a fuller understanding of human experience is turned into something with more disturbing consequences.

This contribution will argue that parallel to the Romantic motif of art leading to madness is the narration of an aesthetic subjectivity that is not so much irrational as governed by sensations that are inadmissible in a strictly rational sense, because they are not capable of being translated into either verbal reasoning or visible messages. By this, I refer to auditory sensations and, more specifically, the experience of music, which seems, in the instance of Kreisler, to be far from irrational in itself. Kreisler does not hover on the verges of sanity simply because he is a composer, but because something about composition pushes him towards a sense of longing that draws him into conflict with his mercenary environment.

It should be noted at the outset, however, that Hoffmann is one of the least theoretically motivated of the Romantic authors and would have had little interest in using music to challenge the framework of Enlightenment reason. Nevertheless, his work narrates subjectivity in a way that is primarily acoustic, and this does have implications for how the borders of the rational/irrational are conceived. Hoffmann's comments on transcendence in his musical writings cannot be taken literally. These writings lack conceptual stringency, and in his contributions to the *Allgemeine Musikalische Zeitung* (The General Music Newspaper) from 1808 onwards, Hoffmann is not always an authoritative commentator. However, it is possible to find in his literary renditions of musical experience some clarification of his thoughts about music. In this essay I discuss Hoffmann's ironic use of musical transcendence and examine the utopian dimension of musical performance. This is followed by a discussion of the rationality of art and how Adorno treats its utopian potential. The final section, returning to Romantic hermeneutics, examines the idea of music as non-verbal reason.

Entertainment versus Utopia: Hoffmann's Johannes Kreisler and the Hazards of Composition

Johannes Kreisler's *Gedanken über den hohen Wert der Musik* (Reflections on the High Value of Music, 1815) from the *Kreisleriana* (Kreisler Papers, 1812–20) begins with a damningly ironic account of how music lessons are essential to good taste in society's better circles. Art, Kreisler comments, is purely about entertainment.[1] It offers us distraction from the serious demands of life. In the case of reading, care has to be taken to avoid "fantastic" literature, where imagination has the unwanted effect that the reader might actually have to think about what he or she is reading. Paintings are harmless, since as soon as the beholder realizes what a painting represents, he or she has lost all interest. Music, Kreisler concludes, is nevertheless the most harmless of all art forms, since, providing it is fairly simple, people can carry on conversations while listening (*FN,* 36). Later, Kreisler refers to Romantic art, and how its pursuit of a "higher principle" seems so abhorrent to the mercenary world around it (*FN,* 39).

The *Kreisleriana* end on a characteristic note of dual identity. Writing his own ironic apprentice's certificate, Kreisler claims that the musician is always surrounded by both melody and harmony. Furthermore, what inspires composition are impulses from other sensual channels: colors, odors, rays — all of which "appear" to the musician as notes (*FN,* 326). Referring to Ritter's *Fragmente aus dem Nachlaß eines jungen Physikers* (Fragments taken from the Literary Estate of a Young Physicist, 1810), Kreisler describes music as an inner seeing:

> So wie, nach dem Ausspruch eines geistreichen Physikers, Hören ein Sehen von innen ist, so wird dem Musiker das Sehen ein Hören von innen, nämlich zum innersten Bewußtsein der Musik, die mit seinem Geiste gleichmäßig vibrierend aus allem ertönt, was sein Auge erfaßt. So würden die plötzlichen Anregungen des Musikers, das Entstehen der Melodien im Innern, das bewußtlose oder vielmehr in Worten nicht

darzulegende Erkennen und Auffassen der geheimen Musik der Natur als Prinzip des Lebens oder alles Wirkens in demselben sein (*FN,* 326).[2]

The last part of the quotation deals with the concept of the secret music of nature, which is seen as an allegory for life. Ritter asks whether there could possibly be such a thing as a thought or an idea without its particular medium and sign.[3] He defines music as a type of composite medium and sees language as an individuation of music that necessarily relates to music.[4] These thoughts echo Schlegel's reflections on the idea of art as formal continuum,[5] which in turn are influenced by Lessing's *Laokoon* (1766).

Hoffmann's figure of Johannes Kreisler should, therefore, not be taken as the type of artist whose work transcends all matter. His work and artistic subjectivity are inherently shifting between the different media of experience. Johannes Kreisler's problem is one of expression and representation. He embodies the eighteenth-century musical debate on the merits of melody or harmony: Rameau, Carl Philipp Emanuel Bach, or Rousseau. Although Hoffmann in his musical essay, *Alte und neue Kirchenmusik* (Ancient and Modern Church Music, 1814), claims that the musical voice is the ultimate triumph of expression over the ambivalence of construction, this is not borne out by the experience of Johannes Kreisler in the novel *Lebens-Ansichten des Katers Murr* (The Life and Opinions of the Tomcat Murr, 1819–21). On a theoretical level, Hoffmann may write of the operatic voice and its promise of transcendence, but there is no escaping the problem that this cannot bypass society. In other words, the alienation described by Jean-Jacques Rousseau in his *Discours sur l'Origine de l'Inégalité parmi les Hommes* (Second Discourse on Inequality, 1755) which was to have such a profound influence on the latter half of the eighteenth century, from Herder to Schiller to the Romantics, is a theme not surprisingly echoed by Hoffmann. If music awakens a longing for the archaic or for something that has been lost in the process of civilization, the question is: what status may we ascribe to this? Is music, therefore, a private experience, solipsistic in its essence, transcendent of time itself, and a disavowal of modernity?

Kater Murr, Hoffmann's second novel, is a parody of bourgeois identity.[6] In line with the caricature of musical taste in *Gedanken über den hohen Wert der Musik,* his novel shows the artist (Kreisler) to be at odds with society. He is an emblem of artistry, which is ambivalent in the bourgeois world. The Kreisler of *Kater Murr* can find neither total expression nor the pure sound to which he aspires. The closest he comes is the momentary promise of transcendence when he hears Julia singing. This turns into an erotic fixation. It is ironic that Julia becomes the object of physical desire, as Kreisler and Julia embody different types of expression: Julia represents unmediated expression, as opposed to Kreisler, who must accommodate himself within the rules of composition. This is made clear in the first meeting between the two. In this early incident Kreisler throws away his guitar in despair because he cannot tune it. Julia, unperturbed by the idio-syncrasies of tuning, picks up the guitar and begins to sing:

> Julia konnte es nicht unterlassen, sie schlug einen Akkord auf dem zier-lichen Instrument an, und erschrak beinahe über den mächtigen vollen Klang, der aus dem kleinen Dinge heraustönte. "O herrlich — herrlich," rief sie aus und spielte weiter. Da sie aber gewohnt, nur ihren Gesang mit der Gitarre zu begleiten, so konnte es nicht fehlen, daß sie bald unwillkürlich zu singen begann, indem sie weiter fortwandelte.[7]

The contrast between Kreisler and Julia is one that underlies all of Hoffmann's writing. Singers like Julia, Antonie in *Rat Krespel* (Councillor Krespel, 1816), or Donna Anna in *Don Juan* (1812) always represent direct, immediate emotion. By contrast to the male composer or musician who has to struggle with the principles of composition, the female singer embodies music as something that is not only pre-reflexive, but defies all need for a reflexive consciousness. As the embodiment of a pure sound, Julia, unlike Kreisler, is able to express her innermost self. The criterion for her spontaneous expression is that she should be outside language. Like so many of Hoffmann's heroines, she is given an arsenal of sighs and gentle sounds to match her particular mood. Meister Abraham, filling Kreisler in on the details of the celebrations on the night of the storm, does not fail to observe Julia's reaction:

> Sowie Pauken und Trompeten schwiegen, fiel Julien unter duftenden Nachtviolen versteckte aufbrechende Rosenknospe in den Schoß, und wie strömender Hauch des Nachtwindes schwammen die Töne deines tief ins Herz dringenden Liedes herüber: Mi lagnèro tacendo della mia sorte amara. — Julie war erschrocken, als aber das Lied, das ich, ich sag es damit du über die Art des Vortrags etwa nicht in bange Zweifel gerätst, von unsern vier vortrefflichen Bassetthornisten ganz in der Ferne spielen ließ — begann; entfloh ein leichtes Ach ihren Lippen [. . .]. (*KM,* 313)

Here Meister Abraham tells how Julia responds with a sigh, "Ach," to the performance of Kreisler's song by distant basset horn players.

"Ach" is the most important word in the female vocabulary. As Friedrich Kittler comments, "Ach" places the female protagonist at the pre-reflexive origin of the Romantic imagination.[8] It echoes a lost unity of conscious-ness that preempts intellectual reflection. "Ach," Julia again later sighs on seeing Kreisler in conversation with her mother, Benzon:

> "Verehrteste," begann Kreisler, aber in dem Augenblick öffnete sich die Türe und Julia trat hinein. Als sie den Kapellmeister gewahrte, verklärte ihr holdes Antlitz ein süßes Lächeln, und ein leises: Ach! hauchte von ihren Lippen. (*KM,* 359)

Hoffmann's reader, seeing the two engaged in a conversation of dubious integrity, is guided towards apprehending Julia as the intruder, the beholder rather than participant, the utopian outsider who has no words for her discomfort with the untruths of conversation. Removed from language, Julia is allowed to appear as a musical ideal, a pure "interior" in a world of linguistic compromise and feigned "exterior." However, on closer examination it turns out that Julia's subjectivity is not an interior in a compact, independent sense, but a transmitter, something that exudes sound, whether this is uttered as the semi-linguistic "ach" or sung.

Another form of transmitter is the Romantic symbol of the Aeolian harp. In *Kater Murr* a variation of this Romantic instrument is used to describe Meister Abraham's longing for the lost Chiara:

> Da schwankte die Glaskugel hin und her und ein melodischer Ton ließ sich vernehmen wie wenn Windeshauch leise hinstreift über die Seiten der Harfe. Aber bald wurde der Ton zu Worten. (*KM*, 620)

On one level this is a metaphor for the Romantic imagination. In the context of Hoffmann's reflection on this in his poetic works, there is, perhaps, a further distinction to be made. Klaus-Dieter Dobat argues that Novalis treats music as a container for a poetic idea, whereas for Hoffmann, musical form is itself the transcendent force.[9] According to Dobat, Novalis's aesthetics imply that musical transcendence relies on the translation into language of the sensations it evokes. In the above example Hoffmann allows Abraham to imagine the musical notes becoming words. What then happens, however, is that the medium does not transcend itself. These words remain medium rather than discarding their materiality. They are not made transparent. Meister Abraham does, of course, interpret the words that ensue from the notes, but in so doing he constructs rather than deciphers a meaning. Abraham himself, therefore, is a clear identity only between music and its transition into language, between language and its interpretation. The ultimate interpretation would rest on his becoming reunited with Chiara, but this does not take place: as in the case of Abraham's constructions for the princess's birthday celebrations, meaning slips away from intention, so that Abraham's mechanical construction of musical instruments and the effects of this become an allegory of Romantic artistry.

Returning to the musical protagonist: Kreisler's dilemma is not to deliver a new and transcendent composition, but to know whether any composition can affect its listener in such a way that he or she transcends a certain predictability of musical composition. As well as expressing Hoffmann's personal frustration and setting out as an ideal what he as a composer did not achieve, this representation of music is made to symbolize a utopian yearning. Kreisler's desire for expression is Romantic, in that the perfect music he almost hears runs parallel to the symbolic relationship with Julia, which is mainly enacted in his imagination. That this depends on a certain level of unfulfillment comes as no surprise to the reader of Romanticism; what is nevertheless uncertain is the status of the attempt to transcend the terms of modern individuality. In the aftermath of Descartes and in the tradition of Scientific Rationalism, the individual is defined by its capacity for cognitive reasoning. Identity is linked to rational understanding and communication takes place between discrete, unconnected intelligences. Kreisler's Romantic aesthetics, and here they represent Hoffmann's, try to capture something different: the merging of feeling and reflection in the experience of music.

Kreisler's need to compose is utopian because it hopes to bring about a unity of consciousness that stretches the terms of European discourse on subjectivity. Clearly, whatever Kreisler *may* compose is not capable of answering the reasons from Descartes onwards for conceiving of individual consciousness as an end in itself. Nevertheless, taking Kreisler's unachieved composition as Hoffmann's rendition of Romantic utopianism, it seems to hold the promise of transcendence and thereby to challenge more philosophical definitions of individual identity. — What if music, even if it destabilizes a rational thought process only momentarily, were to do so repeatedly?

In several cases throughout E. T. A. Hoffmann's literary work, musical performance brings the protagonist to the brink of transcending the solitariness of experience. Herein lies the essence of Hoffmann's musical utopianism, but if it were to be explained in epistemological terms rather than observed as a one-time literary production, it would be difficult to account for this type of experience other than as an instance of personal faith or private madness. In particular, the fictional composer Kreisler is struggling for a form of connection that is impossible; try as he may to achieve this through music, it is not quite attainable. The question therefore arises: does this imply that what can be shown in literature and therefore imagined can be summarily dismissed as "just imagined"?

That human experience is fundamentally solitary is one of the central premises of modern aesthetics, from Cartesian rationalism to German Idealism. Within this paradigm, art is a form of communication, but also a longing to cross the boundaries between two monadic existences. The writings of Hölderlin, Novalis, Schelling, and Friedrich Schlegel all set themselves the goal of providing a corrective to the isolationism of subject philosophy. In conceptions of the Absolute — an imaginative ideal of poetry and a level of consciousness beyond philosophical reflection — these writers endeavored to conceptualize aesthetic subjectivity as a less solitary way of being.[10] While this would be the subject of a separate study and cannot be dealt with adequately here, it is important to point out that the Romantic invention of a "new mythology" should not be misunderstood as a regressive and reactionary call for the mystical dissolution of consciousness and a return to a pre-modern view of existence. Nor can it be identified with the simplifications and monumentalism of Wagner in the second half of the nineteenth century. Andrew Bowie succinctly identifies Schelling's conception of the Absolute as an artistic ideal that motivates the practice of art and holds aesthetic subjectivity to be an immanent engagement with the Other:

> Schelling insists that art is the unity of conscious and unconscious activity, as part of the attempt to make philosophy confront aspects of self-consciousness which philosophers like Kant can only put into a realm to which philosophy has no access. Schelling is convinced that these aspects are accessible, and faces the philosophical consequences of showing how this is the case.[11]

Bowie then argues that the consequences of Schelling's position are that art can articulate thoughts that may be inaccessible to philosophy, and that this influences Theodor Adorno in the twentieth century, even though Adorno insists that artistic expression has to remain incommensurate with public and political expression if it is not to be used as an instrument of oppression.[12] But the consequences of this are, according to Bowie, that Adorno in *Ästhetische Theorie* (1970) conceives of art as a negative relation to what is, and beyond that (since there can be no reconciliation of the individual and the general that is not oppressive) insists that art has to forfeit the epistemological and experiential utopian quality that Schelling had foreseen for it.[13]

The question of how art can be utopian has always been controversial, from Plato's charge in his *Republic* that art subverts rational truth to Adorno's distrust of any modern aesthetics that are not distinguished in a negative dialectical relationship to what is, and to post-structuralism, in which utopian tendencies are dismissed as ideological and totalizing. Adorno's *Ästhetische Theorie,* implicitly responding to the philosophy of Hegel, provides a melancholy account of the utopian potential of art. Art is, in Adorno's view, capable of embodying protest, since it formally withstands antagonisms that have to be repressed in the historical construction of reality.[14] The work of art can resist reality by refusing the universalism of product-based capitalist exchange. Where Hegel chooses to construe the present as a moment in the dialectical progress towards the Ideal, Adorno points to the work of art as something that discredits such premises by showing the very things that they have had to repress. Art's negativity provides its critical potential, its resistance to the ontological claims of a status quo as, for instance, any stage of capitalism. Likewise, Adorno's conception of time as music seems to be influenced by the idea of rhythm and the repetition of selected themes as a negation of empirical time.[15] Music, although thoroughly conceived in time, can also develop from a concentrated displacement of thematic development.[16] In other words, musical themes can awaken expectations in the listener that are then not fulfilled, with the result that the listener has an awareness of the contingency of historical reality. Adorno explains: "Drängt eine Musik die Zeit zusammen, faltet ein Bild Räume ineinander, so konkretisiert sich die Möglichkeit, es könnte auch anders sein."[17] In his contention that art encompasses possibilities beyond the repressions of conscious knowledge, Adorno does, as Bowie contends, show the influence of Schelling. But overall, Adorno's conception of art as utopian possibility has to be linked to the negation of what is. The moment it lays claim to a better reality, art, for Adorno, falls into the trap of positing an idea of the "best possible of all worlds" (Leibniz), and what had started out as an artistic rendering of something that is possible is frozen into a retrospective justification of ethical stagnation. In other words, ethics has failed in Leibnizian terms, since the "best possible of all worlds" is a lame justification of historical developments that lets reason off the hook by pointing to a divine source. This is seen to be the case most notably in Hegel, who in *Phänomenologie des Geistes* (Phenomenology of Spirit, 1810), regards history as the unfolding of stages of dialectical imbalances on the inevitable course of rational perfection. Art, as far as Adorno is concerned, has to be able to nullify the circular arguments of an ethical practice that has its roots in ideas that do not account for what they have repressed in arriving at their respective representations.

Sound as Perception

In his book, *Aesthetics and Subjectivity from Kant to Nietzsche*, Andrew Bowie discusses Hegel's dismissal of music as "feeling" (rather than concept) in relation to Hoffmann's essay on Beethoven's Fifth Symphony, in which Hoffmann refers to music as the "unsayable" ("das Unsagbare"):[18]

> For Hegel the truth of music is eminently sayable in the form of philosophy. As we saw, in discussing the signifier "I," Hegel maintained that the "*Unsayable*, emotion, feeling is not the most excellent, the most true, but rather the most insignificant, most untrue." For Hoffmann music can articulate the "unsayable," which is *not* representable by concepts or verbal language.[19]

Turning to Novalis, Bowie notes that Novalis understands rhythm in language to be the enabling analogous factor that establishes a continuum that is often mistaken for a cognitive, logical continuum:

> Rhythm, like language, is a form of meaningful differentiality; a beat becomes itself by its relation to the other beats, in an analogous way to the way in which the I of reflection is dependent upon the not-I, the signifier on the other signifiers. Rhythm is a form of reflection.[20]

Bowie sees a connection between Schleiermacher's hermeneutics and Hoffmann's essay on Beethoven's Fifth Symphony. For Schleiermacher, as

Bowie has argued in an earlier chapter, the link between music and language is not arbitrary: both show a sequential organization and are therefore linked at an irreducible point of self-consciousness.[21] According to Bowie, Hoffmann "makes music into the means of access to other aspects of self-consciousness because of the way he sees the limitations of conceptual thinking."[22] The question arises, however, as to the purpose of whatever access this may be. Whether the emphasis is on articulation or on the ultimate limits of self-knowledge, art is conceived of here in relation to individuality. In this view of subjectivity, perception is as much defined by "feeling" in the Romantic sense as it is by rational understanding. It is also capable of being more ethically accountable than a form of rationality that is limited to the concept, as is that of Kant and Hegel.

In effect, Bowie's analysis takes issue with deconstruction's rejection of the metaphysics of presence by pointing to alternatives of self-consciousness in German Romanticism. While this is a subtle argument, it nevertheless decouples Romantic subjectivity from the historical and cultural matrix within which, as Michel Foucault shows, the object of knowledge is produced. German Romanticism, including E. T. A. Hoffmann, is a part of this matrix; it can be read in Bowie's sense as the enhancement of thinking of the self. This partially leads in the direction of Adorno, who emphasized music in particular as the zenith of aesthetic autonomy. Romanticism could be read in the context of aesthetic autonomy, albeit departing then from Adorno, as a means of preserving subjectivity. This seems to me to be the thrust of Bowie's defense of Romanticism against Hegel.

Bearing this in mind, it is far from inconceivable that Hoffmann, despite his lack of interest in philosophy, should have understood that music as a form of expression may be a different but no less viable source of individual and cultural identity. Hoffmann's musical transcendence is based on a physical process that has a complex but not subordinate relationship to verbal expression. The fact that there is no direct philosophical explanation for such a phenomenon does not mean — as Bowie's interpretation of Novalis's reading of Fichte shows — that philosophy is uninformed by many types of non-verbal expression.

Hoffmann's first published work, *Ritter Gluck* (Chevalier Gluck, 1809), shows how sound is intrinsic to identity without being transmitted into linguistic reason. The ghostly appearance of the composer Gluck and his trance-like immersion in music links the question of identity to the form of expression. Hoffmann's tale opens with a vivid and detailed description of a late autumn Sunday afternoon in Berlin. The scene is set by the even pacing of the narrative; all sections of society are represented, and the narrator's eye calmly takes in the people passing by. The reader is introduced to this "slice of life" as the narrator lists off the passers-by: "Elegants, Bürger mit der Hausfrau und den lieben Kleinen in Sonntagskleidern, Geistliche, Jüdinnen, Referendare, Freudenmädchen,

Professoren, Tänzer, Offiziere" (*FN*, 14). At first the picture is silent, but as some of the passers-by sit down at a café, they are brought to life. The first addition of sound to the picture is localized. As the people begin to talk and argue at their tables, we become aware of sound as a separate dimension to the pictures in which they had first been presented. As soon as this has been established, sound dominates the narrative in the form of an untuned harp, two discordant violins, a flute, and a bassoon. The narrator walks on until he finds a seat out of earshot of the "cacophony" (*FN*, 14). The sound has been banished, allowing pictures once again to predominate: "Immer bunter und bunter wogt die Masse der Spaziergänger bei mir vorüber, aber nichts stört mich, nichts kann meine phantastische Gesellschaft vescheuchen" (*FN*, 14). With this proclamation we are introduced at an early stage to the tension between interior and exterior, profane reality and the Romantic transcendent imagination. The narrator is at pains to point out his imaginative autonomy. No sooner is this established than it is once again curtailed by the intrusion of badly played music: "Die kreischende Oberstimme der Violine und Flöte und des Fagotts schnarrenden Grundbaß allein höre ich [. . .]" (*FN*, 14). Already there is no reconciliation. Both the narrator's imagination and his sensory experience focus on one thing at a time. Sound and vision do not peacefully coexist, but stamp each other out. In this instance it is the bassoon that drowns out the other noises. The whole business leads to physical pain. From the moment the narrator reports of this physical pain, he has already uttered what will be one of the constant themes of Hoffmann's literary writing: the inadequacy of language to recapture any experience in its underlying form.

The failure of language is only one angle; ironically it draws attention to other ways of showing intelligence, and these ways are innately physical, such as when the narrator's ear is "pierced" by what it hears (*FN*, 14). Whether good or bad, music is actively felt in Hoffmann rather than passively imported. The narrator in *Ritter Gluck* also complains of a burning pain. Both the piercing sound and the burning pain are scarcely what might be termed original metaphors. Like so many other figures in Hoffmann's writing, the narrator of *Ritter Gluck*, with his punctured eardrums and strange burning sensations, is neither rational nor irrational, neither articulate nor inarticulate.

Central to *Ritter Gluck* is the empty page from which the ghostly composer conducts his final performance: it is unclear whether the ghostly composer does not require a score because he is already in the realm of transcendence, or whether we should simply read this as an allegory of all music in performance. Hoffmann seems to imply that all performance rests on harmony and on the designation of notes within a constructed system. Instead of transcendence — or perhaps, as a different way of looking at transcendence — we are left with the unique aesthetic moment: the physical experience of music as a reality that exists in time, not despite it. Gluck, the composer who has returned from the dead to conduct a final performance in Berlin, reads from an empty page. This is in one sense a parody of Rousseau's utopia of original music at the pre-reflexive origin of society. Hoffmann, the writer and composer, is more than aware, as indeed is Rousseau, of the physical reality of the interval. Gluck's presence oddly testifies to the singularity of performance. In a way, performance itself is transcendence. Therefore, though it might hint at utopia, it is characterized by its instantaneous nature. What music is Gluck reading?

From one minute to the next, experience is structured by time. Each interval in frequency between notes implies that nothing is really simultaneous. Simultaneity, carrying this idea a step further, is a manner of expression for a fundamentally incommunicable sensation. The fact that Gluck, a ghost who has cheated on his mortal time-span, is reading invisible notes, could be read as Hoffmann's distortion of time, a reduction of all bodily reality to an atemporal comic utopia. What could instead be concluded, however, is that Gluck's performance stands for the uniqueness of time, not its obliteration; while the notes he reads are invisible, they are nevertheless there, therefore time itself is not transcended. On the contrary, Gluck's rendition of the composition alerts his dumb-struck listener to the singularity of performance. Gluck need not be viewed as a symbol of radical aesthetic autonomy — the solipsistic internal consciousness of a bourgeois performer. He may be seen instead as an altogether more optimistic symbol of the power of performance to outdo the petrification of bourgeois form. If Ritter Gluck, the dead composer, returns to perform for a somewhat smug narrator who is clearly au fait with the contemporary art world, the very singularity of his performance transcends not time itself, but the claim to ownership of art by virtue of its written notation. In other words, though many may read Gluck's invisible notation, possession of the textual product is not the same as the transformation of this product in performance. In relating the language of transcendence to musical performance, E. T. A. Hoffmann differs from other Romantic writers. Although music is as dependent on the medium as a literary text on signification (which inspires the Romantic metaphor of the hieroglyphic for a hermeneutic process) Hoffmann relies on a more psychologically dramatic cliché of music without medium. The genial composer Ritter Gluck surpasses any interpretation of musical notation among his contemporaries by reading from an empty sheet, but that is not to say that the notes are not there. Hoffmann's novella leaves many uncomfortable questions and ultimately allows music to show a transgression of boundaries (Gluck is a ghost) and an *apparent* transcendence of medium; since it is the performance itself which grips, the implication is that the notation, in the manner of all hermeneutic explanation of the world, offers no certainties.

In conclusion, it would seem that Hoffmann understood that expression and desire were not contained in an idealized identity or an absolute textual basis. Romantic transcendence and its path through ambivalence in many ways preempts the psychoanalytic re-thinking of rationality, but also adverts to the less popular and less well understood role of sound in how thought and feeling intertwine. Hoffmann gives this a particular twist in the haunting, music-related themes of his novels and novellas.

Notes

[1] E. T. A. Hoffmann, *Fantasie- und Nachtstücke,* ed. Walter Müller-Seidel., rev. ed. (Munich: Winkler Verlag, 1993), 36: "Es ist nicht zu leugnen, daß in neuerer Zeit, dem Himmel sei's gedankt! der Geschmack an der Musik sich immer mehr verbreitet, so daß es jetzt gewissermaßen zur guten Erziehung gehört, die Kinder auch Musik lehren zu lassen, weshalb man denn in jedem Hause, das nur irgend etwas bedeuten will, ein Klavier, wenigstens eine Guitarre findet." Subsequent references to this edition of the *Fantasiestücke* are cited in the text using the abbreviation *FN.*

[2] Müller-Seidel's commentary to the *Fantasiestücke* quotes Ritter, noting that Ellinger originally traced the quotation. Johann Wilhelm Ritter, *Fragmente aus dem Nachlaß eines jungen Physikers,* ed. Arthur Henkel, 2 vols. in one (1810; facsimile reprint, Heidelberg: Lambert Schneider, 1969), 224: "Das Hören ist ein Sehen von innen, das innerstinnerste Bewußtsein" (cf. *FN,* 794).

[3] Ritter, *Fragmente,* 224.

[4] Ibid., 236.

[5] Particularly in his "Rede über die Mythologie" within *Gespräch über die Poesie* (1800).

[6] See Martin Swales, "'Die Reproduktionskraft der Eidexen.' Überlegungen zum selbstreflexiven Charakter der *Lebens-Ansichten des Katers Murr,*" *E. T. A. Hoffmann-Jahrbuch* 1 (1993): 48–58.

[7] *Die Elixiere des Teufels: Lebens-Ansichten des Katers Murr,* ed. Walter Müller-Seidel, rev. ed. (Munich: Winkler Verlag, 1993), 341. Subsequent references are cited in the text using the abbreviation *KM.*

[8] See Kittler's analysis of Serpentina as a pre-discursive origin of the subject in Hoffmann's *Der goldne Topf:* Friedrich A. Kittler, *Aufschreibesysteme 1800·1900* (Munich: Fink, 1985), 93.

[9] Klaus-Dieter Dobat, *Musik als romantische Illusion: Eine Untersuchung zur Bedeutung der Musikvorstellung E. T. A. Hoffmanns für sein literarisches Werk* (Tübingen: Niemeyer, 1984), 62: "Die musikalische Form gilt nicht mehr als beliebige äußere Hülle für eine poetische Idee, die Form ist insofern selbst 'Geist,' als sie entsprechend der Aussageintention gestaltet und geprägt ist."

[10] The most comprehensive analysis of Romantic aesthetics and philosophy has been carried out by Manfred Frank, *Einführung in die frühromantische Ästhetik* (Frankfurt a. M.: Suhrkamp, 1989), *Die Unhintergehbarkeit von Individualität* (Frankfurt a. M.: Suhrkamp, 1986), and *Der kommende Gott: Vorlesungen über die neue Mythologie* (Frankfurt a. M.: Suhrkamp, 1982).

[11] Andrew Bowie, *Aesthetics and Subjectivity from Kant to Nietzsche* (Manchester: Manchester UP, 1990), 97.

[12] Ibid.

[13] Ibid.: "Art ends up retreating into autonomy in order to resist such a false reconciliation [. . .]."

[14] Theodor Adorno, *Ästhetische Theorie* (Frankfurt a. M.: Suhrkamp, 1970), 28.

[15] Ibid., 207.

[16] Ibid. Adorno mentions Schönberg here, holding Schönberg's notion of music as a "Geschichte der Themen" to be an implicit answer to an empiricist notion of the musical progression of an idea. Although the passage is not entirely clear, it would seem that Adorno reads Schönberg as an answer to the notion of time in Idealist aesthetics of the Absolute, whereby aesthetic time can involve a suspension of empirical time, but does so, as far as Adorno is concerned, with a utopian promise that cannot be fulfilled, and fails to realize that it cannot be fulfilled.

[17] Ibid., 208.

[18] E. T. A. Hoffmann, *Schriften zur Musik: Nachlese,* ed. Friedrich Schnapp (Munich: Winkler, 1963), 34.

[19] Bowie, *Aesthetics and Subjectivity,* 184.

[20] Ibid., 79.

[21] Ibid., 173.

[22] Ibid., 184.

Responses to Goethe

Perceptions of Goethe and Schubert

Lorraine Byrne

OVER THE YEARS GOETHE'S MUSICALITY has been called into question. Ernest Walker calls him "the greatest of the few exceptions" of "unmusical poets";[1] Moritz Bauer describes Goethe as a "man of very limited musical understanding";[2] Elisabeth Schumann writes about his "indifference to music";[3] Calvin Brown speaks about his "rather severe musical limitations";[4] and Lorraine Gorrell portrays a "musically opinionated, but conservative poet."[5] Even where Goethe's musicality has been recognized, it is always qualified. McClain argues that Goethe "was not a person who instinctively understood music as a language or who used it as a means of expression";[6] Claus Canisius attributes the poet's lack of musical competence to his late introduction to the art,[7] and though Kenneth Whitton argues for Goethe's musicality, he concludes that "Goethe was musical in a different sense."[8]

In examining this traditional portrait of Goethe, we find that the term "musical" presents a certain ambiguity in itself. To criticize a person as being "unmusical" implies that he or she is neither fond of nor skilled in music. However, searching through Goethe's work, it is easy to trace an apparent love of music in his activities, thoughts, and writings. As one can show in detail, Goethe's autobiographical writing records a lifelong interest and involvement in music.[9] Throughout his life, Goethe surrounded himself with musicians, and, contrary to the traditional perception, his openness to modern music is revealed in his willingness to be taught by most artists with whom he had personal contact. Goethe's need for music in his life is also illustrated by the fact that he attended concerts regularly. Yet to him music was more than a source of entertainment; his reviews of these musical soirées in his diaries and correspondence reveal a critical and discerning listener. His musical understanding is considered "limited," yet his judgments are often independent and reveal a real understanding of the art. Goethe's fictional work is further proof of his musical appreciation. In his novels and plays the characters frequently sing and accompany themselves, yet music does not merely provide a foil or a musical scene in which his characters partake — its emotional impact is also recognized.[10] Goethe's lyrical proficiency is affirmed through the musical quality of his verse, which has both attracted and taxed composers to the highest degree.

The continual attraction of musicians to Goethe's verse bears testimony to his intrinsic musicality.

So why, in view of the evidence of Goethe's unceasing pursuit of music, the high value he placed on the art, and the innate musical aspect of his writings, is he criticized so acutely? One reason is that the majority of such criticism comes from scholars whose main interest is music. Furthermore, their dismissal of Goethe as a man of limited musicality is founded on the poet's association with Zelter and with the Berlin school of composers, and on his so-called "rejection" of the Schubertian Lied.

Goethe's correspondence with Zelter, which commenced in 1799 and continued until Goethe's death in 1832, imparts further proof of the poet's sincere endeavor to understand the art of music, and testifies to his musical interest and intelligence. His correspondence with Zelter reveals his interest in music as an acoustic phenomenon, yet it also reveals his spiritual response to the art.[11] In his letters to Zelter, Goethe's genuine need for music in his life is apparent. He regularly attends concerts and soirées, and, when approaching sixty, organizes a choir on Sunday mornings in his house, to make music under his direction.[12] However, constant musical activity alone is not enough for Goethe; we also witness his concern to understand the art. After performances he consults Zelter about the music he has heard and seeks his opinion on various composers. The history of music interests Goethe as part of the chronicle of human culture, and his correspondence with Zelter reveals his desire to obtain a picture of musical development in general.[13] In a letter to Zelter from January 1819, he records a series of instructional recitals in Berka given by the composer Schütz:

> da mir denn der Inspector (Schütz)[14] täglich drei bis vier Stunden vor-
> spielte und zwar auf mein Ersuchen, nach historischer Reihe: von Sebastian
> Bach bis zu Beethoven, durch Philipp Emanuel, Händel, Mozart, Haydn
> durch, auch Dusseck, und dergleichen mehr.[15]

In a similar fashion, he urges the twenty-two year old Mendelssohn to play him a number of pieces in chronological order and then to explain what each composer had done in order to further the art.[16] While Goethe's relationship with Zelter and Mendelssohn reveals his search for musical understanding, it also admits a certain reliance on an interpreter to bring music alive to him. Yet Goethe's lack of technical skill in score reading and performance does not result from a lack of musicality, but arises through his late start in learning an instrument. While Goethe grew up with music, he was fourteen before he learned to play the piano, studying flute and cello only in later years. This certainly created in him a degree of dependency on Zelter, yet, conscious of his own inadequacy,[17] he was industrious in acquiring a greater knowledge of the art. Although Zelter is continually hailed as Goethe's musical oracle, many discussions were initiated by the poet, and as his knowledge grew, his dependence on Zelter diminished.

Goethe's letters to Zelter document his musical growth and development from his journey to Italy in 1786 up to the final months of his life. In addition to the wealth of musical activity it contains, the *Italienische Reise* (Italian Journey, 1786–88) also records Goethe's early endeavor in perfecting his skill in the visual arts. While in Italy, however, he realized that he was not particularly gifted in this area and decided to stop painting. Goethe's resolution discloses a clear awareness of his own inadequacies, and in conversation with Eckermann on 20 April 1825 he discusses how detrimental false tendencies can be.[18] In view of this, it is highly unlikely that Goethe would have spent so much time and energy in the field of music had he felt that he was "unmusical."

While Goethe's early acquaintance with the artists of the second Berlin school has encouraged the myth of a musically conservative poet, his lability and eclectic nature are much more apparent in his relationship with this group. Throughout his life Goethe experienced an immense variety of cultural influences; however, he never surrendered himself to any one agency (although he might adopt something of its color). From the second Berlin school he took the idea that the poem should play a dominant, not a subordinate role in music, but he did not adhere totally to all the theories expounded by the school. Rather than rigidly insisting on strophic form as suggested by the Berlin school, Goethe's chief concern was that the inner meaning of his poetry should be clearly reflected in the music. He demanded this from composer and performer alike. Whereas in his early years Goethe's preference for strophic form is apparent, contrary to traditional opinion this did not amount to a dogma. He applauded a song, not because of its strophic setting, but if he felt the artist had recognized the importance of poetry in determining the musical form. In his correspondence he frequently praises through-composed settings such as Zelter's "Johanna Sebus" (1810), and his openness to the nineteenth-century Lied is revealed in his celebration of the composer Tomaschék, whose songs are often through-composed in form.[19]

Goethe's breach with the conventions of the Berlin circle became more apparent towards the end of his life, as he gradually allowed the composer more freedom of interpretation. The poem still played a dominant role, but now the composer was at liberty to portray his own understanding of the text in the music. As early as 1811 Goethe relates to Moritz von Dietrichstein how interesting it is to see how a composer appropriates a poem and enlivens it in his own way,[20] and he repeats these sentiments to Tomaschék on 18 July 1820.[21] A month later he writes to Carl von Schlözer that the composer's setting of a poem is the most sincere sign of its appreciation: the music brings the poem to life, while it is the personality of the composer that individualizes it. He concludes: "Es entsteht dadurch ein neues Poem, welches den Dichter selbst überraschen muß." The end result is, quite simply, a new poem.[22]

Finally, the Swiss composer, Xaver Schnyder von Wartensee, gives us verification of Goethe's convictions.[23] In his memoirs he recalls how he visited Goethe in 1829, presented him with two settings of "Heidenröslein" (Little Heath Rose, 1771) and asked him: "Welche Farbe, die sentimentale oder die humoristische, die rechte sei"? To this Goethe replied that both were correct, and stressed the liberty he granted composers when interpreting his work.[24]

Schubert's fruitless relationship with Goethe is often taken by musicologists as Goethe's rejection of the direction given to nineteenth-century music by Schubert and Beethoven. W. C. R. Hicks considers that "despite any differences in the music of Beethoven and Schubert, it can be said that Goethe's coolness to one explains his coolness to the other,"[25] while other critics connect it with a lack of musicality on Goethe's part.[26] Sheltering the poet from this attack, Romain Rolland argues that perhaps it was unfair to expect Goethe, "a man of the time of Cimarosa, Haydn, and Mozart," to identify with Weber, Schubert and Berlioz, but agrees that Goethe certainly missed the "greatness and originality" of the three later composers.[27] Frederick Sternfeld also defends him, but his argument is clearly mistaken when he says that "there is no evidence whatsoever that Schubert actually wrote to Goethe and that Goethe was aware of him at that time."[28]

The first attempt to interest the poet in Schubert's work was made by the composer's most faithful friend, Josef von Spaun, who on 17 April 1816 sent Goethe a group of Schubert's settings of the poet's verses. The manuscript contained all the finest Goethe songs of the previous two years.[29] It was accompanied by a long letter in which Spaun (on behalf of the ascendant Schubert) asked for permission that the songs might be dedicated to the poet. It was envisaged that the Lieder sent by Spaun would comprise the first volume in an eight-volume collection. The first two volumes would contain settings of Goethe poems, while the remaining six volumes would contain settings of poems by Schiller, Klopstock, Matthisson, Hölty, Salis, Ossian, and others. Spaun expressed Schubert's desire to dedicate the first volume to Goethe:

> dessen so herrlichen Dichtungen er nicht nur allein die Entstehung eines großen Teils derselben, sondern wesentlich auch seine Ausbildung zum deutschen Sänger verdankt. Selbst zu bescheiden jedoch, seine Werke der großen Ehre wert zu halten, einen, so weit deutsche Zungen reichen, so hoch gefeierten Namen an der Stirne zu tragen, hat er nicht den Mut Euer Exzellenz selbst um diese große Gunst zu bitten, und ich, einer seiner Freunde, durchdrungen von seinen Melodien, wage es Euer Exzellenz in seinem Namen darum zu bitten: für eine dieser Gnade würdige Ausgabe wird gesorgt werden. Ich enthalte mich jeder weiteren Anrühmung dieser Lieder, sie mögen selbst für sich sprechen, nur so viel muß ich bemerken, daß die folgenden Hefte dem gegenwärtigen, was die Melodie betrifft, keineswegs nachstehen, sondern selbem vielleicht noch vorgehen dürften,

und daß es dem Klavier-Spieler, der selbe Euer Exzellenz vortragen wird, an Fertigkeit und Ausdruck nicht mangeln dürfe.

Sollte der junge Künstler so glücklich sein auch den Beifall desjenigen zu erlangen, dessen Beifall ihn mehr als der irgend eines Menschen in der weiten Welt ehren würde, so wage ich die Bitte mir die gesuchte Erlaubnis mit zwei Worten gnädigst melden zu lassen.[30]

Spaun's letter is testimony to Schubert's admiration for Goethe. The passage closes with Spaun's praise for Schubert's settings and a sentimental plea for Goethe's consent to the dedication. While awaiting word from Weimar, Schubert began preparing a second volume that he entitled *Lieder von Goethe componiert von Franz Schubert. 2tes Heft.*[31] However, when the manuscript was returned without any written response from the poet, this second book of songs was retained. Nine years later Schubert sent Goethe three more songs, his op. 19, accompanying them with a note that effuses in its veneration of the poet, and again expresses the wish to dedicate the songs to him:

Anfang Juni 1825

Euer Exzellenz!
Wenn es mir gelingen sollte, durch die Widmung dieser Komposition Ihrer Gedichte meine unbegrenzte Verehrung gegen E. Exzellenz an den Tag legen zu können und vielleicht einige Beachtung für meine Unbedeutenheit zu gewinnen, so würde ich den günstigen Erfolg dieses Wunsches als das schönste Ereignis meines Lebens preisen.
  Mit größter Hochachtung
    Ihr
      Ergebenster Diener
      Franz Schubert.[32]

Although Goethe acknowledged receipt of the songs in his diary, noting: "Sendung von Schubert aus Wien, von meinen Liedern Kompositionen,"[33] he made no reply.[34] Yet his failure to respond to Schubert should not be taken as concrete evidence of a lack of musical discernment, or as an example of his musical conservatism. There are, in fact, various reasons for his silence.

Firstly, when one searches through Goethe's letters and diaries, his continual collaboration with musicians reveals his need to bring a score alive. As Spaun points out in his letter to the poet, Schubert's songs require a particular "Fertigkeit und Ausdruck" — dexterity and expression — on the part of the pianist. Yet even if Goethe heard an accomplished performance of Schubert's Lieder and rejected the settings, it still does not confirm a lack of musicality, as is often claimed. In the same year the music publishers Breitkopf & Härtel rejected Schubert's setting of "Erlkönig" (Erl-King, 1782), and returned it to the wrong composer — Franz Schubert of Dresden (not Vienna). The Dresden Schubert, in turn, claimed he would never have composed such trash![35]

A second factor that must be kept in mind is the sheer bulk of music that was dedicated to Goethe. (In his later years it was not unusual for several hundred songs to arrive within a week.) It is safe to assume that the huge majority of these pieces by composers hopeful of the poet's approval were not masterpieces, and that most of the music was quite justly ignored and forgotten. When one takes into account the extent and variety of Goethe's activities, and the fact that music was only one part of these ventures, the context of Goethe's "missing" the significance of Schubert becomes clearer.[36]

A third reason is found in Eckermann's testimony, where he relates how Goethe preferred not replying at all to using empty phrases, and many reasons that explain his reticence towards the composer can be found in each letter. Goethe's disregard of Spaun's letter may have had something to do with the fact that an uncle of Spaun's, the eccentric Franz Seraphicus von Spaun in Munich, had turned from an avid Goethean scholar into a malicious opponent of the poet.[37] Furthermore, Spaun had made a rather undiplomatic reference to the series of publications planned by Schubert: he had noted that while the first two volumes would contain Goethe-poems, the last two volumes — containing poems by Ossian — would surpass all others. This would hardly have enticed the poet into accepting the dedication.

If one examines the political background against which Schubert's first volume was received, the reasons for Goethe's silence become clearer. The political aftermath of the Wars of Liberation, the Congress of Vienna, and in particular, the new democratic constitution, filled Goethe with unease. The dark despair to which he confesses in his diary reflects events in his personal situation that may also have curtailed his response. At the time Goethe received Spaun's consignment, his wife Christiane was critically ill, and she suffered a painful death on 6 June 1816. In his diary Goethe describes the void in his life: "Leere und Todesstille in und außer mir."[38]

Hicks suggests that Schubert was unknown even to the professional musicians in Goethe's circle.[39] Although this is a plausible reason for Goethe's lack of reply to the consignment of songs dated 1816, it is unlikely that Schubert was still unknown to Goethe by 1825. In 1820, in conversation with Schubert's school-friend Max Löwenthal, Goethe reveals he knew nothing of Schubert's compositions, and had forgotten the dedication of 1816,[40] yet the conversation would have triggered an awareness of the composer. By 1821 "Erlkönig" (published eventually by Cappi and Diabelli) had received its first performances, and in 1825 Anna Milder-Hauptmann[41] performed it in Berlin. Eleven of Schubert's Lieder (op. 21–24) had received their first lengthy review in the *Allgemeine Musikalische Zeitung* on 24 June 1824,[42] and from this time the paper acknowledged any subsequent publication of his songs. By July 1825, forty-four of Schubert's songs had been published by various printing companies, eighteen of which were settings of Goethe's verse. Even though there is no mention of Schubert in Goethe's correspondence with Zelter, Marianne von Willemer refers to Schubert's op. 19 Lieder in a letter to Goethe on 16 April 1825 — less than two months before Schubert's letter.[43] The fact that she does not mention the composer's name suggests that Goethe would know to whom she was referring, and this is confirmed by Goethe's acknowledgment of Schubert's dedication in his diary.

In conclusion, while Schubert's songs were widely published and performed, much of the music that has secured his immortality was unknown during his lifetime. In his memoirs Josef von Spaun points to this lack of widespread reception and recognition[44] and his words are confirmed by the fact that Weimar's most prominent musician, Johann Nepomuk Hummel, did not discover Schubert until 1827. And even Mendelssohn, who played a minor role as musical advisor to Goethe in 1830 and later became a great promoter of Schubert's work, was unfamiliar with Schubert's music at this time. Consequently, though Goethe's response to Schubert is usually read as a lack of musical discernment, his recognition of the composer is, in fact, quite remarkable for his time.

Whereas Goethe's silence to Schubert reveals the poet's initial reluctance in accepting the new Lied, he did acknowledge Schubert's achievement at a later date. Towards the end of his life, after hearing Schubert's setting of "Erlkönig" sung by the famous Wilhelmine Schröder-Devrient in 1830,[45] he took her face in his hands and kissed her on the forehead, proclaiming:

> Ich habe diese Komposition früher einmal gehört, wo sie mir gar nicht zusagen wollte, aber so vorgetragen, gestaltet sich das ganze zu einem sichtbaren Bild.[46]

In conversation with J. G. von Quandt[47] in 1830 Goethe referred to an earlier performance she gave:

> Ihre Madame Devrient war auch vor kurzem hier und hat mir eine Romanze vorgesungen — nun, man muß sagen, daß der Komponist das Pferdetrappel vortrefflich ausgedrückt hat. Es ist nicht zu leugnen, daß in der von sehr vielen bewunderten Komposition das Schauerliche bis zum Gräßlichen getrieben wird, zumal wenn die Sängerin die Absicht hat, sich hören zu lassen.[48]

Thus, on hearing "Erlkönig" for the first time, Goethe found favor with Schubert's portrayal of the horse's gallop. Later, when he heard an accomplished performance of the Lied, Goethe recognized the real significance of Schubert's achievement.

Goethe's recognition of Schubert's "Erlkönig" setting dispels three allegations that are frequently made against the poet. First, it illustrates his sanction of the through-composed Lied, when the composer has understood the poetic substance and realized it in his song. Second, it refutes the accusation of a lifelong conservatism on the part of the poet in relation to the nineteenth-century Lied; and, finally, it bears testimony to the fact that Goethe did in fact salute Schubert's achievement in setting his poetry. Before accepting the composer, Goethe clearly needed time to cultivate his ideas on the Lied, and he also needed to hear a good rendition of Schubert's songs. Yet even very recent criticism on Goethe's involvement with the Lied does not recognize this factor. Kenneth Whitton defends the poet, claiming that by the time Goethe received Schubert's op. 19 settings he "was naturally no longer so receptive to requests and suggestions"[49] and in an earlier study Jack Stein states that Goethe was right in rejecting Schubert as a composer of the Lied because "the spirit of 'Erlkönig' is a far remove from the folk-like simplicity and naive characteristic of the poem."[50] In one respect I agree with Stein, for a strophic setting of "Erlkönig" is more appropriate to the character of Dortchen who sings this song in the opening scene of Goethe's *Singspiel, Die Fischerin* (The Fisherwoman, 1782). In previous years Goethe had rejected Beethoven's interpretation of Mignon because he felt a folk-like simplicity was required for the character in the novel.[51] Yet the fact that Goethe did not criticize Schubert's interpretation of "Erlkönig" reveals a change of opinion in relation to the nineteenth-century Lied. While Stein asserts: "Even the most ardent admirers of Schubert would be forced to admit that the simple strophic design is obscured in this through-composed setting,"[52] Goethe overlooked this because he conceded that Schubert's song realizes the dramatic potential in the poem. Consequently, though Goethe's response to Schubert has prompted unqualified criticism about his musical discrimination, the poet's final words of praise for Schubert's "Erlkönig" gives greater attestation to the fact that Goethe's relationship to music — and in particular to the nineteenth-century Lied — has been much misunderstood. Furthermore, when one considers that Goethe was sixty-eight when Spaun wrote to him, seventy-six when he received Schubert's letter, and eighty-one when he recognized the composer's genius, the traditional portrayal of the musically conservative poet should be seen in a new light.

Goethe and Schubert are usually considered as holding different convictions on the nineteenth-century Lied, yet they are closer in their ideas than is traditionally portrayed. The two artists are presented as belonging to opposite schools of thought in their appreciation of the Lied. Goethe has been falsely placed in the conservative traditions of the Berlin school, while Schubert — through his development of the Lied — is not normally associated with this circle. The idea that Schubert revolutionized the Lied is prevalent among scholars from Konrad Volker, Maurice Brown, and A. Craig Bell, to Hans Gál, and Lawrence Kramer,[53] yet to revolutionize implies fundamental change rather than development. However, as Spaun recounts, Schubert's aim was to modernize the Lied,[54] which does not suggest a radical change but a refinement of something already present.

It is not the origins of the Schubertian Lied but the composer's aesthetic consciousness and refusal to write for the popular market that distinguish him from the artists of the Berlin school.

The impact of the piano in society played an important role in the development of the *geselliges Lied,* and, unlike Schubert, Reichardt and Zelter were clever businessmen, socially intelligent, and willing to cater to this market. However, their commercial success worked against them in later years, and their experimentation with the Lied and the quality of some of their settings have become lost in the quantity of songs they composed for the popular audience. Schubert did not have the same business acumen as Reichardt and Zelter. In the early days of his career, it was Schubert's friends who saw the need to get his work published. Spaun's aforementioned letter to Goethe mentions how general praise and the wishes of his friends finally moved Schubert to consider publishing some of his compositions. While Schubert was conscious of an audience, this did not dictate what he wished to compose, and this clearly distinguishes him from Reichardt and Zelter. However if we look at portraits of Schubert, such as Julius Schmid's *Ein Schubert-Abend in einem Wiener Bürgerhaus* (A Schubert evening in a Viennese civilian's house, 1899) or Gustav Klimt's *Schubert am Klavier* (Schubert at the Piano, 1899), we see how these paintings create a wonderful impression of the context in which Schubert's songs were performed. To recreate this original context requires performance in an intimate setting, for the physical proximity of a voice accompanied by fortepiano brings the sonority much more alive than does even a first-rate performance in a large auditorium. Apart from his song settings, Schubert's output includes an immense amount of piano music, which confirms his place in the domain of the popular music of the day, as well as in the art music tradition. In Viennese circles the demand for piano music was very high, and it is frequently overlooked that Schubert was one of the most prolific composers of dance music of his time. Some of Schubert's songs and piano pieces had a public baptism in the musical salon, the most famous of which was the *Schubertiade.* While the context of the *Schubertiade* is recognized in biographies of the composer, Schubert's connections with the *geselliges Lied* are rarely admitted.

Contrary to accepted opinion, Schubert's development of the nineteenth-century Lied and the work of the Berlin school of composers placed him in pre-established sympathy with Goethe. As Goethe's poetry heralds a new development in the *geselliges Lied,* Schubert's Goethe settings mark the pinnacle of this genre. Like Goethe, Schubert was eclectic. Rather than allowing his style to be dominated by any one composer, Schubert took from his forerunners the elements of their musical vocabulary that appealed to him most. Yet his genius and mastery of his art makes Schubert's achievement far superior to the work of his predecessors. Like the second Berlin school of composers, Schubert recognized the importance of

Julius Schmid, "Ein Schubert-Abend in einem Wiener Bürgerhaus" (1899), courtesy of the Museen der Stadt Wien.

Gustav Klimt, "Schubert am Klavier" (1899), courtesy of AKG Berlin.

unifying words and music in the Lied. This was Goethe's main criterion in judging the success of a setting. Not only did Schubert fulfill this criterion, but his whole development of the nineteenth-century Lied centered around this portrayal of poetic meaning in his settings. Like Reichardt and Zelter, Schubert set Goethe's verse extensively and the number of comparative settings, along with striking similarities in some of these settings, suggests that Schubert was influenced by their work. In his Goethe settings Schubert transcends the unity of words and music achieved in Reichardt and Zelter's renditions and creates a new unity: one where poetry and song attain equal artistic value. In this respect Schubert's Goethe settings are distinguished from the work of his musical forebears, for they attain a true unity of form.

In recent years Walther Dürr has traced the unity in a Schubertian song back to Nägeli's conception of how a poem in music engenders a type of polyrhythm where both run side by side.[55] In relation to Schubert's Goethe settings, Dürr's argument is interesting, for Nägeli's perception of how two strands run side by side suggests that each strand is given equal weight. This unity of form in Schubert's Goethe settings also reveals the influence of Goethe's classicism. Beginning with Weimar Classicism, Goethe advocated totality ("Ganzheit") in all matters of creativity, and the Lied was no exception. Goethe's desire for equality between words and music in the Lied reflects his belief that a work of art must reflect the universal harmony and order. It is not modernity of which he disapproved, but lack of classical balance. Contrary to traditional perception, Schubert's "Romantic" Lieder are not in opposition to the poet's classical ideals, but attain the classical balance Goethe sought.

Notes

[1] Ernest Walker, "Goethe and some Composers," *Musical Times* 73 (1932): 497–502 (here, 497).

[2] Moritz Bauer, *Die Lieder Franz Schuberts* (Leipzig: Breitkopf & Härtel, 1915), 12.

[3] Elisabeth Schumann, *German Song* (London: Macmillan, 1948), 10.

[4] Calvin S. Brown, "The Relations between Music and Literature As a Field of Study," *Comparative Literature* 22 (spring 1970:2): 97–107 (here, 105).

[5] Lorraine Gorrell, *The Nineteenth-Century German Lied* (Portland, Oregon: Amadeus Press, 1993), 216.

[6] Meredith McClain, "Goethe and Music: 'Nur wer die Sehnsucht kennt,'" in *Johann Wolfgang von Goethe: One Hundred and Fifty Years of Continuing Vitality*, ed. Ulrich Goebel and Wolodymyr T. Zyla (Texas: Texas Tech. Press, 1984), 201–77 (here, 202).

[7] Claus Canisius, *Goethe und die Musik* (Munich: Piper, 1998), 9.

[8] Kenneth Whitton, *Goethe and Schubert: The Unseen Bond* (Portland, Oregon: Amadeus Press, 1999), 84.

[9] See, for example, Johann Wolfgang von Goethe, *Dichtung und Wahrheit*, ed. Erich Trunz, vol. 9 of *Goethes Werke*, 14 vols. (Hamburg: Christian Wegner Verlag, 1948–60 [hereafter *HA*]), book 1, ch. 4, 115–17; book 2, ch. 8, 338, 381. See also Goethe, *Italienische Reise* (*HA*11): letters of 3 October 1786 (p. 74), 6 October 1786 (p. 85), 1 March 1788 (p. 524), 14 March 1788 (p. 528), and 22 March 1788 (p. 530).

[10] See, for example, the musical scenes in *Die Wahlverwandtschaften*, *Die Leiden des jungen Werthers*, *Wilhelm Meisters Lehrjahre*, *Wilhelm Meisters Wanderjahre*, *Faust I*, and *Egmont*.

[11] *Goethes Werke*, ed. Gustav von Loeper, Erich Schmidt, and Hermann Grimm, 143 vols. (Weimar: Hermann Böhlaus Nachfolger, 1887–1912 [hereafter *WA*]), series IV, vol. 35: letter of 14 October 1821 (p. 140); vol. 37: letter of 24 August 1823 (pp. 189, 191–92).

[12] Letter of 15 September 1807, *HA*3:407–9.

[13] Letter of April 1827, *WA*IV/42:152.

[14] Johann Heinrich Schütz (1779–1829). Schütz studied composition with Zelter.

[15] Letter of 4 January 1819, *WA*IV/31:45; see also letter of 21 June 1827, *WA*IV/42:230.

[16] Letter of 3 June 1830, *WA*IV/47:86.

[17] Letter of 5 February 1822, *HA*4:29–30; see also letter of 8 March 1824, *WA*IV/38:70–71.

[18] Letters of 20 April 1825, 10 April 1829 and 12 April 1829, in Johann Eckermann, *Gespräche mit Goethe*, ed. Hubert Houben, 25th ed. (Wiesbaden: F. A. Brockhaus, 1959), 117, 274, 277–78.

[19] Vaclav Jan Tomaschék (1774–1850), Bohemian composer and pianist. See, for example, Tomaschék's setting of "Nähe des Geliebten," op. 53, no. 2, in Tomaschék, *Gedichte von Goethe für den Gesang mit Begleitung des Pianoforte* (Prague: the composer, 1815).

[20] Letter of 23 June 1811, *WA*IV/22:113–14. Moritz von Dietrichstein (1775–1864) played an important role in the cultural life of Vienna. In 1819 he was appointed *Hofmusikgraf,* and in 1821 director of the court theatres. At a soirée given by Matthäus von Collin in 1820, Schubert was introduced to Dietrichstein, who readily acknowledged Schubert's genius. Dietrichstein himself composed a certain amount of vocal music, both sacred and secular, and was among the musicians invited to contribute to the *Diabelli Variations.*

[21] Cited in Hedwig Walwei-Wiegelmann, ed., *Goethes Gedanken über Musik* (Frankfurt a. M.: Insel Verlag, 1985), 138.

[22] *WA*IV/23:176: letter of 27 August 1820. Carl von Schlözer (1780–1859) was the brother of the historian and publicist August Ludwig von Schlözer. He was a correspondent of Goethe's and provided a Lied setting for Goethe's "Erlkönig."

[23] Xaver Schynder von Wartensee (1786–1868), composer of instrumental and vocal works. Von Wartensee studied music in Vienna but settled in Frankfurt am Main,

where he taught and composed. He was especially known for his recitals on the glass harmonica.

24 Cited in Walwei-Wiegelmann, *Goethes Gedanken,* 139.

25 W. C. R. Hicks, "Was Goethe Musical?" *Publications of the English Goethe Society* 27 (1958): 73–139 (here, 123).

26 See, for example, Konrad Volker, "Schubert and Goethe," *Die Musik* 14 (1915): 128–32 (here, 129).

27· Romain Rolland, "Goethe's Interest in Music," *Music Quarterly* 17 (1931): 157–94 (here, 177, 190). His opinion is shared by O. Linke, "Schubert and Goethe," *Neue Musik Zeitung* 12 (1891).

28 Frederick W. Sternfeld, *Goethe and Music: A List of Parodies and Goethe's Relationship to Music: A List of References* (New York: New York Public Library, 1954), vii.

29 *HA*2:188–90; also in Otto Erich Deutsch, *Schubert: Die Dokumente seines Lebens und Schaffens,* 3rd rev. ed. (Leipzig: Breitkopf & Härtel, 1996), 40. The Goethe songs that accompanied the letter were: "Jägers Abendlied," D. 368, "Der König in Thule," D. 367, "Meeresstille," D. 216, "Schäfers Klagelied," D. 121, "Die Spinnerin," D. 247, "Heidenröslein," D. 257, "Wonne der Wehmut," D. 260, "Wandrers Nachtlied" ("Der du von dem Himmel bist"), D. 224, "Erster Verlust," D. 226, "Der Fischer," D. 225, "An Mignon," D. 161, "Geistesgruß," D. 142, "Nähe des Geliebten," D. 162, "Gretchen am Spinnrade," D. 118, "Rastlose Liebe," D. 138, "Erlkönig," D. 328.

30 Ibid.

31 This contained the following poems: "Sehnsucht" ("Was zieht mir das Herz so?"), D. 123, "Wer kauft Liebesgötter?" D. 261, "Trost in Tränen," D. 120, "Der Gott und die Bajadere," D. 254, "Nachtgesang," D. 119, "Sehnsucht" ("Nur wer die Sehnsucht kennt"), D. 310, "Kennst du das Land?" D. 321, "Bundeslied," D. 258, "Tischlied," D. 234, "An den Mond," D. 259, "Der Rattenfänger," D. 255, "Der Sänger," D. 149.

32 *HA* 2, 407. Quoted in Deutsch, *Dokumente,* 288.

33 Letter of 16 June 1825, *WA*III/10:68–69.

34 While Goethe's failure to reply halted the publication of Schubert's Lieder, most of the first volume and the three op. 19 settings were published during Schubert's lifetime, though in conventional groups of three to five settings.

35 Deutsch, *Dokumente,* 51–52.

36 For further reasons see Willy Tappolet, *Begegnungen mit der Musik in Goethes Leben und Werk* (Bern: Benteli, 1975), 122; Robert Spaethling, *Music and Mozart in the Life of Goethe* (Columbia: Camden House, 1987), 41–42; Angelika Arend, "Goethe and Schubert: An Eclectic Affinity," *Carlton Germanic Papers* 22 (1994): 15–24 (here, 17); Jane Brown, "The Poetry of Schubert's Songs," in *Schubert's Vienna* ed. Raymond Erikson (New Haven: Yale UP, 1997), 188; and Whitton, *Goethe and Schubert,* 140–42.

37 Deutsch, *Dokumente,* 41.

[38] *WAIII/5:189.*

[39] Hicks, "Was Goethe Musical?" 123.

[40] Volker, "Schubert and Goethe," 130.

[41] (Pauline) Anna Milder-Hauptmann (1785–1838), German soprano, studied with Sigismund von Neukomm and Antonio Salieri. She made her début at the Theater an der Wien in 1803 and sang the role of Leonore at the première of Beethoven's *Fidelio* in 1805. She is remembered particularly for her interpretations of Gluck's heroines. Schubert attended a performance of *Iphigenia in Tauris* in 1813 where she appeared in the title role; in later years he exchanged some correspondence with her (1824–25) and dedicated "Suleika II" to her.

[42] Deutsch, *Dokumente,* 244.

[43] Cited in ibid., 123.

[44] Otto Erich Deutsch, *Schubert: Die Erinnerungen seiner Freunde,* 2nd rev. ed. (Leipzig: Breitkopf & Härtel, 1996), 19–20.

[45] Wilhelmine Schröder-Devrient (1804–60) made her début in Vienna in 1821 and sang the role of Leonore in Beethoven's presence one year later. She performed at many prestigious venues throughout Europe and is particularly known for her roles in Wagner's operas *Rienzi, Der fliegende Holländer* (The Flying Dutchman), and *Tannhäuser.*

[46] Eduard Genast, April 1830. Genast's account of the performance was first published by Alfred von Wolzogen in *Wilhelmine Schröder-Devrient: Ein Beitrag zur Geschichte des musikalischen Dramas* (Leipzig: Brockhaus, 1863), 146. It is also quoted in Hans Pless, "Goethe und die Musik," *Musikerziehung* 3 (1949): 73.

[47] Johann Gottlob von Quandt (1787–1859), influential art-lover, patron of the arts, and Goethe-admirer.

[48] Walwei-Wiegelmann, *Goethes Gedanken,* 50.

[49] Whitton, *Goethe and Schubert,* 146.

[50] Jack M. Stein, "Was Goethe Wrong about the Nineteenth-Century *Lied*"? *Publications of the Modern Language Association of America* 77 (1962): 232–39 (here, 235).

[51] Letter of 6 August 1822, Goethe to Tomaschék, *Goethes Gespräche,* ed. Flodoard Biedermann, 3 vols. (Leipzig: Biedermann, 1909–11), 2:592.

[52] Stein, "Was Goethe Wrong?" 235.

[53] Volker, "Schubert and Goethe," 128; Brown, *Schubert: A Critical Biography* (London: Da Capo Press, 1958), 86; Bell, *The Songs of Schubert* (London: Alston Books, 1964), 6; Gál, *Franz Schubert oder die Melodie* (Frankfurt a. M.: Fischer, 1992), 59; and Kramer, *Franz Schubert: Sexuality, Subjectivity, Song* (Cambridge: Cambridge UP, 1998), 9.

[54] Deutsch, *Erinnerungen,* 13–23.

[55] Walther Dürr, "Poesie und Musik: Goethe und Schubert," in *Zeichen-Setzung: Aufsätze zur musikalischen Poetik,* ed. Werner Aderhold and Walpurga Litschauer (Kassel: Bärenreiter, 1992), 114–27 (here, 126–27).

Goethe's *Egmont,* Beethoven's *Egmont*

David Hill

BEETHOVEN'S INCIDENTAL MUSIC to *Egmont,* op. 84, is a paradigmatic illustration of a number of possible relationships between music and ideas. Even when the overture is played by itself, as it was in Beethoven's day too, the title invites us to hear it not as an abstract symphonic movement, but as relating somehow to Goethe's play. Eduard Hanslick's claim that the link between the overture and the play is loose and arbitrary ("lose und willkürlich")[1] is only true in the sense that we would be unable to deduce the plot of the play from the music alone. The F-major coda of the overture reappears at the end of the incidental music as Beethoven's response to Goethe's instructions for a "Siegessymphonie" (3.1:329),[2] so we are presumably intended to hear the end of the overture as in some sense victorious. Each of the four entr'actes takes the audience from the mood at the end of one act to that at the beginning of the next, and towards the end of the play the music is supposed to express details of what is happening on stage more explicitly. Beethoven adopts Goethe's stage directions requiring "eine Musik, Clärchens Tod bezeichnend" ("music for Clärchen's death," 3.1:320), and goes on to indicate the various functions of the music accompanying Egmont's vision: for example, a flute motif headed "bedauernde Empfindung" ("sorrow") or a string passage marked "Egmonts Tod andeutend" ("suggestive of Egmont's death").[3]

Each of these examples raises a different theoretical issue: in some cases the music seems intended to express or underline the mood created by the play; in others, as the use of verbs like "bezeichnen" and "andeuten" indicates, the music is evidently supposed to give expression to particular actions on stage, or, in this last case, the content of the vision of a character on stage — albeit a vision that is displayed so that the audience too can see it. However, it is the Victory Symphony that ends both the overture and the play as a whole that this essay will discuss in particular detail because it is so crucial to an overall interpretation of the play and of the music, appearing to represent the final resolution of the tensions they have in their different ways developed. In what sense does Goethe's *Egmont,* and in what sense does Beethoven's *Egmont,* end with victory? What does each of them mean by the word "Sieg"?

Beethoven's Victory Symphony has commonly been taken as evoking ecstatic heroism. An early formulation of this view is provided by E. T. A. Hoffmann, who writes of "die Apotheose des siegreich für die Freiheit fallenden Helden."[4] Beethoven seems not only to portray a heroic individual, but also to conjure up something of the radicalized Enlightenment enthusiasm that pervades his opera *Fidelio*. In fact, the revision of the 1805 *Leonore* into the 1814 *Fidelio* seems to contain a debt to *Egmont:* Beethoven and his librettist Treitschke added to Florestan's dungeon scene a vision of Leonore as an angel leading Florestan to freedom, not unlike Egmont's vision of Klärchen.[5] There is a range of possible interpretations here. Beethoven may well have seen Egmont, like Florestan, as an image of himself, a visionary imprisoned in his deafness, or an artist excluded from normal social relations, and particularly marriage. Above all, if he is a hero, Egmont is the hero opposing tyranny, and this is, of course, the perspective of Egmont himself, who sees his individual death as a sacrifice necessary for the liberation of the Netherlands: "ich sterbe für die Freiheit, für die ich lebte und focht, und der ich mich jetzt leidend opfre" (3.1:329). Beethoven responded strongly to Goethe's play, quoting it from memory[6] and writing the incidental music, as he says, "bloß aus Liebe zum Dichter" — out of love for Goethe — rather than from commercial considerations,[7] and it seems likely that Egmont's final reference to breaking down tyranny would have stirred him. Indeed, the first page of the Hanover sketches to *Egmont* contains a note that Beethoven evidently wrote in order to help him focus on the essence of the play as he saw it: "Der Hauptpunkt ist, daß die Niederländer die Spanier zuletzt besiegen," that is: the defeat of the Spanish.[8] Similarly, under a motif in an early sketch for an overture in C minor Beethoven wrote the word "victoria."[9]

Hartmut Reinhardt has shown that for the Romantic readers of *Egmont* the ending of the play was an apotheosis in which Egmont's final moments have intimations of transcendence.[10] Even before Beethoven composed his music, Tieck's Joseph Berglinger was made to praise Goethe for ending his play with music, which moves the discourse beyond words: "als Erklärung, als Vollendung des Ganzen."[11] This tradition has retained its power up until the present day and has been sustained by the heroic force of the ending of Beethoven's Victory Symphony. This has come to be what one might call the common-sense interpretation of the play, which, in numerous variations, claims that victory means victory: that is, the Victory Symphony refers to a perspective from outside the play that vindicates Egmont by deeming him — despite his execution — as in some higher sense victorious.

Egmont may want to persuade himself that his death is an apotheosis, but does the play as a whole confirm this? Since the collapse of the tradition of heroic nationalism and heroic individualism, scholars have tended to see *Egmont* as a more problematic play and Egmont as a more problematic character. His interview with his secretary and his ensuing discussion with Oranien both show that he is warm-hearted and generous but also that he is impulsive and incapable of the longer-term planning that might produce real results. He is truly himself in the midst of battle or in the arms of Klärchen, but in the world of politics he is out of his depth. He misjudges people; he puts misplaced trust in King Philip and the order of the Golden Fleece; he even misjudges Klärchen to the point of entrusting her to Ferdinand just after we, the audience, have seen how circumstances have driven her to suicide. There seem indeed to be good reasons for Schiller's criticism of Egmont for his "leichtsinniges Vertrauen" (his naivety).[12]

Schiller's review of 1788 criticized precisely those aspects of *Egmont* that the Romantics were to admire. Schiller saw a discrepancy between the casualness of Egmont in political matters, his noble naivety, and the apotheosis that the vision and the Victory Symphony seemed to imply. He felt the ending was insufficiently integrated and therefore described it famously as a *salto mortale* into the world of opera.[13] When Goethe asked him to provide a revised performing version of the play in 1796, Schiller therefore developed the "stoical resistance"[14] of Egmont and at the same time relativized the validity of the final apotheosis by making the vision something Egmont reports rather than something the audience sees.[15]

Scholars, such as Sammons,[16] who extend this interpretation of Egmont regard with suspicion his supposed development from a happy-go-lucky aristocrat into a freedom fighter laying down his life for his people's liberation. In the review of a 1975 Cologne production, Ulrich Schreiber described the Egmont figure as someone concerned less with the fight for liberation than with his class privileges: "Er ist ganz strahlende Hohlheit, ein Playboy, der sich mehr um die Erhaltung seiner Standesprivilegien als um die Freiheit der Niederländer kümmert."[17] There is indeed a case for arguing that Egmont, faced by the inevitability of death, is desperately trying to make sense of life, styling himself as a Dutch hero when in fact his arrogance and his blindness to reality and to other people have allowed him to walk into trap after trap. By this interpretation, Egmont's vision, in which he sees himself crowned by Klärchen as the embodiment of freedom, is the fantasy of a deluded, or self-deluding mind. In the interpretation by Daniel Wilson it is even an attempt to impose on Klärchen — the only character who engages in real political activity — the traditional female role, decorously rewarding the male for his heroic sacrifice.[18] Behind the words Egmont uses to announce his sacrifice we hear resonating a slightly different emphasis: "ich sterbe für *die* Freiheit, für die ich lebte und focht, und der ich mich jetzt leidend opfre" (3.1:329, my emphasis). There are different kinds of freedom and by his use of the one abstract word, "Freiheit," Egmont is able to legitimize himself and his search for personal freedom by associating it with the idea of popular liberation.

Earlier scenes showed Egmont amongst the crowd as a man of the people, but when he dies — supposedly for the sake of their freedom — he is separated from them, in prison. Egmont's life has indeed been devoted to an ideal of freedom, but not to popular liberation. He has benefited from his privileged position, which allows him to indulge himself in a life dedicated to spontaneity, a life free from care, "Sorge," and his idea of sacrifice is his way of imagining he can escape the self-referentiality of a life dedicated merely to living. His focus on himself prevents him from taking the political initiative in the way that even Klärchen does, and behind the word " leidend" ("suffering") we begin to hear not only Egmont's self-designation as a martyr re-enacting the passion of Christ, but also the reality of his passivity.

Even at the level of the political implications of the plot there is ambiguity. In the uproar following the death of the historical Egmont, only the northern Netherlands (the united provinces) eventually gained their independence, albeit eighty years later. Yet the southern provinces, where the play is exclusively set, remained under Habsburg control; Goethe's first readers would have been reminded of this by the unrest there in 1787.[19] Beethoven's idea of the ultimate liberation of the Netherlands may therefore have been wrong. Schiller seems to have thought that Egmont's death made no effective contribution to it.[20]

If — following this interpretation — Egmont is ineffectual and deluded, what kind of Victory Symphony would be appropriate? One, presumably, that emphasizes the one-sidedness, the illusory nature of his victory. We can imagine a march, perhaps, full of empty clichés underlined by dissonances and an edgy instrumentation: we imagine Mahler. This is how we imagine it today — but is this what Goethe imagined when he asked his friend Philipp Kayser to compose the music in 1788? It is uncertain whether or not Kayser's setting of the incidental music was ever completed and performed, but one wonders whether he or Reichardt — whose music for the play was first performed in 1801 and which has also, for the most part, been lost — would have been capable of ironic victory music, or if Goethe were capable of imagining it. What would ironized heroism have sounded like? Would it have been something like the muted and rather out-of-kilter march that accompanies the entrance of Pizarro in *Fidelio*?[21]

Or might it indeed be the heady enthusiasm of the Victory Symphony that concludes Beethoven's *Egmont*? This seems to be the view of that expert on subversive texts, Adorno. He argues that Beethoven's *Egmont* Overture, and especially its concluding Victory Symphony, is forced and has a kind of emptiness or false simplicity, a "falsche, der Substanz widersprechende Simplizität" that is typical of the Restoration, and he finds that the lack of symphonic material produces "etwas Brutales, Deutsches, Auftrumpfendes."[22] Can one argue therefore that this alleged brutal triumphalism of the music expresses the hollowness of Egmont's claims to victory? Or could it also at some level express the victory of the sinister

Alba? Either way, Adorno's interpretation would allow us to claim that Beethoven's music expressed the failures embodied in Egmont. Conversely, Ernst Oster's Schenkerian analysis denies the simplicity of the Victory Symphony by showing its motivic connection to the earlier parts of the overture.[23] More fundamentally, it seems, Adorno does not distinguish sufficiently between his argument that there is something inherently repressive about the German tradition of idealism, which in some respects Beethoven represents, and the argument that Beethoven's intervention in the tradition in this specific case is an attempt to say something about repression. A comparison with the emptiness of his *Wellingtons Sieg*, op. 91 (Wellington's Victory, 1813), which Carl Dahlhaus rightly describes as a "Petrifakt" or even a parody of Beethoven's heroic style,[24] draws attention by contrast to the vitality and intensity of the Victory Symphony.

And is there not, similarly, too much cynicism in a reading of Goethe's *Egmont* that looks only for irony in his directions for a concluding Victory Symphony? A more charitable view of Egmont is that he embodies a system of values, a philosophy of life that is the antithesis of the deathly, calculating Alba, one that is in many ways the spirit of the Dutch people in its purest form, but also one that has a positive value in its own right. Egmont is a charismatic hero with a vision and a zest for life that far transcends that of any other character on stage, except perhaps Klärchen. He is at ease amongst the people and with Klärchen, but he feels out of place at the court of Margarete, and his only serious engagement with political issues (in Act IV) is irrelevant to the action of the play, because the outcome has been determined in advance. Egmont compares himself with a sleepwalker who would fall if he were called by name; that is, if Egmont's secretary made him confront the cares of the day: "Daß ich fröhlich bin, die Sachen leicht nehme, rasch lebe, das ist mein Glück und ich vertausch es nicht gegen die Sicherheit eines Toten-Gewölbes" (3.1:275). Specifically, he would not exchange this carefree existence for the security of a burial chamber. Egmont, we may say, represents one way of life. From the point of view of those who live by "Sorge" (a life of care), of course — Alba, Oranien, Graf Oliva, and Klärchen's mother — it is a devotion to the moment that can be criticized as short-sighted and impractical, even as self-deluding. These are the criticisms that some scholars make of Egmont, and they may not be wrong as long as effectiveness remains the only criterion.[25] But this is not the whole story. It may be more satisfactory to interpret *Egmont* as an experiment with a philosophy of life, one that on the one hand is shown to be lacking in certain situations and unable to meet certain of the demands placed on it, but that on the other hand reflects a warmth and intensity of living that we cannot help admiring. Egmont's weakness has been shown to be planned activity, his strength has been intensity of being for the moment. As in other plays of his, Goethe's version of tragic guilt involves counterposing alternative modes of existence.

A destructive principle of rational control is seen to be victorious over an individual who is closer to nature and his own nature, a hero who struggles to remain true to a way of life or philosophy of life that is inexorably being eroded from inside and out. In the words of Elizabeth Wilkinson:

> The contrast is between thought, and self-propagating activity of the mind, turning over its few fragments of data, inferring, elaborating, combining, speculating; and knowledge derived from intuitive contemplation and dependent on ever-renewed contact with the objects of the outer world.[26]

By the end of the play Alba and all he represents are victorious, in that they succeed in killing Egmont and repressing the popular expression of discontent. Even Klärchen has killed herself in despair. However, Egmont has inspired Alba's son, Ferdinand, and his vision (nicely complementing the blindness or short-sightedness he has been identified with throughout the play[27]) shows that he is aware of other dimensions of existence in which Alba cannot in the end hold sway. His premonition of ultimate vindication should be read not only as a psychological event, revealing what goes on in the mind of this character in this situation, but also as a comment on the play as a whole, revealing the verdict of poetic justice, namely that the values Egmont stands for cannot in the end be suppressed by the cold-blooded Alba.[28] It is appropriate that while the "real" events on stage present Egmont's defeat and his death, a different medium — music — intervenes to present the case for the principles for which Egmont stands.[29] Goethe uses the Victory Symphony in order to balance the ostensible victory of Alba, and to show the relative, not the absolute, validity of Egmont's principles.

This approach to Goethe's *Egmont* remembers the political failures, but it also remembers and celebrates Egmont's force of personality and the philosophical position it represents. It regards the concluding Victory Symphony neither as simply affirming the apotheosis of Egmont nor as a sarcastic reference to the purely imaginary nature of his victory. Egmont as a character has many merits that deserve celebration, even if they are inseparable from aspects of his personality that prevent the realization of his ideals in the real world. Paradoxical as it may seem, Egmont's thirst for life is, in a way, victorious over Alba's plans for his execution. There is a sense in which the intensity with which he lives the moment represents a way of life that cannot be overcome by death. The values by which Egmont lives condemn him in one sense to failure, but in another, make him immune to failure. At the same time it is important to recall the suspicions of transcendence that distinguished Goethe from the Romantics and that are reflected in the realism of the world he has conjured up. The crowd scenes in the earlier part of the play, the scenes with Margareta von Parma, and even the scenes with Klärchen, locate the values of Egmont and the debate about freedom in the real world of sixteenth-century Flanders. It is this social and political world that gives rise to the values of Egmont — but also prevents their realization. The tragedy that Goethe addresses is the impossibility of the realization of unconditional values like freedom and vitality in a conditional world.

If we turn now from the sense in which Goethe meant the term "Siegessymphonie" to Beethoven's realization of this instruction, we find that very similar arguments can be used, although one may want to apply them in slightly different ways. First, one can argue that it does represent a potentially transcendent culmination of the play, but that the victory is less that of Egmont himself than of the values for which he stands. Second, however, Dahlhaus, writing of the *Egmont* Overture, emphasizes that the meaning of a piece of music cannot be reduced to its final bars, and that the F-major coda does not subsume the preceding conflicts. He points out that the dramatic structure shows the precarious balance between the real and the ideal, power and hope:

> Die "Sieges-Symphonie" als "Quintessenz" der Ouvertüre zu verstehen, wäre [. . .] eine Verzerrung der dramatischen Struktur, die kein "Resultat" präsentiert, sondern in der sich die Realität der Gewalt und die Idealität der Hoffnung [. . .] im Gleichgewicht halten [. . .].[30]

The same argument can be applied to the ending of the play: our final vision of a heroic Egmont — both Goethe's Egmont and Beethoven's Egmont — need not eradicate our knowledge of his weaknesses, or at least his one-sidedness, and a celebration of liberation does not imply denial of the problems associated with turning the idea of liberation into reality.

We have, then, two arguments that can be applied to both Goethe and Beethoven, and which can be used to support the contention that the conclusion of *Egmont* embodies a problematic and qualified victory. The first argument focuses on the ideas of the play and emphasizes that, despite Egmont's execution, the conclusion is a victory for certain ideas that are only partially manifest in the person of Egmont. The second, which can refer either to the ideas or to Egmont as an individual, doubts that the concluding Victory Symphony is to be read as a summation and resolution of the problems that have been explored in the play; it implies that the audience take a more distanced perspective, weighing up the mixture of positive and negative, victory and defeat — in the words of Dahlhaus: "die Realität der Gewalt und die Idealität der Hoffnung." Both arguments can be applied to Goethe's play as well as to Beethoven's music. Moreover, they are not incompatible with each other: they are coordinates against which the two conceptions of a Victory Symphony can be plotted. Goethe's, it seems, would have lain more in the direction of realism and balance, and Beethoven's more in the direction of idealism and culmination.

In political terms, Goethe is commonly regarded as a conservative and Beethoven as a radical. When they met in 1812, Beethoven saw in Goethe

the courtier, while Goethe saw in Beethoven elements of that unsociability and disorder that in the end threatened life.[31] In both cases, though, their political positions are more complex than these assessments might suggest.

Goethe was well aware of the parallels between the intervention of Philip II in the Netherlands and the attempts of absolutist rulers in his own day to impose their values on subject peoples. When he returned to the composition of *Egmont* while in Italy in 1787 he realized that the play he had begun to write some twelve years earlier could be regarded as exactly prefiguring current events in Brussels, where the troops of that archetype of enlightened absolutism, Joseph II, were attempting to enforce the abolition of the estates (3.1:838), and he could express sympathy with those who feared Joseph's similarly despotic designs for expansion in Italy (15:232). His conception of Egmont goes back to a time when his political thinking was strongly indebted to the writings of Justus Möser, who countered such absolutist tendencies with the idea of organic communities held together by local traditions, and in Weimar he remained critical of the excessively centralized planning of Prussia. Thus many aspects of Egmont's opposition to centralized control were attractive to Goethe.[32] At the same time, he was equally aware of the need for an ordered response. In his diary entry for 13 May 1780, he states that governance is predicated on self-denial: "Niemand als wer sich ganz verläugnet ist wert, zu herrschen, und kan herrschen."[33] This renunciation is, of course, exactly what Egmont rejects in his zest for living life to the full.

Beethoven, too, in Vienna at the end of the first decade of the nineteenth century, knew all about the attempts of powerful nations to impose centralized order. Austria declared war on France on 9 April 1809; Napoleon's troops besieged Vienna and a month later occupied the city.[34] It seems likely that Beethoven's enthusiasm for Goethe's play goes back at least in part to the connections he made between it and his own situation. This was, after all, a period of enormous intensification and politicization of German feelings of national identity. Beethoven himself had the reputation of being a Francophobe, and was dependent on Francophobe Viennese aristocrats like Lobkowitz. His "Landsberg 5" sketchbook contains a number of drafts of patriotic compositions dating from the spring of 1809, including a setting of Collin's "Österreich über Alles" ("Austria above all") and, probably, "Freudvoll und leidvoll" ("Joyful and Sorrowful") from *Egmont*.[35]

Beethoven's attitude was, however, profoundly ambivalent, as Maynard Solomon has shown, torn between, on the one hand, a belief that Napoleon had inherited moral legitimacy from the ideals of the French Revolution, and, on the other, the reality of French expansionism:

> Beethoven regarded Bonaparte as an embodiment of Enlightened leadership; but, simultaneously, he felt betrayed by Bonaparte's Caesaristic actions. Beethoven's ambivalence mirrored a central contradiction of his age. [. . .] As an artist and a man, Beethoven could no longer accept

unmediated conceptions of progress, innate human goodness, reason, and faith. His affirmations were now leavened by an acknowledgement of the frailty of human leadership and a consciousness of the regressive and brutalizing components in all forward-thrusting stages in social evolution.[36]

There were still signs of a faith in Napoleon, hints that he would have liked recognition from him,[37] and it may well be that Beethoven detected this ambivalence, "the conflict between faith and skepticism, the struggle between belief and disbelief,"[38] in Goethe's play. However, Beethoven did not need to choose between belief and skepticism any more than Goethe did. The ambivalences of art allowed the Victory Symphony to express belief in the idea of liberation and progress, without needing specifically to confirm or deny the problems that the play had revealed.

If both Goethe and Beethoven felt and articulated some ambivalence towards the enthusiasm with which *Egmont* appears to end, the quality of this ambivalence is nevertheless different in each case. They are distinguished by their aesthetics and by their understanding of the idea of freedom. With the radicalization of Enlightenment ideas in the French Revolution, the tragic idealism of the *Sturm und Drang* (Storm and Stress) gave way to heroic idealism, the idea of organic community to the idea of nation, and a pre-Romantic aesthetic that counterposed blocks of ideas to an aesthetic of transcendence. There is no indication that Goethe was able to understand this development, least of all in Beethoven's music. He did not, as far as we know, respond to Beethoven's request for a critique of his *Egmont*-music,[39] and seems to have been evasive in his response to Marianne von Willemer's enthusiasm for it.[40]

The entry in his diary for 29 January 1814, after he first witnessed a performance of *Egmont* with Beethoven's incidental music, is eloquent in all that it does not say: it contains the one word "Egmont."[41]

Notes

[1] Eduard Hanslick, *Vom Musikalisch-Schönen*, 13th ed. (Leipzig: Breitkopf & Härtel, 1922), 156. See also Martha Calhoun, "Music as Subversive Text: Beethoven, Goethe and the Overture to *Egmont*," *Mosaic* 20 (1987): 46. See also Eugen Kilian, "Beethovens Egmont-Musik und das Theater," *Allgemeine Musik-Zeitung* 48:3 (1921): 35–36; Kilian, *Goethes Egmont auf der Bühne: Zur Inszenierung und Darstellung des Trauerspiels: Ein Handbuch der Regie* (Munich: Müller, 1925); Johanna Rudolph, "Realismus und Antizipation in Werken Ludwig van Beethovens: Zur Wechselwirkung der Künste am Beispiel der 'Egmont'-Musik und des 'Fidelio'-Problems in Shakespeares 'Cymbeline,'" in *Bericht über den internationalen Beethoven-Kongress 10.-12. Dezember 1970 in Berlin*, ed. Heinz Alfred Brockhaus and Konrad Niemann (Berlin: Neue Musik, 1971), 249–68.

[2] References in this form in the text are to volume and page of Johann Wolfgang Goethe, *Sämtliche Werke nach Epochen seines Schaffens*, ed. Karl Richter et al.,

21 vols. (Munich: Hanser, 1985–99). Beethoven was insistent that his publisher should not omit the word "Siegessymphonie" from the score: see letter to Breitkopf & Härtel of 15 October 1810, in Ludwig van Beethoven, *Briefwechsel: Gesamtausgabe,* ed. Sieghard Brandenburg, 8 vols. (Munich: Henle, 1996), 1:162 (hereafter abbreviated to *BB* with volume and page numbers).

[3] Ludwig van Beethoven, *Musik zu Egmont und andere Schauspielmusiken,* ed. Helmut Hell, vol. 9.7 of *Werke: Gesamtausgabe* (Munich: Henle, 1998), 115, 121, 124.

[4] E. T. A. Hoffmann, *Musikalische Novellen und Schriften,* ed. Paul Friedrich Scherber (Munich: Goldmann, n.d.), 175.

[5] Ludwig van Beethoven, *Fidelio in Full Score* (Leipzig: Peters, 1870; reprint New York: Dover, 1984), 160. At this point in Florestan's aria, Beethoven modulates from F minor to F major, as do the coda of the *Egmont* Overture and his song setting "Die Trommel gerühret!"

[6] Letter to Therese Malfatti, May 1810, *BB*2:122.

[7] Letter to Breitkopf & Härtel, 21 August 1810, *BB*2:150. The same phrase occurs in a letter to Bettina Brentano of 10 February 1811, *BB*2:178.

[8] Adolf Fecker, *Die Entstehung von Beethovens Musik zu Goethes Trauerspiel Egmont: Eine Abhandlung über die Skizzen,* vol. 18 of *Hamburger Beiträge zur Musikwissenschaft* (Hamburg: Wagner, 1978), 17.

[9] Fecker, *Beethovens Musik zu Goethes Trauerspiel,* 108.

[10] "'. . . jene tiefere, echt romantische Tendenz.' Goethes Egmont und seine Rezeption bei den Romantikern," in *Schnittpunkt Romantik: Text- und Quellenstudien zur Literatur des 19. Jahrhunderts: Festschrift für Sibylle von Steinsdorff,* ed. Wolfgang Bunzel, Konrad Feilchenfeldt, and Walter Schmitz (Tübingen: Niemeyer, 1997), 1–22.

[11] Wilhelm Heinrich Wackenroder, *Sämtliche Werke: Historisch-kritische Ausgabe,* ed. Silvio Vietta and Richard Littlejohns (Heidelberg: Winter, 1991), vol. 1: *Phantasien über die Kunst, für Freunde der Kunst,* 246. This section, "Symphonien," is almost certainly by Tieck.

[12] "Über Goethes Egmont," *Schillers Werke: Nationalausgabe,* ed. Julius Petersen et al., 41 vols. (Weimar: Böhlau, 1943ff.), 22:201.

[13] Ibid., 208.

[14] Lesley Sharpe, "Schiller and Goethe's 'Egmont,'" *Modern Language Review* 77 (1982): 629–45 (here, 637).

[15] Goethe in turn felt that Schiller's version was too brutally logical and insisted on his original (3.1:862). Although Schiller's revised version does not fit, either in its conception or in the practicalities of its execution, it was nevertheless common in performance to combine Beethoven's music with Schiller's version of the play, or else with Goethe's subsequent compromising revision of Schiller's version: see Kilian, *Goethes Egmont auf der Bühne,* 47–53; Sigrid Siedhoff, *Der Dramaturg Schiller: "Egmont": Goethes Text — Schillers Bearbeitung,* vol. 6 of *Mitteilungen zur Theatergeschichte der Goethezeit* (Bonn: Bouvier, 1983), 260. Heinrich Laube was at least consistent in preferring Schiller's version of the play and at the same time

thinking that Beethoven's music was too heroic for it (see Kilian, *Goethes Egmont*, 53). See also Karl Konrad Polheim, *Zwischen Goethe und Beethoven: Verbindende Texte zu Beethovens Egmont-Musik: Mit Einführung und Kommentar* (Bonn: Bouvier, 1982), 15.

[16] Jeffrey L. Sammons, "On the Structure of Goethe's *Egmont*," *Journal of English and Germanic Philology* 62 (1963): 241–51. See also: Robert T. Ittner, "Klärchen in Goethe's *Egmont*," *Journal of English and Germanic Philology* 62 (1963): 252–61, and, more moderately, M. W. Swales, "A Questionable Politician: A Discussion of the Ending to Goethe's 'Egmont,'" *Modern Language Review* 66 (1971): 832–40, also Edward T. Larkin, "Goethe's *Egmont*: Political Revolution and Personal Transformation," *Michigan German Studies* 17 (1991): 28–50. The source of this line of argument is the brilliant essay by Elizabeth M. Wilkinson, "The Relation of Form and Meaning in 'Egmont,'" in *Publications of the English Goethe Society* 18 (1949): 149–82, reprinted in Elizabeth M. Wilkinson and Leonard A. Willoughby, *Goethe: Poet and Thinker* (London: Arnold, 1962), 55–74.

[17] Quoted in Johann Wolfgang von Goethe, *Egmont: Ein Trauerspiel in fünf Aufzügen*, ed. Irmgard and Bernhard Nagl (Stuttgart: Klett, 1986), 131.

[18] W. Daniel Wilson, "Amazon, Agitator, Allegory: Political and Gender Cross (-Dress)ing in Goethe's *Egmont*," in *Outing Goethe & His Age*, ed. Alice A. Kuzniar (Stanford: Stanford UP, 1996), 125–46.

[19] See Hans Reiss, "Goethe, Moser and the Aufklärung: The Holy Roman Empire in *Götz von Berlichingen* and *Egmont*," *Deutsche Vierteljahresschrift für Literaturwissenschaft und Geistesgeschichte* 60 (1986): 609–44 (here, 641).

[20] Sharpe, "Schiller and Goethe's 'Egmont,'" 636.

[21] This strange march was not Beethoven's first response. The 1805 version contains a quite different march that has more of the straightforward pomp one might have expected for Pizarro, and is in the key of D, with which he tends to be associated.

[22] Theodor W. Adorno, *Beethoven: Philosophie der Musik: Fragmente und Texte*, ed. Rolf Tiedemann, in Adorno, *Nachgelassene Schriften* (Frankfurt a. M.: Suhrkamp, 1993), 1.1:134, 121.

[23] Ernst Oster, "The Dramatic Character of the *Egmont* Overture," in *Aspects of Schenkerian Theory*, ed. David Beach (New Haven and London: Yale UP, 1983), 209–22, esp. 220–22.

[24] Carl Dahlhaus, *Ludwig van Beethoven und seine Zeit* (Laaber: Laaber, 1987), 45.

[25] Some critics claim even that the case for Egmont's political ineptitude has been exaggerated; for example, H. G. Haile, "Goethe's Political Thinking and *Egmont*," *Germanic Review* 42 (1967): 96–107; John M. Ellis, "The vexed question of Egmont's political judgement," in *Tradition and Creation: Essays in Honour of Elizabeth Mary Wilkinson*, ed. C. P. Magill et al. (Leeds: Maney, 1978), 116–30.

[26] Wilkinson, "The Relation of Form and Meaning in 'Egmont,'" *Publications of the English Goethe Society* 18 (1949): 165, and in Wilkinson and Willoughby, *Goethe*, 64. For variations on this argument see Hans-Jürgen Schings, "Freiheit in der Geschichte: Egmont und Marquis Posa im Vergleich," *Goethe-Jahrbuch* 110 (1993): 61–76; see also Roger A. Nicholls, "*Egmont* and the Vision of Freedom,"

German Quarterly 43 (1970): 188–98. Both of these emphasize how Egmont is contrasted with characters like Alba and Vansen, who are in different ways in thrall to abstract ideas.

[27] The point is made by Goethe himself in his report of Angelika Kauffmann's response to the play (3.1:842).

[28] His name is derived from *albus* (white), an association also found in the naming of other "bloodless" characters like Albert and Weislingen. See also Margareta's description of Alba: "der hohläugige Toledaner mit der ehrnen Stirne und dem tiefen Feuerblick[,] murmelt zwischen den Zähnen. . ." (3.1:284).

[29] Steffen Martus argues in this context that Goethe's concept of aesthetic totality is inherently musical. "Sinn und Form in Goethe's 'Egmont,'" *Goethe-Jahrbuch* 115 (1998): 45–61 (here, 47).

[30] Dahlhaus, *Ludwig van Beethoven*, 42.

[31] Beethoven writes: "Göthe behagt die Hofluft zu sehr mehr als es einem Dichter ziemt, Es ist nicht vielmehr über die lächerlichkeiten der Virtuosen hier zu reden, wenn Dichter, die als die ersten Lehrer der Nation angesehn seyn sollten, über diesem schimmer alles andere vergessen können" (*BB*2:287). Less than a month later Goethe gave a report on Beethoven to Zelter in a letter of 2 September 1812: "Sein Talent hat mich in Erstaunen gesetzt; allein er ist leider eine ganz ungebändigte Persönlichkeit" (20.1:282).

[32] Volkmar Braunbehrens relates Goethe's ambivalence towards Egmont to his ambivalence towards Karl August: "Egmont, das lang vertrödelte Stück," in *Johann Wolfgang von Goethe*, ed. Heinz Ludwig Arnold, special vol. of Text + Kritik (Munich: Text + Kritik, 1982), 84–100.

[33] *Goethes Werke*, ed. Gustav von Loeper, Erich Schmidt, and Hermann Grimm, 143 vols. (Weimar: Hermann Böhlaus Nachfolger, 1887–1912), 3.1:118.

[34] See Andreas Ballstaedt, "Musik zu 'Egmont,' op. 84," in *Beethoven: Interpretationen seiner Werke*, ed. Albrecht Riethmüller et al., vol. 1 (Laaber: Laaber, 1994), 649–60, esp. 649–50.

[35] *The Beethoven Sketchbooks: History, Reconstruction, Inventory*, ed. Douglas Johnson (Oxford: Clarendon, 1985), 188. See also Beethoven, *Werke*, 9.7:205.

[36] Maynard Solomon, *Beethoven* (London: Cassell, 1977), 141.

[37] There is evidence that in 1810 Beethoven was thinking he might dedicate his Mass in C Major to Napoleon.

[38] Solomon, *Beethoven*, 142.

[39] Letter of 12 April 1811, *BB*2:185.

[40] Jochen Golz, "Goethe in seinem Verhältnis zu Beethoven," in *"Meine Harmonie mit der Ihrigen verbunden": Beethoven und Goethe*, ed. Jochen Golz and Michael Ladenburger (Bonn and Weimar: Beethoven-Haus Bonn and Stiftung Weimarer Klassik, 1999), 9–22 (here, 13).

[41] *Goethes Werke*, 3.5:94.

A Tale of Two *Fausts:* An Examination of Reciprocal Influence in the Responses of Liszt and Wagner to Goethe's *Faust*

David Larkin

ONE OF THE MAJOR DIFFERENCES between the music of the classical period (late eighteenth century) and that of the nineteenth century was the tendency of Romantic composers to resort explicitly to external, non-musical sources to form the basis for the creation of new instrumental compositions. Nature proved valuable in this regard; examples include such works as Liszt's piano piece *Au lac de Wallenstadt* (*Années de Pèlerinage* I) (At the Wallenstadt Lake, Years of Pilgrimage I, 1858), or Mendelssohn's *Hebrides* Overture (1832), which consciously try to reproduce in sonic terms a visual phenomenon — or, at least, an emotional recollection of the scene. However, with famous examples by Vivaldi (*Le quattro stagione,* The Four Seasons, 1725) and Beethoven (Symphony No. 6, "Pastoral," 1808) providing precedents, nature depiction was not really a new departure in the nineteenth century, but rather the continuation of an existing tradition on a more widespread basis. For many composers, including Schumann and Liszt, the impetus that other art forms could give to the production of musical works was even more important than nature, and truly constituted one of the major innovations of the period. If few in the nineteenth century went as far as Wagner in advocating a *Gesamtkunstwerk* — a union of all arts to the service of music-based drama — virtually all musicians were conscious of being part of a broader cultural movement. The stimulus provided by literature proved hugely important for many composers, even in the field of purely instrumental music. Schumann's piano music, for instance, would have been very different were it not for his fascination with the writings of Hoffmann and Jean Paul, visible in his works and acknowledged by him. Shakespeare and contemporary Romantic writers such as Novalis, Byron, and Hugo proved rich sources.

However, the single most important literary subject in the nineteenth century for the musician was unquestionably the "Faust" legend. It appealed to the Romantic sensibility in many ways: a heroic central character (the eponymous Faust), an agreeable touch of the diabolic in Mephistopheles, a redeeming woman figure (Gretchen), and a titanic struggle between good and evil impulses in the breast of the protagonist. Johann Wolfgang von Goethe's tragedy *Faust* (part 1: 1808, part 2: 1833) stimulated the imagination of literally hundreds of artists, including writers such as Nikolaus Lenau and Gérard de Nerval, musicians as varied as Schubert, Berlioz, Wagner, Liszt, and Gounod, and painters such as Delacroix, Alma-Tadema, and Tissot. Both Wagner's *Faust* Overture (1840, revised 1855) and Liszt's *Faust* Symphony (1854, revised 1857) were inspired by and explicitly relate to Goethe's work — but the composers' reactions to the drama were not solely responsible for shaping these orchestral compositions. Another huge factor was the mutual interaction between the two composers; their almost symbiotic relationship played a large role in the evolution of the works as we know them today. This paper will first examine the gestation of Liszt's work and Wagner's role in shaping this project (the final three-movement design of Liszt's symphony stems in all likelihood from Wagner). The fundamental features of this symphony will also be briefly described in this section. Secondly, a study of the music of Liszt's symphony will reveal that certain important thematic shapes are musical quotations from Wagner's overture. This thematic citation undoubtedly derived from Liszt's study of Wagner's 1840 score of the overture and their subsequent correspondence. Finally, Wagner's work will be scrutinized to see how Liszt's suggestions can be said to have influenced its 1855 revision.

Liszt's *Faust* Symphony: Conception and Structure

In 1830 Liszt was introduced by Berlioz to Goethe's *Faust* I in Gérard de Nerval's French translation.[1] From sketches he made in the 1840s, he was contemplating an instrumental composition based on *Faust,* but — probably due to his hectic touring lifestyle — nothing came of it at that time. On 14 October 1849, having seen a set of short pieces Liszt had written for Goethe's centenary, the so-called *Goethealbum* (1849), Wagner suggested that Liszt should write an opera. He felt Liszt needed the stimulus that a larger project would provide, and in this regard alluded to the complete *Faust* as an adequate (if impossible) subject. In connection with his operatic recommendation, Wagner's mention of the *Faust* subject proved prophetic.[2] Less than a year later, in August 1850, Nerval arrived in Weimar to meet Liszt, whom he knew slightly from their Parisian days. He suggested to Liszt that they should collaborate on a *Faust* opera, based not on Goethe's *Faust,* but on a French-style treatment of the legendary exploits. This suggestion found a ready echo in Liszt, whose attitude to Goethe was not one of unmixed admiration, as we shall see, and the project must have sounded particularly appealing when Nerval, an unsure dramatist, suggested working with the enormously successful Alexandre

Dumas on the libretto. Liszt wrote to Nerval on 25 December 1850, confessing that in composing a *Faust* opera, he was realizing one of his goals.[3] Dumas had to flee France in 1852 in order to escape his creditors, which threw the burden of the project firmly on Nerval's shoulders. During the course of 1852, Liszt conducted a large number of works on the subject of *Faust,* including the Weimar première of Wagner's *Faust* Overture in its original (1840) form.[4] It seems logical that such activities would have stirred Liszt's creative impulses for the *Faust* opera-project into life, causing him to review his earlier sketches, although he had not yet received any text with which to work. Admittedly, in the initial stages the absence of a text would not have inhibited the creation of music suitable to an archetypal story like *Faust;* and in any case, Liszt did not have Wagner's scruples about the overriding importance of a true word-tone synthesis.

The plan had not been formally abandoned by the time of Liszt's visit to Wagner in Zurich in July 1853. Jensen suggests that during the visit Liszt played Wagner excerpts from the opera *Faust* (presumably improvising on sketches), passages that eventually were incorporated into the *Faust* Symphony.[5] However, there is a distinct possibility that even before this visit, Liszt had already begun to revert to his original idea of an instrumental work based on the legend. He must have realized that the plan was not going to amount to anything, due to Nerval's procrastination in supplying him with even a scenario, let alone a libretto. In the course of their correspondence in November 1852, Wagner had described to Liszt the plan of his own abandoned *Faust* Symphony[6] with its "Faust" first movement and its second movement depicting Gretchen — of which the *Faust* Overture represented the first movement (the only one completed). It is very probable that this directed Liszt's own *Faust* project into the same mold, whether he was conscious of it or not. Whether Liszt came to Zurich resolved on this scheme, or whether it emerged when the two of them were discussing Wagner's *Faust* Overture (with its early symphonic plan), cannot be ascertained.[7] It can be surmised that when Liszt left Zurich, Wagner was certain that his friend was going to work on a *Faust* Symphony, as Wagner made an unprompted allusion to it early in 1854, casually asking about Liszt's progress with the work.[8] Wagner's own account of this first meeting in his autobiography (admittedly written much later, and not always reliable as a source) supports this, describing the eagerness with which they went through Liszt's completed symphonic poems, in particular his *Faust* Symphony.[9]

The symphony was written in the astonishingly short period between August and October 1854, which again suggests that Liszt was working with a very familiar plan. Though dedicated to Berlioz, it really owed its symphonic layout to Wagner: what could be more obvious than the links between Wagner's abandoned character-depicting symphony and Liszt's symphony, whose full title is *Eine Faust-Symphonie in drei Charakterbildern für Tenor, Männerchor und Orchester* (A Faust-Symphony in Three Character-Portraits for Tenor, Male-voice Choir, and Orchestra)? As we shall see in the next section, Liszt chose to pay this debt internally.

Since space precludes a detailed analysis of this symphony, possibly Liszt's masterpiece, only some of the more important features can be pointed out. With a few exceptions, Liszt by and large eschewed any attempt at narrative of the Faust plot (a rare approach in his programmatic instrumental music) in favor of musical character-depiction. While this seems to follow Wagner's lead, it is also in line with the procedure Liszt generally followed; other examples include the symphonic poem *Hamlet* (1858), where a sound picture of the gloomy Dane is drawn in preference to the depiction of specific incidents of Shakespeare's play. By following this approach Liszt was able to come to terms with his ambivalent attitude towards Goethe — and his *Faust* in particular. He seemingly had more empathy for a great, if flawed, character such as Byron's Manfred, as opposed to the *petit bourgeois* mentality he detected in Faust. On one occasion, Liszt commented disparagingly on Faust's vacillation and his weakness in putting up with Mephistopheles, contrasting him to a more decisive character like Manfred, who Liszt believed would have been able to kill Gretchen, but who would never have deserted her cravenly like Goethe's protagonist.[10]

While Liszt avoided depicting any incidents or aspects in Faust's character that did not appeal to him (for instance, his desertion of Gretchen), one or two passages follow the action of the drama more closely: for example, one passage in the second movement supposedly represents Gretchen plucking the flower petals to "er liebt mich — liebt mich nicht" (101). Richard Pohl, a member of Liszt's inner circle, identified the various themes in the first movement ("Faust"): for example, one represents Faust's brooding (see example 1b below), another his passion or urge for life (example 2b), a third supposedly represents Faust in love (example 8b), yet another the famous line "Im Anfang war die Tat" ("In the beginning was the act," 44).[11] Gretchen's two themes are of total simplicity; some of Faust's themes also occur in "her" movement, a device that not only is programmatically apt, but also fulfils the Romantic penchant for unity of thematic material right across a composition. Liszt's brilliant idea for the last movement ("Mephistopheles") was to use grotesque variants of Faust's themes. Mephistopheles is there only to pervert, not to create: "Ich bin der Geist, der stets verneint" — the spirit of negation (47). This masterstroke (admittedly, merely an instance of his favorite device of thematic transformation) may have been gained from the similar distortion of the theme of the beloved (the *idée fixe*) in the final movement of Berlioz's *Symphonie Fantastique* (1830), a work that Liszt knew well and had transcribed for piano solo. The theme that initially represented Faust in love, for example, is treated as a cacophonous fugato — perhaps in order to depict the multiple passions that Mephisto can provide for Faust as a substitute for true love.

The later addition (1857) of the "Chorus Mysticus" and tenor solo singing the last octet of the whole *Faust* drama ("Alles Vergängliche": "all that is transient," 364), rounds off the symphony in a very satisfying fashion, for all that Wagner disliked this new ending;[12] it gives the impression of having progressed through the course of the drama. The thematic material here is drawn from Gretchen's movement. Only her themes remained uncorrupted when they appeared in the course of the third movement[13] — in keeping with Mephistopheles's own admission that he has no hold over her: "über die habe ich keine Gewalt" (84) — and their reappearance in the beatific finale testifies to her redemptive role: "Das Ewig-Weibliche / Zieht uns hinan" (364).

In sum, Liszt wisely eschewed the philosophical preoccupations of Goethe's text in favor of a more straightforward depiction of the three principal characters. In this symphony he balanced the most ingenious formal manipulations with a liveliness of imagination that resulted in brilliantly realized musical pictures — true *Charakterbilder* — worthy of the drama that generated them.

Musical Quotation in Liszt's *Faust* Symphony

Not only does Liszt model his symphonic layout on Wagner's abandoned plan, but he also makes clear his debt to Wagner in the use he makes of themes from Wagner's *Faust* Overture. Musical quotation, which Rosen has defined as the "thematic allusion to a previous work,"[14] was very common in the Romantic period. Such importations are generally inserted either as gestures of homage or because there is some extra-musical link between the theme in its original setting and the allusion to it in its new setting. For example, Schumann quoted a theme from Beethoven's song-cycle *An die ferne Geliebte* (To My Distant Beloved, 1815/16) when writing the piano Fantasy for *his* beloved, Clara, who was at that time separated from him. In the third movement of the *Faust* Symphony, Liszt even quotes a motif from one of his own earlier works, the *Malédiction* Concerto (1833), which in its new setting is presumably also used to represent a curse. From both of the above examples, it can be seen that this is a rather esoteric process, very much dependent on a fund of shared knowledge between "quoter" and "listener," particularly if the quotation is not signposted. Liszt, for one, was very much attracted by secret understandings; the "half-talk code of mysteries"[15] restricted to the select few had an abiding attraction for him.[16] To some degree, this trait was carried into his musical compositions also. His frequent references to Wagner's works in his own compositions are to be comprehended in this light — gestures of appreciation to the composer he admired above any of his contemporaries, and intended only to be understood by Wagner himself and their immediate circle. In actual fact, in many of Liszt's quotations from Wagner an extra-musical reason for the borrowing can also be found. What can surely be dismissed out of hand is the contention that Liszt was drawn into the Wagnerian atmosphere unconsciously; Liszt was one of the great innovators in the nineteenth century, with a clear notion of how and where he was developing the musical language of his day. He was far from being the archetypal instinctive composer, and his use of the works of others was a deliberate and calculated device on his part.

In the case of the *Faust* Symphony, the borrowings from the *Faust* Overture are obviously inspired by both the extra-musical connection and his personal regard for Wagner. However, in keeping with Liszt's penchant for transforming his own themes, the importations are not simple "cut-and-paste" jobs, but rather are manipulations of basic cells or figures from Wagner's overture. All the resemblances I have noted occur in the "Faust" movement of Liszt's symphony: neither of Gretchen's themes has any parallel in Wagner's overture (Liszt himself recognized that this aspect was missing in Wagner's work, as we shall see in the next section), and the material in the "Mephistopheles" movement is, as indicated earlier, a parody of the themes belonging to Faust.

In Wagner's *Faust* Overture there are seven independent motifs or figures, of varying importance.[17] Two of the most prominent have visible counterparts in the symphony:

Ex. 1: a) Faust *Overture: mm. 1–3*   *b)* Faust *Symphony I: mm. 646–51*[18]

Ex. 2: a) Faust *Overture: m. 3*   *b)* Faust *Symphony: mm. 71–74*

As can easily be seen, neither of the above cases involves exact quotation: in example 1, the feature in common is merely the opening cell, a descending seventh followed by a rising third. It would be unwise to rule out coincidence, but when viewed together with the rest of the evidence, it is probably an appropriation on Liszt's part. The second pair of illustrations shows a repeated note texture, which in the overture generally serves as an accompaniment; by contrast, it forms part of the main theme in Liszt's symphony. In the next example, one of the more intertextually-rich similarities, Wagner takes part of the secondary theme, and uses it independently of its original setting:

Ex. 3: a) Faust *Overture: mm. 123–26*   *b)* Faust *Overture: mm. 370–73*

This figure, whose associated rhythmic pattern was sometimes altered in the revision (see table 1 below), bears a distinct resemblance to the shape of the famous "Blickmotiv" from *Tristan und Isolde* (1865) (example 4a). Liszt uses a very similarly contoured motif in his work. In the three works, it is sometimes used sequentially:

Ex. 4: a) Tristan *Prelude: mm. 17–19*   *b)* Faust *Symphony I: mm. 84–87*

To the best of my knowledge, Liszt's pupil August Göllerich was the first person to make this connection. He quotes Liszt: "Wir — Wagner und ich — wüßten nichts voneinander — ich gebe Ihnen mein Wort — und nahmen beide für Faust ein gleiches Thema," thus asserting complete independence from Wagner, and in his own footnote he compares this idea to the "Blickmotiv" from *Tristan und Isolde*.[19] However, this may not be the theme identified by Liszt — there certainly are plenty of alternatives! Another possibility is the pair of themes in example 1 above. This descending seventh/ascending third figure, appearing initially in the introductory section of the first movement of the symphony, forms the basis of the principal theme in the second subject group (insofar as we can use the terminology of sonata form to describe the procedures of this movement), as shown in example 8b. It is far more prominent than the *"Tristan"* phrase in Liszt's symphony, and as such, Liszt was more probably referring to this idea. There is no direct evidence to back up Liszt's claim that he came up with this theme before he knew Wagner's work (he had the score from 1849, but the Weimar performance in 1852 may represent the first time he really studied the piece). However, on one of the few surviving sketch sheets for this work, the opening passage containing this germinal motif is written almost note for note as it occurs in the score — which may confirm his claim that the two themes evolved independently.[20]

Returning to the incontrovertible evidence, Wagner's principal idea — a chromatic passage with constant octave displacements — also occurs in a transitionary role in Liszt's work: it is heard in the lower strings leading to the rather bombastic music for "Im Anfang war die Tat" (44).

Ex. 5: a) Faust *Overture: mm. 63–67*

Ex. 5: b) Faust *Symphony I: mm. 217–22*

Besides melodic correlation, other types of influence can be deduced. Wagner's "second ending" to his overture — actually dating from sometime later in 1840, and thus part of the version Liszt had studied and conducted — consists of a chromatic passage leading into the final triad (with the standard "Picardy third"). Liszt's final cadence is an even more tortuous affair, with semitonal linear movement resolving an F-sharp minor chord onto C major. In place of Wagner's seraphic upper woodwind and string confirmation of D major, there are repeated chromatic runs from the dominant (G) up to the tonic (C) in the symphony; the writing from here on is all in unison. A final recitative in the celli and basses, hinting darkly at F minor, removes any possibility of retrospectively seeing the earlier C-major resolution as "upbeat." The difference is probably related to the fact that Wagner's work ends at this point, while Liszt has two further movements to resolve the tensions inherent in this enigmatic close.

Ex. 6: a) Faust *Overture: mm. 427–43*

Ex. 6: b) Faust *Symphony I: mm. 637–43*

Another similarity is the device used in both works whereby important themes serve as accompaniments, while hitherto subordinate patterns are superimposed and brought prominently into the foreground. Whether one could infer a Wagnerian influence on Liszt in this case is doubtful; in Liszt's earlier Sonata in B minor, motifs are used in a far more plastic fashion than this:

Ex. 7: a) Faust *Overture: mm. 280–84*

Ex. 7: b) Faust *Symphony I: mm. 382–84*

One further point of resemblance might be noted, although it is so tenuous that it is probably nothing more than two composers using a figuration that was part of the common vocabulary in the mid-nineteenth century. This concerns the use of a similarly shaped accompanimental pattern — almost as a commentary — during an important, tonally stable melody. In Wagner's case, the busy string passage-work under the long held notes in the woodwind melody is a hyper-accelerated version of Liszt's leisurely, pleading viola line (to which violins are later added) that recurs as a regular interjection during the "love" motif:

Ex. 8: a) Faust *Overture: m. 19*   *b)* Faust *Symphony: mm. 179–80*

Wagner's *Faust* Overture: Correspondence and Revision

Wagner's symphonic work known as the *Faust* Overture [*Eine Faust Ouvertüre*] (WWV 59) was composed in Paris in the winter of 1839/40, and finished on 12 January 1840. I say "known as" advisedly: Wagner himself saw it as being the first movement of a projected *Faust* Symphony, and there are at least three other titles for it.[21] Wagner intended his overture for Paris, but it was not premièred until 22 July 1844 in Dresden; by this stage a number of revisions had already been undertaken, most significantly a refashioning of the ending (as mentioned above). After one other performance in the same year, the work was not performed again until 1852.

Wagner sent the score to Liszt in January 1849, and it was the one work Liszt reserved when asked to return Wagner his scores in July of the same year. No more is heard of this work for over two years, until Wagner writes to his young friend Hans von Bülow (who at that time was studying with Liszt in Weimar), asking him to retrieve the score and send it to Zürich.[22] The phrase Wagner used — "Die Partitur meiner Faustouvertüre, die Liszt doch wohl nicht gebraucht" — accuses Liszt of a lack of interest and would seem to have stung the latter into action: apparently in response to this pressure, the work was programmed for the *Gesangverein* concert of 11 May, and was a success.[23] Liszt finally returned the overture on 7 October 1852. The covering letter is extremely interesting, representing one of the few occasions when Liszt ventures on specific criticism of one of Wagner's works (the numbers in square brackets have been added for convenience of reference later):

> Dies Werk ist ganz Deiner würdig — wenn Du mir jedoch erlaubst, Dir eine Bemerkung zu machen, so verhehle ich Dir nicht, daß mir entweder [1a] ein zweiter Mittelsatz (bei Buchstabe E oder F) [that is, the sections beginning at measures 120 or 150 in the first version] oder [1b] eine ruhigere, in anmutiger Färbung gehaltene Führung des Mittelsatzes willkommen sein würde [here in the letter he quotes measures 120–23]. [2] Die Blasinstrumente treten da etwas *massiv* auf — und, verzeihe mir diese Meinung, [3] das Motiv in F-dur halte ich für ungenügend [by this, Liszt could have referred either to that beginning at measure 120, quoted above, or that *at* F (measure 150), also *in* F!] — es fehlt ihm gewissermaßen an *Grazie* und bildet da eine Art von Zwischending, nicht recht Fisch, nicht recht Fleisch, welches mit dem Vorhergehenden und dem *Nachfolgenden* nicht in dem richtigen Verhältnis oder Kontraste steht und folglich das Interesse hemmt. [4] Wenn Du anstatt dem einen weichen, zarten, gretchenhaft modulierten, melodischen Satz hineinbringst, so glaube ich Dich versichern zu können, daß Dein Werk sehr gewinnt. — Überlege es Dir, und falls ich Dir eine Dummheit gesagt hätte, so sei mir nicht böse.[24]

In summary, Liszt proposes here composing an extra "Gretchen" movement, which he feels would enhance the already promising work.

Liszt's unusual precision can perhaps be put down to the fact that this work was in a genre with which he was more confident: an instrumental rather than operatic work, although the knowledge that Wagner himself was not fully satisfied with it and proposed altering it may also have contributed to his frankness.[25] Liszt wrote again on 27 December 1852, and further remarked that [5] he felt the work could do with a few extensions (Verlängerungen). Although Wagner agreed with Liszt's remarks and was pleased by them, it would have been very uncharacteristic had he not tried to justify himself — and indeed, he had some very good excuses to make. On 9 November 1852 he revealed why there was no "Gretchen" section: the overture as it existed was supposed to be only a portrait of Faust (in the abandoned symphonic plan the overture was, of course, initially just the first movement). The second movement was to have introduced Gretchen, but he had no more than a theme for her — he wrote instead the opera, *Der fliegende Holländer* (The Flying Dutchman, 1843).[26] Although Wagner's symphonic claims have been doubted in the past,[27] principally because the work is referred to as an overture in all the sources from the 1840s, there is some empirical evidence for his statement. On the other side of the sheet with the "Gretchen" theme there are sketches for *Der fliegende Holländer*.[28] This verifies Wagner's symphonic claims, for we know that Wagner began work on this opera in the Parisian period. John Deathridge makes the connection between the two projects when suggesting that the figure of Senta, who first appears in *Der fliegende Holländer* sitting at a spinning wheel with a sorrowful air, is related to that of Goethe's heroine, and the parallels extend beyond just the "Gretchen am Spinnrade" pose.[29] A musico-dramatic realization rather than a purely instrumental treatment of a similar idea would have appealed more to Wagner.

Liszt's criticism sparked off Wagner's interest in this old composition, and he wrote to the publishers Breitkopf & Härtel proposing it for publication, but the firm was unwilling to meet his financial demands. In the letter to "Härtels" (as he invariably referred to them), he made his revisions contingent on their agreeing to publish the work.[30] In fact, it was under another stimulus from Liszt that Wagner finally began his revisions of the overture: on learning in January 1855 that Liszt had completed his *Faust* Symphony.[31]

It is difficult to speculate just why Liszt delayed telling Wagner of the completion of the *Faust* Symphony for over two months, when he actually finished it on 19 October 1854.[32] Despite the fact that there is a large five-month gap during this crucial period of the correspondence for which none of Liszt's letters have survived (from 28 July 1854 to 1 January 1855), Wagner's reaction to this announcement makes it hard to believe that Liszt could have mentioned it in any missing letters. He was delighted to hear that Liszt had finished it, and looked forward to seeing the work and especially to hearing it performed, if not by an orchestra, then by Liszt at the piano.

Even more significantly — "ridiculously," as he told Liszt — Wagner decided to remodel his score at this time; this is almost certainly as a result of hearing Liszt's news, even though the reworking was finished very quickly (by 17 January). In his own words: "ich hab' eine ganz neue Partitur geschrieben; die Instrumentation durchgehends neu gearbeitet, manches ganz geändert, auch in der Mitte etwas mehr Ausdehnung und Bedeutung (2tes Motiv)," that is: taking all changes into consideration, he has effectively written a new score.[33] Also, he prefixed the work with a quotation from *Faust* I, depicting the world-weariness and interior struggle of the protagonist, with which the overture is now solely concerned:

> Der Gott, der mir im Busen wohnt
> Kann tief mein Innerstes erregen,
> Der über allen meinen Kräften thront,
> Er kann nach Außen nichts bewegen;
> Und so ist mir das Dasein eine Last,
> Der Tod erwünscht, das Leben mir verhaßt. (53)

However, his earlier intention of changing the title (9 November 1852) had been altered: "in einigen Tagen führe ich mir's in einem hiesigen Konzerte auf und nenne es 'Eine *Faust* Ouvertüre.' "[34] Not to be out-done, Liszt expressed immediate interest in performing the revised work.[35] Wagner sent it to him soon afterwards, expressing pride in the reworking and asking him to compare it with the first version. He felt sure that Liszt would particularly enjoy the revised middle section, which was developed, but could not introduce Gretchen herself.[36]

Following Wagner's own instructions, let us now examine the two versions of the overture a little more closely. It can be easily seen that Liszt's five recommendations, made in October and December 1852, were obviously at the forefront of Wagner's mind when he made the revisions (although some would surely have occurred to him independently). First, the orchestration is refined throughout: excess doublings are eradicated; for example, in measure 75 (**73**) [the bold measure numbers refer to the revised edition, the roman type to the 1840 version] ten-part brass writing is cut to six parts, and in measures 65–69 (**63–67**) all instruments were originally hammering out the principle rhythmic figure (♩ ♩. ♪), but now variety is introduced through the use of sustained writing in some lower parts. However, in his revisions of *Der fliegende Holländer* and *Tannhäuser* (1845), Wagner made similar changes unprompted, so in this respect Liszt's suggestion was probably superfluous. Much more importantly,

Wagner remolded the central section considerably, as outlined in the following table:

Table 1. Alterations to the central section of the *Faust* Overture

1840 mm.	1855 mm.	Alterations
120–27	118–25	Orchestra slightly thinned, but otherwise the same.
/128–31	/126–29	Antiphonal writing introduced, different groups answering each other. Squareness of the original figure ♩∞♩. ♪|♩ ♩ is somewhat alleviated by avoiding entry on the strong first beat (it is anticipated) ♪⌐|♩ ♩. ♪|♩ ♩, and entries overlap.
132–35	130–33	Prosaic cadence changed; new chromatic voice leading in top part. Modulation to A major much more subtle.
/143–46	/141–44	Again, antiphonal writing: woodwind choir answers string figure. Rhythmic modifications as before.
/147–49	/145–47	Much more adventurous, chromatic modulation back to F major.
———	148–66	New, very serene passage. The use of suspensions and chromatic notes give it the feel of "later Wagner." It is at first based thematically on the retrograde of the *"Tristan"*-figure (example 4a above), with a similar rhythmic profile. It might be said to be *"gretchenhaft moduliert,"* without the programmatic concomitants.
150-	167-	Parallel again (until coda).

We can see how these alterations correspond almost directly to Liszt's suggestions: the whole section is extended [5]; the instrumentation is thinned, and refined [1b, 2]; a new modulatory (or at least, chromatically decorated) section is introduced [1a, 4]. Liszt's comment on the unsatisfactory nature of the motif in F [3] is a little unclear, but in any case Wagner did not alter either of the themes to which it could have referred, as this would have entailed not revision, but recomposition. The reworkings in the main are great improvements on the original (especially where thematic shapes are incorporated into the accompaniment, as in the new leaping octaves in the double bass part in measures **45–49**, in place of plain sustained notes in the original measures 47–51), and the composition is a worthy ancestor of a genre that includes works such as Liszt's *Symphonische Dichtungen* and Strauss's *Tondichtungen,* by virtue of the satisfyingly original formal design and its vividness in representing the extra-musical content.

It is undeniable that the interaction between Wagner and Liszt had profound implications for the development of both overture and symphony. Liszt's intervention may have come long after the initial composition of Wagner's *Faust* Overture, but his suggestions and advice had far-reaching implications for the work as we know it today. Many of the revisions Wagner undertook followed Liszt's suggestions directly, and Wagner was finally motivated to alter the work on hearing that Liszt had finished his *Faust* Symphony. Liszt's debts to Wagner are even more profound. Liszt took the symphony's three-movement design from the abandoned plan Wagner disclosed to him, and a close examination of the music reveals that certain motivic shapes occur in both works. So prominent are these in both compositions that some surely were quotations on Liszt's part. However, I purposely included some resemblances between the symphony and overture that were probably *not* borrowings, but were rather part of the common musical currency of the period. This illustrates the important fact that the use of similar motifs by Wagner and Liszt would tend to imply not only musical interaction and mutual admiration, but also that in both composers Goethe's great drama aroused similar musical responses.

Notes

[1] *The Memoirs of Hector Berlioz,* trans. and ed. David Cairns (London: Panther, 1970), 166. In 1849 Liszt set "Rosen ihr blendenden" as part of a *Goethealbum* (Hamburg: Schuberth, 1849), proving that he must have been acquainted with part 2 of the tragedy by that time (though possibly only after he settled in Weimar in 1847). This work for chorus and piano is based on the words of the Angels' Chorus in part 2, act 5, Johann Wolfgang von Goethe, *Faust: Eine Tragödie,* ed. Erich Trunz, rev. ed. (Hamburg: Christian Wegner, 1967), 352–55. Further quotations are from this edition of the drama, and are indicated by page number in the text.

[2] Letter of 14 October 1849 in *Franz Liszt — Richard Wagner: Briefwechsel,* ed. Hanjo Kesting (Frankfurt a. M.: Insel, 1988 [hereafter *LW*]), 87.

[3] Cited in Eric Jensen, "Liszt, Nerval and *Faust*," *19th-Century Music* 6 (fall 1982): 151–58 (here, 153). I am indebted to this article for much of the information concerning Liszt's *Faust* opera plans.

[4] Other *Faust*-inspired works conducted by Liszt in Weimar in 1852 were by Schumann (part 3 of *Scenen zu Goethes Faust,* 11 May), Spohr (opera *Faust,* 24 October), and Berlioz (*La Damnation de Faust,* 21 November). See Alan Walker, *Franz Liszt,* vol. 2: *The Weimar Years 1848–1861* (London: Faber and Faber, 1994), 286–88, 326–28, and *Orchesterwerke* 2, ed. Egon Voss, vol. 18 of *Richard Wagner: Sämtliche Werke,* ed. Carl Dahlhaus (Mainz: Schott, 1997), xxxviii.

[5] Jensen, "Liszt, Nerval and *Faust*," 157.

[6] Letter of 9 November 1852, Wagner to Liszt, *LW,* 248.

[7] There is a precedent for Wagner trying to interest Liszt in his cast-off plans — in 1850, he wished Liszt to use his unrealized opera sketch *Wieland der Schmied* (Wieland the Blacksmith). Letter of 8 October 1850, *LW,* 147–48. After some further pressure from Wagner on the subject, Liszt had to decline firmly, claiming he would never write a German opera. Letter of 3 January 1851, *LW,* 161.

[8] Letter of 7 February 1854, Liszt to Wagner, *LW,* 363.

[9] "Jetzt genoß ich denn zum ersten Male die Freude, meinen Freund auch als Komponist näher kennenzulernen. Neben manchen berühmt gewordenen neueren Klavierstücken von ihm, gingen wir auch mehrere seiner soeben vollendeten Symphonischen Dichtungen, vor allem seine Faust-Symphonie mit großem Eifer durch." Richard Wagner, *Mein Leben* (complete and annotated edition), ed. Martin Gregor-Dellin (Munich: List Verlag, 1976), 508. A good English translation is the one by Andrew Gray and Mary Whittall (Cambridge: Cambridge UP, 1983). Some sketches for the *Faust* Symphony can be dated to the 1840s and early 1850s; it is not impossible — in fact, it is quite probable — that Liszt improvised on the fragmentary material from this period.

[10] Liszt to Therese von Helldorff, 22 September 1869; complete letter in original French published in Peter Raabe, *Franz Liszt,* vol. 2: *Liszts Schaffen,* rev. ed. (Tutzing: Hans Schneider, 1968), 82. This was not the first anti-Goethe sentiment he expressed: earlier in November 1853, Liszt scandalized and mortally insulted Bettina von Arnim when, according to Peter Cornelius's eyewitness account, he said that he preferred the very worst Jesuit to the whole of her beloved Goethe. This came at the end of a heated debate; Liszt was defending Schiller, whom Bettina had just called "Jesuitical" (Cornelius to his sister Susanne, 5 December 1853, cited in *Portrait of Liszt: By Himself and His Contemporaries,* ed. Adrian Williams [Oxford: Clarendon Press, 1990], 301). In 1856 Wagner also testified to the strength of Liszt's passion on the subject of Goethe; the two nearly had a fight over *Egmont,* which Liszt pretended to despise (*Mein Leben,* 554).

[11] For a complete list of identifications see Walker, *Franz Liszt,* 2:329–32.

[12] Liszt's son-in-law, Emile Ollivier, who attended the first performance along with Wagner, recorded in his diary their mutual dissatisfaction with the choral finale: see Williams, *Portrait of Liszt,* 379 (diary entry for 6 August 1861). In *Mein Leben* Wagner, writing with the benefit of hindsight, praised the original ending as one of the clearest evidences of Liszt's musicality, and complained that it was under the influence of Liszt's companion, Carolyne Sayn-Wittgenstein, that the new vulgar ending was substituted (*Mein Leben,* 551).

[13] Lawrence Kramer takes issue with this point. He shows that the theme does undergo some alteration, and concludes: "Far from being untouched by Mephistopheles' wild and obscene ado, Gretchen is demystified by it," and earlier: "She is roused from her rigid sweetness, released into self-transformation, imbued with a restless eroticism." *Music as Cultural Practice, 1800–1900* (Berkeley: U of California P, 1990), 125–28, especially 127.

[14] Charles Rosen, "Influence, Plagiarism and Inspiration," *19th-Century Music* 4 (fall 1980): 87–101 (here, 87).

[15] In the Irish poet Patrick Kavanagh's poem "Inniskeen Road: July Evening," the poet is represented as being outside the activities of the other young people, bonded by "the half-talk code of mysteries / And the wink-and-elbow language of delight." Kavanagh, *The Complete Poems,* ed. Peter Kavanagh (Newbridge, Kildare: Goldsmith Press, 1984), 18–19.

[16] This partly explains his Masonic affiliation, his involvement in clerical life in Rome (however peripheral), and the frequent "in-house" allusions to musical societies when dealing with other initiates.

[17] In this section, measure numbers are taken from the second (1855) version of the *Faust* Overture. Although Liszt knew only the first version when writing his symphony, the two editions are parallel in all the passages under discussion, and it is more practical to refer to the definitive and more easily available edition.

[18] This figure occurs as early as m. 4, but the example at the end of the movement shown above is the clearest parallel to Wagner's opening statement, as both are monodic and in the bass register.

[19] August Göllerich, *Franz Liszt* (Berlin: Marquardt & Co., 1908), 172.

[20] In two excellent articles — "Die musikalischen Gestaltwandlungen der *Faust*-Symphonie von Liszt," *Studia Musicologica* 2 (1962): 87–137, and "Die Metamorphose von der 'Faust-Symphonie' von Liszt," *Studia Musicologica* 5 (1963): 283–93 — Laszlo Somfai traces the development of the *Faust* Symphony from its inception (although he never touches on the opera plans). Two sketches in particular, which are reproduced in the 1962 article (p. 113), are pertinent here. The first, from a sketchbook dating from the mid-1840s, gives a primitive version of the dodecaphonic theme; the second, on an undated sheet, consists of this theme, now almost exactly as in the final score, followed here by the familiar descending seventh "answering" phrase (an octave too low, and lacking the sighing figure continuation). Obviously, there is some way to go before the finished product, and I am thus inclined to believe that Liszt's first workings on the *Faust* Symphony could date from as early as 1850, when Nerval made his proposition, or possibly even earlier. Rena Charnin Mueller refers to some *Faust* sketches dating from 1850–51, though she does not reproduce them: "Liszt's *Tasso* Sketchbook: Studies in Sources and Revisions" (Ann Arbor, Michigan: University Microfilms International, 1986 [Ph.D. diss.: New York University, 1986]), 320).

[21] Including *Ouvertüre zu Goethes Faust Teil I, Der einsame Faust,* and *Faust in der Einsamkeit.* In the last two cases it is described as *Ein Tongedicht für Orchester.*

[22] Wagner to Bülow, 14 December 1851, *Richard Wagner: Briefe an Hans von Bülow,* ed. D. Thode (Jena: Eugen Diedrichs, 1916), 16–17.

[23] "Deine Faust-Ouvertüre hat Sensation gemacht und ist gut gegangen." Letter to Wagner written soon after the Weimar première, i.e., mid-May 1852, *LW,* 218. Liszt has been criticized for the diplomatic reports he sent back to Wagner of performances of his friend's works, but, unlike the case of the *Lohengrin* première, he never subsequently revised this opinion.

[24] Letter of 7 October 1852, Liszt to Wagner, *LW,* 241.

[25] Wagner, when presenting Liszt with the work in 1849, said that he no longer liked it. Letter of 30 January 1849, *LW,* 60. By 12 September 1852 Wagner's

earlier vague plans for the work had crystallized somewhat: "Mich reizt es sie zu überarbeiten, und bei Härtels herauszugeben." *LW*, 237.

26 "[. . .] schon hatte ich das Thema für sie — — es war aber eben ein Thema: das Ganze blieb liegen — ich schrieb meinen 'fliegenden Holländer.' " Letter of 9 November 1852, Wagner to Liszt, *LW*, 248.

27 See, for example, Gerald Abraham, "Wagner's Early Overtures," in *Romanticism 1830–1890*, vol. 9 of *The New Oxford History of Music*, ed. Abraham (Oxford: Oxford UP, 1990), 12–14 (here, 14). See also Ernest Newman, *The Life of Richard Wagner*, vol. 1: 1813–1848 (Cambridge: Cambridge UP, 1976 [originally New York: Alfred A. Knopf, 1937]), 321. Indeed, at first sight the case *against* the symphony is very plausible. For instance, opponents of the "symphonic" origin of the work could cite a letter Wagner wrote on 18 January 1840 (only six days after completing the score) to his then respected friend and quasi-patron, the composer Giocomo Meyerbeer, where he already called it an "Ouvertüre, *Faust*, erster Teil" (quoted in *Orchesterwerke* 2, xxxii). It is referred to in similar terms in the *Autobiographische Skizze* of 1842/43 in *Richard Wagner: Sämtliche Briefe*, ed. Gertrud Strobel and Werner Wolf, vol. 1: 1830–1842, rev. ed. (Leipzig: VEB Deutscher Verlag für Musik, 1979), 107. Only in later sources is the symphonic plan revealed; for example, *Eine Mittheilung an Meine Freunde* (1851) in Richard Wagner, *Sämtliche Schriften und Dichtungen*, Volksausgabe, vol. 4 (Leipzig: Breitkopf & Härtel, [1911–1916]), 230–344 (here, 261), and *Mein Leben* (186), when conscious myth-making adds to the normal unreliability of dated evidence. Even the first page of the manuscript bears this title, although closer examination shows that it was added later, indirectly confirming Wagner's statement. See the editorial reading of this title page in *Orchesterwerke* 2, xxxii–xxxiii. A much clearer color reproduction of this page is available in Herbert Barth, Dietrich Mack, Egon Voss, *Wagner: sein Leben und seine Welt in zeitgenössischen Bildern und Texten* (Vienna: Universal Edition AG, 1975), plate 36.

28 See *Wagner-Werke-Verzeichnis (WWV): Verzeichnis der musikalischen Werke Richard Wagners und ihrer Quellen*, ed. John Deathridge, Martin Geck, and Egon Voss (Mainz: Schott, 1986), 206, §Id.

29 John Deathridge, "Richard Wagners Kompositionen zu Goethes *Faust*," *Jahrbuch der Bayerischen Staatsoper 1982*: 90–99 (here, 98–99). Here the sketches for the "Gretchen" movement are reproduced in facsimile.

30 Cited in *Orchesterwerke* 2, lix.

31 Letter of 1 January 1855, Liszt to Wagner, *LW*, 397.

32 On 19 October 1854, Liszt wrote to Anton Rubinstein saying that he had finished his *Faust* and was having it copied. Cited in Somfai, "Die musikalischen Gestaltwandlungen," 101.

33 Letter of 19 January 1855, Wagner to Liszt, *LW*, 398.

34 Ibid.

35 Letter of 25 January 1855, Liszt to Wagner, *LW*, 401.

36 "[ich bin] so kindisch Dich zu bitten, sie einmal recht genau mit der ersten Abfassung zu vergleichen, weil es mich reizt, in dieser Kundgebung meiner Erfahrung und meines gewonnenen feineren Gefühles mich Dir mitzuteilen. [. . .]. Der Mittelsatz wird Dir jetzt besser gefallen: natürlich konnte ich kein neues Motiv

einführen, weil ich dann fast alles hätte neu machen müssen; ich konnte hier nur, gleichsam in weiter Kadenzform, die Stimmung etwas breiter entwickeln. Von *Gretchen* kann natürlich nichte die Rede sein, vielmehr immer nur von Faust selbst: *"ein unbegreiflich holder Drang / trieb mich durch Wald und Wiesen hin."* Letter of 15 February 1855, Wagner to Liszt, *LW*, 403. The quotation in the letter is actually an inaccurate version of lines 775–76 from *Faust* (31).

Musical Gypsies and Anti-Classical Aesthetics: The Romantic Reception of Goethe's Mignon Character in Brentano's *Die mehreren Wehmüller und ungarische Nationalgesichter*

Stefanie Bach

THE IMAGE OF THE GYPSY[1] was a rich source of association that attracted many Romantic writers to lend it their own interpretation. This undeniable fascination with the traditional Gypsy character and lifestyle, which evoked notions of freedom from social norms, disregard for boundaries (both geographical and social), and an apparent closeness to nature, initiated a plethora of literary manifestations of Gypsy characters, particularly in German Romantic literature. In the image of the Gypsy, Romantic artists found a motif that could express a variety of preoccupations. However, the use of musical Gypsies in Brentano's novella *Die mehreren Wehmüller und ungarische Nationalgesichter*[2] (The Multiple Wehmüllers and Hungarian National Faces, 1817) amounts to more than a Romantic motif; it situates the presentation of the crossroad-dweller character at the writer's own crossroads of literary taste and contemporary aesthetic discourse. Through the use of Gypsy figures and the notions of musicality attributed to them, the portrayal of the brother/sister Gypsy pair Mitidika and Michaly offers an aesthetic counter-argument to Goethe's classical aesthetic discourse. The objective of this paper is to show that Mitidika and Michaly, the musical Gypsies of Brentano's novella, are a criticism of another musical Gypsy, Goethe's "Mignon" figure in *Wilhelm Meisters Lehrjahre* (Wilhelm Meister's Apprenticeship Years, 1796).[3] Brentano revives Mignon in the form of Mitidika and Michaly, while making a statement in favor of music as the guiding aesthetic principle for literature and art in general.[4] These characters are, then, symbols for artistic inspiration and genius. Mignon has to die because she can only express herself through the mode of music. Music, in this interpretation, is both intuitive and sensual but also contrasts with art forms based on reason and reflection. The direct and sensual expression of music establishes this art form as essentially non-classical in nature. Mignon's lack of linguistic and thus structural form-giving abilities dooms her artistic being; conversely, Wilhelm Meister places form over intuition. Brentano reverses this argument, favoring music over language by means of an ironic play on existing notions of the literary Gypsy figure through the characters of Mitidika and Michaly, and thus transforms them into a viable aesthetic alternative. Therefore, central elements of Goethe's novel — androgyny, antagonistic artist figures, and music — undergo a Romantic reinterpretation.

Gypsy figures have been used as symbolic characters from German classical literature onwards. Representations of them draw on sources such as the ethnographic treatment of the Romanies by Grellmann in 1783[5] and the fictional representation in Cervantes' exemplary novella *La Gitanilla* (The Little Gypsy Girl, 1613).[6] Grellmann stresses the musicality of Gypsies, mentioning in particular the unsurpassed musical talent of a fiddler by the name of Mihaly whom he compares to Orpheus[7] — one of the rare instances of a positive value judgment on the Gypsy character and lifestyle under analysis. Grellmann also introduces the basis for an androgynous perception of female Gypsies when he refers to female Romanies as "Bastardes des männlichen Geschlechts"[8] because they wear trousers, smoke, and generally exhibit masculine features. Similarly, in *La Gitanilla* the protagonist Preciosa is characterized by an explicit musical ability. She combines a talent in music, song, dance, and literature with intuitive art and masterly skill, and this is complemented by her beauty of countenance and character. She therefore embodies an idealized image of woman.[9] Both Goethe and Brentano draw on these sources, but while Goethe uses aspects of this image in an indirect way,[10] Brentano copies boldly from Grellmann and bases his female Gypsy, Mitidika, firmly on the female ideal as encountered in Cervantes' novella.

Although Goethe's Mignon and Brentano's Mitidika and Michaly are based on the contemporary image of the Gypsy, their subsequent interpretations differ considerably. The reception and reworking of the Mignon figure by Brentano among others has to be understood within the Romantic discourse on the Gypsy, which appropriated aspects associated with Gypsies, using them as symbolic sites and illustrations of Romantic aesthetics. While Gypsies were endowed with negative attributes in classical literature, the same traits were seen in a very different light in Romantic literature. In a marked contrast to classical authors, the Romantics were attracted by the Gypsy character, which represented an uncivilized and ethnically pure group at the edge of society, unalienated from themselves and their existence in a paradisiacal notion of the noble human being prior to the Fall from Grace. The image of the Gypsy was invoked to express ideas of simple folk, of exoticism and danger, and of uncontrolled sexuality — in particular, female sexuality. In this context, Gypsy characters are particularly adept in expressing a male fear of women. They are thus essentially the image of the dangerous yet fascinating Other, and of everything that is lacking and wished for. Not fully understood by the civilized and industrialized bourgeois society of the nineteenth century, they are feared for their potential to undermine the basis of this society through an incompatible set of mores and customs. As they are seen as being close to the unalienated pre-capitalist society, they are also the bearers of folk knowledge and culture, of folk music and oral poetry, of occultism and supernatural forces.

Mignon's ambivalent character has produced numerous interpretations for her significance within Goethe's Bildungsroman *Wilhelm Meisters Lehrjahre*.[11] For the purpose of this paper, however, Mignon's significance lies in the fact that her image as it is reappropriated by German Romanticism seems to be even more enduring than the original.[12] Her association with contemporary descriptions of Romanies or Gypsies, her musicality, and her androgynous appearance are the threads that link Goethe's Mignon and the Mignon of German Romanticism. Already contemporary readers saw Mignon as a Romantic character, as Friedrich Schlegel's essay, "Über Goethes Meister" (On Goethe's Meister, 1798), shows: there he describes Mignon as a character who lends the whole novel an aura of Romantic magic and music.[13]

Mignon possesses many features common to the contemporary image of the Gypsy. We do not discover until after her death that she is not a Gypsy at all, but actually the daughter of an aristocrat.[14] Her presentation gives rise to different images for the reader: in the first half of the novel she is presented through the eyes of Wilhelm Meister, and in the closing part through the narration of Natalie and Therese. Mignon's description is very much in keeping with the traditional image of a Gypsy: she is dark (*WML*, 92) and mysterious, her "growth [. . .] has been stunted,"[15] yet she is attractive: "Ihre Bildung war nicht regelmäßig; aber auffallend, ihre Stirne geheimnisvoll, ihre Nase außerordentlich schön [. . .] und reizend genug" (*WML*, 99–100); she speaks in broken German interpolated with snippets of French and Italian, but knows no language correctly (*WML*, 111); she is part of a group of traveling acrobats, but her provenance is shrouded in mystery; and, above all, she can only express her innermost feelings through music. When she does so, however, the music seems to come from a primeval locus, unmediated and beyond (linguistic) representation, the prototype of Romantic inspiration.[16] Through her musical expression, she gives voice to unformed and unrepressed feeling — in complete contrast to Wilhelm Meister, whose aim in life is to gain rational control over his feelings and thus succeed in his development as an individual. Mignon's music encompasses both song and dance, and both are equally significant. The character of her music is expressed either in the form of the folk song — thus a naïve art form — or in a wild and immoderate dance accompanied by her playing on the tambourine:

> Sie schlug das Tamburin mit aller möglichen Zierlichkeit und Lebhaftigkeit, indem sie bald mit druckendem Finger auf dem Felle schnell hin und her schnurrte, bald mit dem Rücken der Hand, bald mit den Knöcheln darauf

pochte, ja mit abwechselnden Rhythmen das Pergament bald wider die
Kniee, bald wieder den Kopf schlug, bald schüttelnd die Schellen allein
klingen ließ und so aus dem einfachsten Instrumente gar verschiedene
Töne hervorlockte. (*WML,* 336–37)

Here her musicality is linked to the body. Music is expressed through
bodily movements by means of rhythmic expression. The whole body itself
becomes a musical instrument when not only her hands and fingers but
also her knees and head create the sounds on the tambourine. Her body
instills the instrument with life and sound, governed by the unmediated
expression of her emotions — emotions that are spellbinding and uncontrolled, and that seem to originate in a locus preceding representation. The
effect of her musical expression is thus situated beyond rationalization and
linguistic representation. The directness of her music is established
through the primarily sensual character of the musical performance, which
relies on touch, aural sense, vibrating vocal chords, and a specific and
evanescent moment in time. The latter means that music is irreconcilably
beyond representation; the physical musical act is truly impossible to copy
or represent. As its physical effects on the body cease, it fades completely,
leaving only the memory of the experience.

The sexual character of her musical performance, as expressed through
her dance and her manner of playing the tambourine, links her musicality
with her androgyny. Both are statements about her ambivalent sensuality
and, indeed, sexuality. Her being revolves around her erotic but repressed
relationship to Wilhelm Meister. Like other female characters in the novel
who have amorous intentions towards Wilhelm Meister, she too has to die
in order that her dangerous sexuality and musicality be controlled; in contrast, Wilhelm's unconsummated union with Therese is one of reason.
Although Mignon is much more ambivalent than this sketch indicates,
these are the aspects that were to be central for the Romantic rewriting of
her character.

The two main and intertwined characteristics of Mignon's Gypsy soul
for both Goethe and Brentano are her androgynous nature and her musicality. At no point in the novel is her gender ascertained beyond doubt.
She is referred to by the narrator with neuter or abstract generic nouns,
such as "Wesen," "Geschöpf," "Gestalt," and "Kind."[17] Her very name is
masculine (the female version being "mignonne"). She remains an asexual
child throughout; her sexuality in general and her femininity in particular
are denied her, as is adulthood. At the same time, both her femininity and
her sexuality are suppressed in a language that is highly sexually charged,
so that her sexuality is indeed manifest in the text through the act of narration.[18] Wilhelm Meister is attracted to her mysterious and androgynous
nature, just as he is attracted to other sexually ambivalent characters:
Therese and Natalie as well as Marianne all appear at some instance in male
clothes, as amazons, or are even mistaken for men by Wilhelm Meister.[19]

His attraction to the sexually uncertain is intertwined with his attraction to the emotive powers of its mode of expression — namely music and dance —, which are difficult to contain or control and which threaten his rational development.

In Brentano's novella, the two musical Gypsy figures of Michaly and Mitidika present another notion of the androgynous. Brentano's two characters are Mignon (or: the androgyne) split into two halves, and it is only through their union at the fake border of the *Pestkordon* — the symbolic location of the human state of *Zerrissenheit,* or inner conflict — that the narrative knot is disentangled and order achieved.

The origins of the hermaphrodite or androgyne are, of course, mythological. Their first literary expression is in Plato's *Symposium,* where, during the banquet, Aristophanes introduces the androgyne in his speech about the original unity of man and woman in this mythological figure.[20] Similar to a round Yin Yang and moving about quickly and in all directions with the help of eight limbs, this being is a symbol for the harmony between all things universal: the harmony at the essence of the world. To weaken this strong and harmonious being, Zeus spliced it into two. While the outer appearance of this cut was successfully hidden by the gods, the inner or emotional split is beyond healing.[21] As a consequence, man and woman have an insatiable desire for the other half in an attempt to re-establish their primordial unity. This desire and longing is the basis for all love between man and woman. Androgyny, as Inge Stephan defines it, is thus the ideal of a holistic existence, and due to its intrinsically erotic nature it is associated with the transgression of moral and social conventions and boundaries.[22]

This combination of the ideal of a harmonious unity between man and woman and an increase in the erotic attraction of the androgynous character accounts both for Mignon's treatment in Goethe's novel and the positive portrayal of the androgynous musical Gypsies in Brentano's novella. Mignon's immoderate and erotic exuberance is best exemplified by means of her self-expression through music and dance. Wilhelm describes the performance of her egg-dance as strict, well delineated, and violent (*WML,* 117), and this is mirrored and developed in the description of the playful nature of this dance and her banging on the tambourine. Here, she bares her innermost emotion with childish boisterousness and vigorous joyfulness (*WML,* 336). Similarly, when reciting her songs to the harpist's accompaniment, she touches a chord with Wilhelm, lending expression to his feelings in a way that opposes indirect linguistic representation. The nature of the music of the harpist and Mignon conceptually opposes that of language: music is formless, direct, and unalienated, while language is structured, indirect, and definite. The narrator's description of their recital stresses the originality of Mignon's expression, that is: the unmediated and direct nature of her expression of feeling. Mignon succeeds in expressing Wilhelm's emotional state directly as opposed to the indirect expression that is the narrative transformation of the original event. At the same time, the song that expresses both Wilhelm's and Mignon's nostalgia has an element of unruliness and irregularity, linking it to her androgynous eroticism: the Lied sung by Mignon and the harpist is an "unregelmäßiges Duett" characterized by the warmest expression (*WML*, 250).

It is through music, then, that Mignon reaches depth of feeling. She does this both in a manner appreciated by Wilhelm, when she lends expression to his emotional conflicts, and in a manner that also disconcerts him; for example, her unruliness and wild androgynous eroticism threaten his control over his feelings, thus putting him in touch with aspects of his character he strives to suppress through reason. Mignon, however, upholds her motto that "Die Vernunft ist grausam, [. . .] das Herz ist besser" — feelings are superior to reason (*WML*, 504). In *Wilhelm Meisters Lehrjahre* Mignon's emotional being — her eroticism, her childishness and refusal of gender-specific adulthood, her wildness and indulgence in unmediated forms of expression — is condemned to death, while Wilhelm is the epitome of successful character development through temperance, moderation, and reason.

Brentano, however, chooses to perceive Mignon's musicality and androgyny in a different way, and reappropriates her in the two characters of Mitidika and Michaly. Unlike Mignon, who is forever trapped in childhood and in uncontrolled emotions, and who fails when measured against the ideal process of character development as exemplified by Wilhelm Meister, Brentano's Gypsies stand for the original state of humanity before the split into male and female — reason and emotion — that placed man and woman on a never-ending quest for the Other and for their primeval, unalienated state of unity. Kleist, in his essay "Über das Marionettentheater," has a similar argument:[23] in an original, childlike, paradisiacal, and harmonious state of mankind, human beings lack self-awareness and self-knowledge and are thus characterized by natural grace. From an ontological perspective this stage describes the childhood of the individual person, while from a phylogenetic perspective it refers to humanity before the Fall from Grace.[24] In a second stage, after tasting the fruit of the tree of knowledge and thus reaching self-awareness, mankind is in a state of affectedness or "Zierde." This state can only be overcome in the third and final phase where infinite knowledge and divine existence — unachievable during our limited human existence — are finally attainable:

> So findet sich auch, wenn die Erkenntnis gleichsam durch ein Unendliches gegangen ist, die Grazie wieder ein; so, daß sie, zu gleicher Zeit, in demjenigen menschlichen Körperbau am reinsten erscheint, der entweder gar keins, oder ein unendliches Bewußtsein hat, d. h. in dem Gliedermann, oder in dem Gott. (*ÜdM*, 189)

This state of grace finds its expression in dance too, in the combination of music and bodily movement. For Kleist, it is the puppet on the string that symbolizes the possibility of this regained state of grace. Its perfection stems from its independence from the laws of gravity (*ÜdM*, 185) and thus frees it from social affectedness. In fact, compared to a human dancer, who needs the ground for rest and support, the marionette performs a superior dance, only touching the ground occasionally:

> Die Puppen brauchen den Boden nur, wie die Elfen, um ihn zu *streifen*, und den Schwung der Glieder, durch die augenblickliche Hemmung neu zu beleben; wir brauchen ihn, um darauf zu *ruhen*, und uns von der Anstrengung des Tanzes zu erholen: ein Moment, der offenbar selber kein Tanz ist. (*ÜdM*, 185)

The puppet on the string thus offers the opportunity of free play in art and an independence from norms and conventions (that is: gravity) encountered in everyday life. The puppet is the embodiment of perfect art, of utopia, and of the childlike and divine state of grace, best symbolized and illustrated in dance. Unsurprisingly then, this gravity-defying dancing marionette displays angelic characteristics similar to those of Mignon: they are both creatures of the air rather than the earth, and their character is best expressed through dance.

Let us reconsider Mignon in this light: she is androgynous and child-like, resembling a puppet on a string,[25] she is unaware of her attractiveness, she is graceful when performing her egg-dance, and she is in touch with ineffable inspiration when expressing herself through music. In Mignon's dance, Kleist's marionette seems to have come alive: she defies physical laws as she dances blindly around the eggs without touching a single one. She appears to be guided by a force outside herself. This description resembles Wilhelm Meister's own childhood puppet theatre.[26] Her dance is simultaneously both highly artistic and artificial: "Künstlich abgemessen schritt sie nunmehr auf dem Teppich hin und her" (*WML*, 116), yet in spite of, or rather because of, this artificial character,[27] it is graceful and erotic, and arouses Wilhelm's paternal affections towards Mignon:

> Er [Wilhelm Meister] empfand, was er schon für Mignon gefühlt, in diesem Augenblicke auf einmal. Er sehnte sich, dieses verlassene Wesen an Kindestatt seinem Herzen einzuverleiben, es in seine Arme zu nehmen und mit der Liebe eines Vaters Freude des Lebens in ihm zu erwecken. (*WML*, 117)

Like the marionette in Kleist's essay, Mignon seems only to touch the ground occasionally; she is part of the "springende Gesellschaft," and eventually loses all contact with the ground in her transformation to an angel. It can be said of her that: "die Kraft, die sie in die Lüfte erhebt, größer ist, als jene, die sie an die Erde fesselt," that is: she is a child of the air (*ÜdM*, 185). Furthermore, her lack of self-awareness reveals itself in her general inability to use the first-person pronoun,[28] hence her intro-duction: "man nennt mich Mignon" (*WML,* 99). She acts as a mirror for Wilhelm Meister by wanting to wear clothes of the same color as his and by expressing his feelings in her songs.[29] However, she is unable to reflect her own feelings or put them into any form other than the non-verbal language of music. Her music fails to be deciphered into words because it is so true to human nature and feelings that any non-musical mediation of it is doomed. Transcribing it means imperfectly reflecting it.[30] When the original is transcribed or copied, when it is given form by the artist, its intuitive and formless character is lost. The distance between direct utterance and poetic transcription cannot be bridged.[31] In *Wilhelm Meisters Lehrjahre* this is the characteristic that condemns Mignon. As she is unable to give form to her feelings, she cannot live.[32] Kleist delivers the counter-argument: being conscious of our actions and able to reflect our existence has alienated us from nature and God, and we have to die or else eat the apple of temptation for a second time in order to rediscover our unalienated and harmonious state of existence. Although condemned by Goethe's novel, Mignon is therefore the primeval marionette that was to become the muse for the Romantic artist as a promise for paradise regained.

In *Die mehreren Wehmüller und ungarische Nationalgesichter* we are presented with Mignon split in two.[33] This is the existential split into two spheres of experience — the curse of humanity —, which can only be mastered through and in poetry. Thus the Romantic artist is offered the utopian possibility of overcoming obstacles of gender and social status in the same way that the narrative eventually transgresses both geographical and symbolic boundaries. In Brentano's novella then, the same character-istics and values that eventually proved Mignon's unsuitability for devel-opment and integration into society and adulthood are reinterpreted in a positive light in the characters of Mitidika and Michaly. The similarities of outer appearance and character are striking: Mignon and Mitidika do not only share the same name (both names mean "little one"[34]), but just like Mignon, Mitidika appears in male clothing. Yet unlike her, she combines physical beauty with virtue (*MW,* 299), and dance with courage, but is also modest: "[. . .] sie war ein wunderschönes, frei, kühn, scheu und züchtig bewegtes Menschenbild" (*MW,* 295). She is symbolically situated in a childlike proximity to nature. She dwells in the forest and exhibits a child-like fascination with all things shiny and with make-up. Most significant, however, is her art of dance where she demonstrates a Dionysian wild exuberance. Clemens Brentano comments on the sublime attractions of dance as an art form in a letter to Bettina in 1802: "Tanz ist doch edel! — ja gewiß mit die reinste, die erhabenste der Künste."[35] Combined with the repeated linking of Mitidika's appearance with the description of a princess or, indeed, a queen (*MW,* 294, 295) her symbolic relevance as an incarnation of pure art becomes apparent. The symbolic use of both music and androgyny are thus approximations of an unalienated poetic existence.

Mignon *redivivus* in Mitidika and her male counterpart Michaly are characterized by an idealized beauty and purity that articulate their symbolic status as the allegory of pure and perfect poetry.[36] Mitidika's dance to her brother Michaly's violin music — whose playing is compared by the narrator to Orpheus's (after Grellmann) — is a mirror image of Mignon's egg-dance: both dance on a carpet, and both transfix their audience, expressing the ineffable. While Mignon's musical and androgynous nature with its erotic connotations can only be controlled through her death and transformation into an embalmed artifact and icon — "das Wunder der Kunst" (*WML*, 592) —, Mitidika's and Michaly's music and androgyny are celebrated as the promised return to a better society. "So ward der Friede gestiftet" (*MW*, 310) is the narrator's comment on the calming effect Mitidika's and Michaly's music has on the party. Mitidika's dancing and singing are full of magic; she is in fact a "Zauberin" (*MW*, 299, 310), and her playing of the tambourine while Michaly accompanies her on the fiddle mirrors the scene where Mignon was accompanied by a violinist during her egg-dance. In the novella their music is the missing link capable of reuniting representatives of all lifestyles, social class, and gender. In this way, through those arts that are both social and individual in nature, namely music and storytelling, borders are crossed, communities established, and confusion cleared, while the arts simultaneously provide joy and entertainment in a worrisome and threateningly chaotic situation. The explicit association of Michaly with Orpheus in this context is more than a quotation from Grellmann: Michaly's music succeeds in appeasing the tensions present, just as Orpheus pacified the demons of the underworld by his singing.

This positive impact on society through the musical Gypsies Michaly and Mitidika is further emphasized by the potency of their art and actions. Thus it is through the narrative event on the one hand and the musical event on the other that chaos is controlled and characters are united in *Die mehreren Wehmüller*. The Gypsies play an essential role in this. Just like Mignon, Mitidika and Michaly are artist figures through their use of music, and they offer the Romantic artist a potential for identification. In the novella they are counterpointed with Wehmüller and Froschauer, two painters who succeed in mass-producing their art, which is subsequently devoid of any individuality, so that, as a curse, their own individuality is denied; this is achieved through the witty use of the *Doppelgänger* motif.[37] Brentano juxtaposes this industrialized, mass-produced art with two forms of folk art: the art of storytelling and the art of music.[38] These oral arts do not materially enrich their practitioners, but they do spiritually enrich the traveling group of people who, with their variety of backgrounds, represent contemporary society in miniature. Consequently, while Wehmüller is a problematic artist, Michaly is not, and while Wehmüller represents perverted art, Michaly represents authentic art. Brentano's argument in favor of the authentic folk arts, though delivered with the wink of an eye, incorporates the storytelling of the Italian fireworks' artist Baciochi, Mitidika's dance, and Michaly's fiddling. All three involve their audience, and it is no coincidence that the storyteller's name echoes that of the master of the genre, Giovanni Boccaccio.

More than merely involving their audience in the process of their performance, however,[39] Michaly links the internal story to the frame narrative through his musical interpretation of the song, just as Mitidika performs her dance in both the internal and frame narrative. Thus they link the past with the present, and this culminates in Mitidika's appearance in the frame narrative during the narration of her story. As Mitidika and Michaly unite Wehmüller and his wife Tonerl, themselves, Froschauer (the fake Wehmüller impersonator) and his bride, Devillier (the French fireworks' artist) and Mitidika, and, of course, the two Wehmüllers, they break down the geographic frontier of the *Pestkordon* that had been the cause of all divisions. Thus, it is eventually Mitidika who concludes the narration of the internal story on the external level of the novella, and in so doing unites the two levels.[40] Identities are therefore found and established, and through music and narration truth, unity, and order are created. Poetry, that is: music and storytelling, succeeds in distinguishing appearance from reality, and creates peace among nationalities. In fact, brother and sister Michaly and Mitidika appear as the family of poetry and music because of their extraordinary beauty, which, of course, in physiognomic terms guarantees the beauty of the soul. This ideal beauty of body and mind is expressed in their singing and dancing, and in their transcendence of frontiers as Gypsies.

Finally, Michaly's tune, like Mignon's song, defies written notation. In its originality and individuality, his art (his music, that is) is pure expression, signified without the need of a signifier.[41] Its essence is to be found in its articulation and depends on the moment and situation, the social context, and its emotional adequacy for the listener: "so was diktirt sich nicht, ich wüßte es auch jetzt nicht mehr und wenn Sie mir den Hals abschnitten; wenn ich einmal wieder eine schöne Jungfer betrübt habe, wird es mir auch wieder einfallen" (*MW*, 276). Such evanescent oral, and indeed, aural arts, present an aesthetic contrast to the favored visual and plastic arts of classicism: "visual reality is so equivocal that even love's discrimination must be based on aural evidence";[42] identities have to be confirmed by aural recognition. Michaly and Mitidika thus represent natural, naïve, and oral folk poetry. The holy family of nature poetry — "die heilige Familie der Naturpoesie," as Friedrich Schlegel christened Mignon, Sperata and Augustino[43] — has indeed come alive again in Michaly and Mitidika. The union between Devillier, the representative of enlightened France, and Mitidika, is then, while essentially problematic, also a union of the sensual art of music with reason, the union of the Dionysian and Apolline principles. Through music, the age of reason can be transcended to a higher, possibly poetic existence. The enlightened representative of reason (Devillier) is allowed to cry like a child (*MW,* 311).

The Romantics interpreted Mignon as the embodiment of what music stands for in their aesthetics. Her being is led by emotions and feelings; she is the naïve but direct gateway to poetry and the human soul, a symbol for artistic genius and inspirational intuition. Her death thus has to be reversed,[44] and all she stands for has to be celebrated in a lively picture — which is just what Brentano attempts in his portrayal of the two Gypsies Mitidika and Michaly. In *Wilhelm Meisters Lehrjahre,* their sister in androgyny and Gypsyhood, Mignon, is transformed into an icon and embalmed artifact through an act of narration which, while transforming her into art and thus controlling her and her erotic attraction, also kills her, the narratee.[45] Her character has to be killed for the image to live. Michaly and Mitidika, conversely, are a celebration of life, poetry, and music, brought to life through the narrative process and the impact of music in the novella. The aesthetic implications of the poetics of music have, like Mignon's revival in Mitidika and Michaly, come of age and can enter the world confident in their significance and power. Mignon has been resurrected and is wearing a new gown.

Notes

[1] The problematic nature of the term "Gypsy" cannot be overlooked, as it denotes a semantic construction and classification of an ideological concept with real implications. Here, however, it refers both to the literary and the real image — i.e. it is a term carrying connotations of features real people attributed to a particular group of people (regardless of the actual character and lifestyle of itinerant groups such as the Romanies).

[2] In vol. 3 of Clemens Brentano, *Sämtliche Werke und Briefe: Historisch-kritische Ausgabe,* ed. Jürgen Behrens and Gerhard Kluge (Stuttgart: Kohlhammer, 1975ff.), 251–311. Subsequent references to this work are cited in the text using the abbreviation *MW.*

[3] Johann Wolfgang von Goethe, *Wilhelm Meisters Lehrjahre,* ed. Erich Schmidt (Frankfurt a. M.: Insel, 1980). Subsequent references to this work are cited in the text using the abbreviation *WML.*

[4] See David B. Dickens, "Brentanos Erzählung 'Die mehreren Wehmüller und ungarische Nationalgesichter': Ein Deutungsversuch," *Germanic Review* 58 (1983): 12–20. On p. 15 Dickens maintains that Brentano's treatment of music, which was for the Romantics the highest art form ("die den Romantikern die höchste Kunst überhaupt war"), is satirical, however, because the battle song delivered by Michaly is described as "moving." Dickens overlooks the fact that the battle

song is not aimed at exciting people to battle, but that it is about the loss of many lives. Therefore the adjective is not a satirical commentary on the song.

5 Heinrich Moritz Gottlieb Grellmann, *Historischer Versuch über die Zigeuner*, 2nd ed. (Göttingen: Dieterich, 1787).

6 In vol. 1 of Miguel de Cervantes, *Novelas Ejemplares*, ed. Harry Sieber (Madrid: Catedra, 1992).

7 Grellmann, *Historischer Versuch*, 103: "Ein solcher Orpheus war ein gewisser Barna Mihaly, [. . .] der sich gegen die Mitte dieses Jahrhunderts auf besagte Weise [i.e. his violin-playing] auszeichnete."

8 Ibid., 67.

9 "Salió la tal Preciosa, y la más única bailadora que se hallaba en todo el gitanismo, y la más hermosa y discreta que pudiera hallarse, no entre los gitanos, sino entre cuantas hermosas y discretas pudiera pregonar la fama. [. . .] y lo que es más, que la crianza tosca en que se criaba no descubría en ella sino ser nacida de mayores prendas que de gitana, porque era en extremo cortés y bien razonada" (Cervantes, *Novelas Ejemplares*, 61–62).

10 See Carolyn Steedman, "New Time: Mignon and her meanings," in *Fin de Siècle/Fin du Globe: Fears and Fantasies of the Late Nineteenth Century*, ed. John Stokes (Basingstoke, London: Macmillan, 1992), 102–16 (here, 109), who has argued that however indirect Goethe's use of these sources, Mignon's *Urbild* is indeed to be found in Cervantes' Preciosa.

11 She has been interpreted as Wilhelm Meister's intuition, as his genius, his imagination (in this context, see Hellmut Ammerlahn, "Puppe-Tänzer-Dämon-Genius-Engel: Naturkind, Poesiekind und Kunstwerdung bei Goethe," *German Quarterly* 54:1 [1981]: 19–32; also William Gilby, "The structural significance of Mignon in *Wilhelm Meisters Lehrjahre*," *Seminar: A Journal of Germanic Studies* 16 [1980]: 136–50), as a child of nature and poetry (see again Ammerlahn, "Puppe-Tänzer-Dämon-Genius-Engel"), as an abused child (see Ursula Mahlendorf, "The Mystery of Mignon: Object Relations, Abandonment, Child Abuse and Narrative Structure," *Goethe Yearbook* 7 [1994]: 23–39), and as connected to dark forces (see Gilby, "The structural significance of Mignon"). Her repressed erotic feelings for Wilhelm Meister have been analyzed psychoanalytically (see Mahlendorf, "The mystery of Mignon").

12 As Gerhart Hoffmeister in his work *Goethes Mignon und ihre Schwestern* (New York: Peter Lang, 1993), has outlined, Mignon was interpreted by the Romantics as the incarnation of absolute poetry. Her death had thus to be reversed by reappropriating her from a Romantic perspective.

13 Friedrich Schlegel, "Über Goethes Meister," in *Schriften zur Literatur*, ed. Wolfdietrich Rasch (Munich: dtv, 1972), 278.

14 She shares this feature of aristocratic parentage with Cervantes' Preciosa in *La Gitanilla*.

15 Gilby, "The structural significance of Mignon," 138.

16 See Rudolf Schottlaender, "Das Kindeslied der Mignon," *Jahrbuch des freien deutschen Hochstifts* 41 (1979): 71–89 (here, 77).

[17] In this context, see Hellmut Ammerlahn, "Wilhelm Meisters Mignon — ein offenbares Rätsel," *Deutsche Vierteljahresschrift für Literaturwissenschaft und Geistesgeschichte* 42 (1968): 89–116 (here, 93).

[18] For example *WML*, 148–49.

[19] See Robert Tobin, "The Medicinalization of Mignon," in *Goethes Mignon und ihre Schwestern,* ed. Hoffmeister, 56; see also Inge Stephan, "Mignon und Penthesilea: Androgynie und erotischer Diskurs bei Goethe und Kleist," in *Annäherungsversuche: Zur Geschichte und Ästhetik des Erotischen in der Literatur,* ed. Horst Albert Glaser (Bern: Haupt, 1993), 183–208.

[20] See Stephan, "Mignon und Penthesilea," 185.

[21] Ibid., 186–87.

[22] "[. . .] ist harmonische Ganzheitsvorstellung und zugleich ist sie Steigerung des Erotischen und wird mit Unmäßigkeit, Gesetzesübertretung und Treulosigkeit assoziiert." Ibid., 189.

[23] Heinrich von Kleist, "Über das Marionettentheater," in *Novellen und Ästhetische Schriften,* ed. Robert E. Helbling (New York: Oxford UP, 1967), 180–89. Subsequent references to this work are cited in the text using the abbreviation *ÜdM*. See also Erika Tunner, "'L'Esprit de Mignon': Mignon-Bilder von der Klassik bis zur Gegenwart," *Goethe Jahrbuch* 106 (1989): 11–21 (here, 16). Tunner asks how Goethe's Mignon may be interpreted in the positive sense of Kleist, but does not pursue this query.

[24] The early Romantics were preoccupied with the myth of the child (state of grace). Compared to adults, the child is superior because genius manifests itself in the unreflected nature of the child's thoughts.

[25] See *WML,* 337: "Mignon machte den schnarrenden Ton sehr artig nach, und sie [Mignon and Felix] stießen zuletzt die Köpfe dergestalt zusammen und auf die Tischkante, wie es eigentlich nur Holzpuppen aushalten können. [. . .] Ihre Haare flogen, und indem sie den Kopf zurück und alle ihre Glieder gleichsam in die Luft warf, schien sie einer Mänade ähnlich."

[26] In this context it is interesting to recall that Clemens and Bettina Brentano were fascinated by puppet theatre and theatre in general, which may account for their fascination with the Mignon character: see Angela Thamm, *Romantische Inszenierungen in Briefen: Der Lebenstext der Bettine von Arnim geborene Brentano* (Berlin: Saint Albin, 2000), 159. For an in-depth analysis of Mignon as a character from Wilhelm Meister's puppet theatre come to life see Ammerlahn, "Wilhelm Meisters Mignon."

[27] See again Ammerlahn "Wilhelm Meisters Mignon," 94, who compares the precision of her body when performing the egg-dance to a machine and a marionette.

[28] See Mahlendorf, "The Mystery of Mignon," for a psychoanalytical interpretation of Mignon's repressed feelings for Wilhelm.

[29] "Er [Wilhelm Meister] verfiel in eine träumende Sehnsucht, und wie einstimmend mit seinen Empfindungen war das Lied, das eben in dieser Stunde Mignon und der Harfner [. . .] sangen" (*WML*, 250).

³⁰ Oskar Seidlin, in his article "Zur Mignon-Ballade," *Euphorion* 45 (1950): 83–99, further argues that Mignon is ineffable, a genius, and a messenger from the realm of poetry: this is why she appears as an angel at the end of the novel.

³¹ "Aber die Originalität der Wendungen konnte er nur von ferne nachahmen. Die kindliche Unschuld des Ausdrucks verschwand, indem die gebrochene Sprache übereinstimmend und das Unzusammenhängende verbunden ward" (*WML,* 152).

³² In this context, Ammerlahn ("Puppe-Tänzer-Dämon-Genius-Engel," 12) argues that Mignon's authentic and original inspiration and poetry need to be given form by the talent of the poet.

³³ Tunner suggests in her article " 'L'Esprit de Mignon,' " (14) a similar split of the androgynous Mignon character into two characters in Brentano's *Godwi*.

³⁴ See Adolf Heltmann, "Rumänische Verse in Klemens Brentanos Novelle 'Die mehreren Wehmüller oder [*sic*] ungarische Nationalgesichter,' " *Korrespondenzblatt des Vereins für Siebenbürgische Landeskunde* 49 (1926): 81–104 (here, 83). He translates the Romanian word Mitidika as "Kleine" (the meaning of "Mignon").

³⁵ *Bettina von Arnims Sämtliche Werke,* ed. Waldemar Oehlke, 7 vols. (Berlin: Propyläen, 1920–22), 1:235.

³⁶ Gerhard Schaub argues that Mitidika is an embodiment of poetry: "eine Art lebendiges Kunstwerk" — "sie ist darüber hinaus die vitalste, charmanteste Verkörperung der Poesie im Werk Brentanos." "Mitidika und ihre Schwestern," in *Zwischen den Wissenschaften: Beiträge zur deutschen Literaturgeschichte,* ed. Gerhard Hahn and Ernst Weber (Regensburg: Pustet, 1994), 304–19 (here, 310).

³⁷ "Der falsche Wehmüller sei wohl nur eine Strafe Gottes für den echten Wehmüller, weil dieser alle Ungarn über einen Leisten male; so gäbe es jetzt auch mehrere Wehmüller über einen Leisten" (*MW,* 258). See also Peter Hasubeck, "Spielraum des Humors: Humoristisch-komische Strukturen in Clemens Brentanos Erzählung 'Die mehreren Wehmüller und ungarische Nationalgesichter,' " in *"Stets wird die Wahrheit hadern mit dem Schönen": Festschrift für Manfred Windfuhr zum 60. Geburtstag,* ed. Gertrude Cepl-Kaufmann (Cologne: Böhlau, 1990), 71–101 (here, 76); also Gordon Birrell, "Everything is e(x)ternally related: Brentano's 'Wehmüller,' " *German Quarterly* 66 (1993): 71–86 (here, 79).

³⁸ See Konrad Feilchenfeldt, "Erzählen im journalistischen Kontext: Clemens Brentanos 'Die mehreren Wehmüller und ungarische Nationalgesichter,' " in *Texte, Motive und Gestalten der Goethezeit: Festschrift für Hans Reiss,* ed. John L. Hibberd and H. B. Nisbet (Tübingen: Niemeyer, 1989), 202–23 (here, 219): "In den 'mehreren Wehmüllern' ist der Gegensatz zwischen mündlicher und schriftlicher Überlieferung der Dichtung durch die musikalischen Darbietungen des Zigeunerpaars, Mitidikas Gesang und Michalys Geigenspiel, wo nicht durch die Erzählsituation der Reisegesellschaft, ausreichend anschaulich gemacht."

³⁹ See Birrell, " 'Everything is e(x)ternally related,' " 80: "So great is the immediacy of this narrated reality, in fact, that Baciochi's audience itself, and more than once, spontaneously reenacts the events of the story."

⁴⁰ See Dickens, "Brentanos Erzählung," 13.

⁴¹ Lindpeindler comments on the character of the song performed by Michaly: "O, das ist groß, das ist ursprünglich" (*MW,* 276). Although this is a tongue-in-cheek

parody of the Romantic collector of folklore, it nevertheless points towards the perception of the Gypsy's music as an original and unalienated art form.

[42] Birrell, " 'Everything is e(x)ternally related,' " 83.

[43] Schlegel, "Über Goethes Meister," 278.

[44] See Steedman, "New Time: Mignon and her meanings," 107–8, on the Romantics' search for an anti-Meister narrative that prevents the death of the child that is Mignon.

[45] See Ammerlahn, "Puppe-Tänzer-Dämon-Genius-Engel," 26, 28. Through the act of embalming, Mignon becomes an artifact, living on as an image, but not as a real person. Her being is as an ideal — if lifeless — symbol for art: "Im Körper großer Kunst tritt uns ein ideales aber totes Gebilde, in der Natur ein lebendiges, aber bedingtes Geschöpf entgegen." See also Stephan, "Mignon und Penthesilea," 200: "der Tod der Figur [Mignons] ist die Geburt des Bildes."

Sounds of Hoffmann

Stages of Imagination in Music and Literature: E. T. A. Hoffmann and Hector Berlioz

Andrea Hübener

> "Ich möchte nur," sprach Giglio endlich, "daß die Reiche, die wir künftig beherrschen werden, fein aneinandergrenzten, damit wir gute Nachbarschaft halten könnten; aber irr ich nicht, so liegt das Fürstentum meiner angebeteten Prinzessin über Indien weg, gleich linker Hand um die Erde nach Persien zu."[1]

WITH THESE WORDS the penniless actor Giglio in E. T. A. Hoffmann's capriccio *Prinzessin Brambilla* (1821) evokes the fantastic topography of the two theatrical, fairy-tale kingdoms where Giglio and his lady Giacinta will respectively reign as prince and princess. As Giacinta's appearance in her princess's attire at the beginning of this fairy-tale novella has already implied, and as the novella's end eventually confirms, both kingdoms flout all petty reason. They do not simply border one another, but actually converge within a shared theatrical frame. Thus the stage comes to represent the world of the imagination, where the symbiotic realms of interior and exterior are as one. This magical world of the theater, which brings together music, poetry, and visual images, reaches a similar poetic apotheosis in many other works of Hoffmann, especially in his final narrative tableaux reminiscent of actual stage sets.[2]

Many of Hoffmann's tales take their subjects from drama and opera, and their often histrionic character is emphasized by the use of dramatic devices such as dialogue or *tableau vivant*. In *Don Juan* (1813), one of the *Fantasiestücke in Callots Manier* (Fantasies in the Manner of Callot, 1814/15), music's demonic power to open up the spirit-realm for those in the real world is manifested in the characters of Donna Anna and the traveling enthusiast. In the fourth essay of the *Kreisleriana*, "Beethovens Instrumental-Musik" (1810/14), Kapellmeister Kreisler emphasizes the theatrical qualities of music.

This dramatic interpretation of Beethoven's instrumental music and the ennobling of the musical genres associated with it were of special importance to Hector Berlioz. Not only in his literary works and critical writings on music, but also in his decidedly dramatic musical compositions,

Berlioz drew either directly or indirectly on literature. A highly dramatic scenery with its recourse to patterns of the sublime and a poignant expression of loss are recurring features in Berlioz's work, especially in his early musical compositions of all genres. In fact, Berlioz's compositions can be regarded as a varied series of musico-dramatic answers to the questions of music and language Hoffmann had raised in his literary works.[3] The *Huit scènes de Faust* (1828), later reworked into *La Damnation de Faust* (1845/46), and the melologue *Le retour à la vie* (The Return to Life, 1831/32), which became the monodrama *Lélio, ou le retour à la vie* (1855) are examples of this.[4] Among Berlioz's own literary writings, his collections of music novellas show many similarities to Hoffmann's. The latter's works, which since 1830 have appeared in French translation in two competing editions, inaugurated the vogue of the "conte fantastique" (fantastic tale).

A famous passage from "Beethovens Instrumental-Musik" endows Beethoven's music with the power to awaken fear, horror, terror, and pain in the hearts of his listeners. Though reminiscent of Aristotle's definition of tragedy, this passage describes the unleashing of infinite yearning, which for the narrator is the essence of Romanticism.[5] The "Geisterreich des Unendlichen" (spirit-world of the eternal) evoked by the narrator is a world cut off from the real world.[6] Music is defined as the heightened language of fantasy, a language beyond everyday speech — a type of meta-language.[7] As the example of Chevalier Gluck (from the eponymous *Fantasiestück*) shows, this concept is always linked in Hoffmann's works with the pre-classical concept of a *lingua franca* of loosely organized affect formulae,[8] a concept expressed in music with the object of producing a similar mood among its listeners. Thus, music gives expression to the extreme subjectivity of the composer, while functioning as the self-appointed harmonizing medium between the extremes. This dichotomy is typical of the paradoxes that confront both the fictional characters in and the readers of Hoffmann's literary works. Characters and readers alike see themselves reflected in the necessarily verbal music of his tales, whose genre titles are often derived directly from music.

Tension between the musical spirit-realm, removed from everyday reality, and the competing demands of technical or formal doctrine, is also the subject of Hoffmann's *Alte und neue Kirchenmusik* (Ancient and Modern Church Music, 1814) and *Der Dichter und der Komponist* (The Poet and the Composer, 1813), both included in the *Serapionsbrüder* (Serapion-Brethren, 1819–21) in slightly altered versions. In the first case, music's religious purity is threatened by its intrinsic artistic value, while in the second, the notion of a musical spirit-realm — which for Hoffmann is expressed only through harmony — is incompatible with the fundamental definition of a musico-dramatic (and thus conflict-laden) work. It is in this sense that in *Der Dichter und der Komponist* Ludwig describes to Ferdinand by means of rhetorical questions and answers the essence and effect of Romantic opera. For him the only "true opera" is one whose music is a necessary and direct consequence of the text.[9] Ludwig then goes on to define a desideratum for the transcending of ordinary life — the declared goal of Romantic opera — as the magical power of poetic truth that the poet must possess in order to facilitate the transformation of speech into song, plot into music. The examples he has in mind are operas to texts by Ariosto, Tasso, and Gozzi, whose works contain fantastic and fairy-tale elements. Written either wholly or partly in verse, their meter and rhythm are most fitting for the musical transformation that is to take place on the stage. Alongside examples of *tragédie lyrique* by composers such as Gluck and Piccini — where, according to Ludwig, the world of the Gods assumes responsibility for such a transformation — it is the adventurous and fantastic in *opera buffa* that make for bizarrerie and confusion.[10] Ludwig's comparison of Romantic opera with the performance of Italian actors, whose job it is to bring to life the skeletal structure created by the poet, echoes the commedia dell'arte, where a given narrative frame, the *canevas*, forms the starting-point for the *lazzi*, a game of improvisation with masks. In Romantic opera, however, the work reaches completion not by means of such improvisation, but through the music and the imaginative powers of the audience. The comparison underlines the relative freedom for the composer implicit in the notion of improvisation, and it also stresses every artistic creation's never-ending quest for completion.

The musings of Hoffmann's fictional artists and art enthusiasts opened up for Romantic composers like Berlioz new perspectives of an imaginary stage in the minds of the audience, and, as we shall see, the stage of the real theatre as an imaginary space. The poetic origins of these perspectives may well explain the close ties between poetic and musical scenes in Berlioz's compositions. Any composition that highlights its literary antecedents avows its character as a work of art. In the face of the seemingly direct mediation of language by the Romantic artist, this can easily be overlooked. Berlioz and Hoffmann were experts at this compositional-poetic puzzle game. They constantly prevent an unambiguous interpretation through the invention of new perspectives and in so doing render unambiguity a utopian goal.[11]

One of the many literary features to be found in Berlioz's music is the re-introduction of genres that combine music and language programmatically. One such genre is represented by the melologue *Le retour à la vie* of 1831/32. Berlioz came across this genre through a note in the French edition of Thomas Moore's *Irish Melodies*, which refers to his *Melologue upon National Music*.[12] The word "melologue" implies a mixture of music and language, but the genre was renamed *monodrame lyrique* in 1855, thus hinting at both the *tragédie lyrique* of the revered master Spontini, and at Gluck's reform of opera that traced its origins back to antique tragedy. There is also Berlioz's *Symphonie fantastique* of 1830 (whose title recalls the *contes fantastiques* of Hoffmann), the dramatic symphony *Roméo et Juliette* (1839), the dramatic legend *La Damnation de Faust,* and its prototype, the *Huit scènes de Faust.*

To be sure, Berlioz emphasized the autonomous literary quality of his *Symphonie fantastique* by supplying its first listeners with a detailed program — the minutiae of which exasperated even Robert Schumann, who was soon to write an enthusiastic article on this drama in music. But alongside this, Berlioz wanted to illustrate his indebtedness to established works of drama and literature. What are we to make, for instance, of the quotations from Shakespeare's tragedies *Hamlet* and *Romeo and Juliet* heading each of the nine pieces of music of the *Huit scènes de Faust,* Berlioz's opus 1, whose text follows Gérard de Nerval's 1827 translation of Goethe's *Faust* I?[13] The biographical facts surrounding this composition are well-known: successful performances of Shakespeare's tragedies in France around this time by a British troupe — among them the Irish actress Harriet Smithson whom Berlioz later married — signaled the beginning of Berlioz's lifelong fascination for Shakespeare's works; these were followed closely by the deep impression made on the composer by Nerval's translation of Goethe's *Faust.*[14] Yet the aesthetic impact of forcing together two very different authors in the *Huit scènes* cannot be explained in mere biographical terms. Berlioz has something greater in mind.[15]

The enthusiastic reception of Shakespeare in France, which only a few years earlier would have been inconceivable, owed much to a debate on literature and art opened up by Charles Nodier.[16] Shakespeare, and subsequently Goethe and Hoffmann, formed the backbone of a Romantic protest against doctrinaire classicism in art. With his *Huit scènes* Berlioz composed a work that, in its iconoclastic gesture, decisively overshadowed earlier important works of the Romantic movement, such as the paintings of Eugène Delacroix and the writings of Victor Hugo.[17]

Differences in orchestration between the individual movements of the *Huit scènes* have provoked Julian Rushton to issue an editorial warning that a complete performance may perhaps come across as "somewhat imbalanced." This musical heterogeneity reflects the loosely-connected content: "The collection must be regarded as a miscellany, comparable to the later *Irlande et Tristia*."[18] Berlioz's early withdrawal of his op. 1 and his own subsequent criticism of the work would seem to support Rushton's judgment, but that judgment is questionable with respect to the dramatic-poetic coherence of the *Huit scènes,* and does not take into account the conception of the work.[19] The *Huit scènes* and the later *Le retour à la vie* are similar not only by virtue of their obvious close ties to literature, but also in their mixing of musical genres. If understood programmatically, this mixing can

Table 1. Literary quotations framing each of the *Huit scènes*

Scene numbers and titles	Shakespeare motto at the start of each scene	*Faust* quotation opening each scene	*Faust* quotation closing each scene
No. 1 Chants de la Fête de Pâques	Ophelia: "Heavenly powers, restore him." (*Hamlet*)	Faust: "Voici une Liqueur que je dois boire pieusement; je l'ai préparée, je l'ai choisie, elle sera ma boisson dernière, et je la consacre avec toute mon âme, comme libation solennelle à l'aurore d'un jour plus beau." (Il porte la Coupe à sa bouche. Son de Cloches et chants de Chœurs.)	Faust: "Quels murmures sourds, quels sons éclatants, arrachent puissamment la Coupe à mes lèvres altérées? etc."
No. 2 Paysans sous les Tilleuls. Danse et Chant	Capulet: "Who'll now deny to dance? She that makes dainty, I'll swear hath corns." (*Romeo and Juliet*)	Vagner: "Monsieur le Docteur, il est honorable et avantageux de se promener avec vous, cependant je ne voudrais pas me confondre dans ce monde-là, car je suis ennemi de tout ce qui est grossier. Leurs violons, leurs cris, leurs amusements bruyants, je hais tout cela à la mort. Ils hurlent comme des possédés et appellent cela de la joie et de la danse."	Un vieux paysan: "Monsieur le Docteur, il est beau de votre part de ne point nous mépriser aujourd'hui, et, savant comme vous l'êtes, de venir vous mêler à toute cette cohue, etc."

Table 1. (Continued)

Scene numbers and titles	Shakespeare motto at the start of each scene	*Faust* quotation opening each scene	*Faust* quotation closing each scene
No. 3 Concert de Sylphes. Sextuor	Mercutio: "I talk of dreams, which are the children of an airy brain, begot of nothing but vain fantasy; which is as thin of substance as the air, and more inconstant than the wind." *(Romeo and Juliet)*	Méphistophélès: "De vains préparatifs ne sont point nécessaires, nous voici rassemblés, commencez."	Méphistophélès: "Il dort. C'est bien, jeunes esprits de l'air! vous l'avez fidèlement enchanté! c'est un concert que je vous redois."
No. 4 Écot de joyeux Compagnons. Histoire d'un Rat	Hamlet: "How now? a rat? dead, for a ducat, dead." *(Hamlet)*	Brander, frappant sur la table: "Attention! une Chanson de la plus nouvelle facture! et répétez bien haut le refrain avec moi!"	Siebel: "Comme ces plats coquins se réjouissent! c'est un beau chef-d'oeuvre à citer que l'empoisonnement d'un pauvre Rat!"
No. 5 Chanson de Méphistophélès. Histoire d'une Puce	Hamlet: "Miching mallecho: it means mischief." *(Hamlet)*	Frosch: "Donnez nous une Chanson." Méphistophélès: "Tant que vous en voudrez." Siebel: "Mais quelque chose de nouveau." Méphistophélès: "Nous revenons d'Espagne, c'est l'aimable Pays du Vin et des Chansons."	Siebel: "Ainsi soit-il de toutes les puces!"

Table 1. (Continued)

Scene numbers and titles	Shakespeare motto at the start of each scene	*Faust* quotation opening each scene	*Faust* quotation closing each scene
No. 6 Le Roi de Thulé. Chanson Gothique	Ophelia: "He is dead and gone; at his head a grass green turf, at his heels a stone." (*Hamlet*)	Marguerite: "Un frisson me court par tout le corps . . . ah! je suis une femme bien follement craintive."	
No. 7 Romance de Marguerite	Romeo: "Ah me! sad hours seem long." (*Romeo and Juliet*)		
Choeurs de Soldats. (Passant sous les fenêtres de la Maison de Marguerite)	Mercutio: "Come, let's be gone, the sport is over." (*Romeo and Juliet*)		
No. 8 Sérénade de Méphistophélès	Hamlet: "It is a damned ghost." (*Hamlet*)	Méphistophélès: "Maintenant que le Ciel brille tout plein d'étoiles, vous allez entendre un vrai chef d'oeuvre; je lui chanterai une chanson morale, pour la séduire plus sûrement."	Valentin s'avance: "Qui leurres-tu là? Par le feu! maudit preneur de Rats! . . . Au diable d'abord l'instrument! et au diable ensuite le chanteur!"

give the work a unity that seems to be missing from the apparently external incongruities of musical ambience and literary subject.

A double motto in the form of quotations from Nerval's *Faust* translation (from the pact scene) and Thomas Moore's *Irish Melodies* precedes the *Huit scènes:*

> Je me consacre au tumulte, aux jouissances les plus douloureuses,
> à l'amour qui sent la haine, à la paix qui sent le désespoir.
>
> Goethe, Faust

> One fatal remembrance, one sorrow that throws
> Its bleak shade alike o'er our joys and our woes.
>
> Th. Moore, Irish Melodies

As shown in the table, each of the nine movements or scenes (the seventh is presented in two parts) has a title referring to a scene in *Faust,* which itself is preceded by an English motto from *Hamlet* or *Romeo and Juliet.* In addition, quotations from the French translation of *Faust* frame the individual scenes. (There are exceptions: the end of the sixth scene has no quotation, and both parts of the seventh scene are preceded by a quotation from *Romeo and Juliet* only, with none from *Faust.*) Berlioz appended to the score notes containing precise performance suggestions for the orchestra and singers: these are obviously intended to help the performers form a clearer understanding of the character and direction of the music.

The first quotation in the opening motto is taken, as already mentioned, from the pact scene between Faust and the devil in Goethe's *Faust* (*HS,* 2).[20] The connection between this quotation and the *Huit scènes* becomes all the clearer when one considers exactly what Berlioz has cut out. The devil permits Faust to abandon himself completely to his desires without a thought for the ultimate goal: "Il ne vous est assigné aucune limite, aucun but." Faust's answer shows that he is aware of the dialectical nature of this relentless striving: "Tu sens bien qu'il ne s'agit pas là d'amusemens. Je me consacre au tumulte [. . .]" (Goethe, 1765–67; Nerval, 77). Coming at the very start of the *Huit scènes,* Faust's answer can be read as an aesthetic program of Berlioz's that extends beyond the scope of the work itself. The oxymorons obvious in the words spoken by Faust: "schmerzlichster Genuß" ("most painful enjoyment"), "verliebter Haß" ("amorous hate"), "erquickender Verdruß" ("exhilarating frustration"), define both the poetic and musically heterogeneous shaping of the *Huit scènes.* Faust's contradictory reply to Méphistophélès's suggestion that moderation and intent should have nothing to do with the fulfillment of his desires also says something about the character of the work under discussion here: seemingly lawless, it does nonetheless follow its own regulations.

Berlioz's identification with Faust is emphasized from the very start by the second motto quotation from Moore's *Irish Melodies* (*HS*, 2). While all the associated *dramatis personae* — Faust, Romeo, and Hamlet — are rather arbitrarily connected by their shared sorrow, Moore's words do not appear to have a direct relevance for the *Huit scènes*.[21] The enigmatic quotation, "one fatal remembrance, one sorrow," however, may be an allusion to the consuming love the young Berlioz had for Harriet Smithson and the Shakespearean heroines she played.[22] The following examples will illustrate the dramatic double scenario conjured up in different ways by Berlioz's literary quotations.

The quotations placed before the second and fourth scenes seem at first glance to do little more than give the cue for the music about to be heard: the words pronounced by the lord of the manor at the commencement of the ball in the house of Capulet, "Who'll now deny to dance? She that makes dainty, I'll swear hath corns" (*HS*, 22; *Romeo and Juliet*, I/v, 17–18),[23] introduce Berlioz's second scene, a peasants' dance, while Hamlet's words uttered on his stabbing of Polonius, eavesdropping behind the drape, "How now? a rat? dead, for a ducat, dead" (*HS*, 68; *Hamlet*, II/iv, 23–24), affixed to the fourth scene, recall the drinking song of the rat sung by the merry gathering in Auerbach's cellar in *Faust*.

In the first, third, and fifth scenes, the quotations from Shakespeare permit a closer association with those from *Faust* in that all are abstractions from the concrete dramatic situation. Only in this way is the link between Ophelia's and Faust's words at the opening of Berlioz's first scene clear. Ophelia's plea to the heavens to restore reason to Hamlet (*Hamlet*, III/i, 141) equally applies to Faust, about to poison himself: "Voici une Liqueur que je dois boire pieusement [. . .]" (*HS*, 3; Goethe, 732–36; Nerval, 38–39). Ophelia's words at the start of this scene show what Hamlet and Faust have in common: Hamlet wishes to escape — be it through madness or death — a world gone awry, and Faust, world-weary and convinced of his own nothingness, longs for a final release in death.

Berlioz links the third scene (Mercutio's description of the fairy Mab), which in Shakespeare is set in the context of Romeo's dreams of impending doom ("I talk of dreams, which are the children of an airy brain, begot of nothing but vain fantasy; which is as thin of substance as the air, and more inconstant than the wind," *Romeo and Juliet*, I/iv, 96–100) with the spirits of the air that are conjured up when Méphistophélès casts a spell on Faust. Here the devil seems to adopt the role of *spiritus rector* for the ensuing music, denying the necessity for any preparation: "De vains préparatifs ne sont point nécessaires, [. . .]" (*HS*, 26; Goethe, 1445–46; Nerval, 66). The end of the sextet cites Méphistophélès's praise for the power of this music felt by both Faust and the listeners: "[. . .] vous l'avez fidèlement enchanté! c'est un concert que je vous redois" (*HS*, 67; Goethe, 1506–7; Nerval, 68). In *Faust* this quotation is preceded by words that could apply equally well to both Méphistophélès and Berlioz, to magic as well as to music:

> Ton esprit, mon ami, va gagner davantage dans cette heure seulement que dans l'uniformité d'une année entière. Ce que te chantent les esprits subtils, les belles images qu'ils apportent, ne sont pas une vaine magie. (Goethe, 1436–41; Nerval, 66)

Faust's demand, prior to this, that Méphisto entertain him[24] — which he does with music that sends Faust to sleep — can also be interpreted as an ironic comment by Berlioz on the unreasonable demands placed on his art. It recalls too Boïeldieu's remark about Berlioz's failed third attempt at winning the *Prix de Rome,* this time with his lyric scene, *La mort de Cléopâtre* (The Death of Cleopatra, 1829): "Comment pourrais-je approuver de telles choses, moi qui aime par-dessus tout la musique qui me berce?"[25] Here we see Boïeldieu (himself a composer of operas and a member of the jury for the *Prix de Rome* at the conservatory) wanting to be soothed by music — in stark contrast to Berlioz, who is constantly striving to unsettle the audience by his music. Similarly, Méphisto's provocative words to the sleeping Faust (which Berlioz omits): "Tu n'es pas encore homme à bien tenir le diable!" (Goethe, 1509; Nerval, 68), can be understood as a failed attempt by the musical traditionalists to tie a composer down to musical rules, to make him follow the path of convention.

Given this background, it might be expected that the *Faust* quotations that preface the second and fourth scenes do more than merely provide a context for the music about to be heard. Yet these quotations are the words of minor figures, whom Goethe has already established as poor judges of art and character. Wagner's words at the start of the second scene reveal him as the servile character and bore that Goethe intends him to be (*HS*, 22; Goethe, 941–48; Nerval, 47–48). Not only is the pretentious and affected behavior of Wagner juxtaposed with the old peasant's words that Berlioz transfers to the end of his scene, but the vivacious dance composed by Berlioz itself belies Wagner's resentful words.

The situation is reversed in the song of the rat: here it is Brander who announces his song as "Chanson de la plus nouvelle facture," the newest composition (*HS*, 68). In *La Damnation de Faust* Berlioz adds at this point a stereotypical "Amen" fugue to heighten the ironic effect of the scene, but even in the earlier version in the *Huit scènes,* the song succeeds in giving expression to the brutality and mental torpor of the singer and his drinking companions. Thus, from the very outset there exists a tension in the relationship between the text and the music. The text does not primarily reflect the music: rather, the music questions the preceding text.

The quotation placed at the start of the fifth scene, Méphisto's song of the flea, is Hamlet's answer to Ophelia's question about the meaning of the actors' pantomime: "Miching mallecho: it means mischief" (*HS,* 72;

Hamlet, III/ii, 132). As in the scene in *Hamlet* where the audience (both in real terms and within the play itself) is initiated into the deeper meaning of the masque, so too is the deeper meaning of Méphisto's song revealed to the audience of the *Huit scènes.* Conversely, the irony in pronouncing revenge on the flea should it bite — "Et, dès qu'une nous pique, / Écrasons-la soudain!" (Goethe, 2237–38; Nerval, 99) — is lost on the merry drinking companions of Auerbach's cellar. Furthermore, Hamlet's words can be seen to allude to the ominous role being played by Méphisto, especially in respect of Gretchen.

The eighth scene, Méphisto's serenade, is preceded by Hamlet's reaction to the appearance of his father: "It is a damned ghost" (*HS,* 97; *Hamlet,* I/v, 138: "honest ghost"). Valentin turns to Méphisto at the end of the serenade (in Goethe's drama these are practically his final words) and condemns him, asking him whom he thinks he is deceiving (*HS,* 99; Goethe, 3698–701; Nerval, 170). Thus an association is set up between the "damned ghost" and Méphisto, whom he has to fight, but whose power is out of his reach. Placed as they are at the end of the eighth scene, and thus at the close of the work, these words do more than frame the song just heard. They are to be read as a double-edged ironic commentary of his op. 1, aimed both at Berlioz and at Méphisto (in the latter's role as musician).

Together with the rather ironic disjointedness of Valentin's speech, the dramatic irony (it is Valentin who dies, not the "rat-catcher") has relevance also for the composer about to triumph over his critics. In the words with which Méphisto has just introduced his song, "Maintenant [. . .] vous allez entendre un vrai chef d'oeuvre; je lui chanterai une chanson morale, pour la séduire plus sûrement" (Goethe, 3678–82; Nerval, 169) — a song of moral seduction — Berlioz adds an ironic touch to the practice of placing actual, or even alleged, moral demands on music. In the same way that Valentin's words anticipate the criticism of Berlioz's compositions (Valentin identifies the musician with the rat-catcher), so too can Faust's words in the dedication to the *Huit scènes* be interpreted as referring to Berlioz's lifelong struggle for recognition. In addition they are an indictment on the specific character of his compositions. By bringing together genres hitherto deemed incompatible, it seems that Berlioz's intent on the bumpy compositional road is to let the listener participate in the musically adapted oxymorons in *Faust.* Himself a "nouveau Faust," one of the role models of the artist in *Le retour à la vie* (*Lélio,* 239), Berlioz carries on searching for new possibilities of musical interpretation.

Berlioz sent the score of his op. 1 to Goethe, enclosing a letter in which he describes the genesis of the composition and the music's seductive hold on him:

Depuis quelques années, *Faust* étant devenu ma lecture habituelle, à force de méditer cet étonnant ouvrage [. . .] il a fini par opérer sur mon esprit une espèce de charme; [. . .] peu à peu la séduction a été si forte, le charme si violent, que la musique de plusieurs scènes s'est trouvée faite presque à mon insu [. . .]. (10.4.1829, *CG*, 247)

The magical effect that *Faust* had on Berlioz is doubly emphasized. The resulting musical work is the fulfillment of the poetic magic in that it has grown out of the composer's mind in a manner almost beyond his control. Berlioz truly believed that his musical ideas had joined forces in his mind with Goethe's poetic ideas; if this is interpreted as a *de facto* explanation of how the work came into being, rather than merely flattering Goethe, then the unusual synthesis of literature and music in the score can be seen as forming the actual shape of the composition. This in turn makes the essence of each subsequent scene more meaningful and comprehensible to the performers. Berlioz thus achieves something quite new: an extension of the process of artistic evolution to embrace all performers and listeners who know the score and its introductory quotations.

This marriage of quotations and music in Berlioz's *Huit scènes* can be compared with Hoffmann's custom of establishing a narrative framework for his stories. But whereas Hoffmann counterbalances his fantastic tales by reflecting on these very narratives, thus creating within the text itself a distance between the work and its readers, Berlioz seems to go in two different directions at the same time. In other words, through the poetic framing of his music — the ironic fusion of music and language — he imbues his work with a high degree of reflexivity. By combining quotations from Shakespeare and Goethe, Berlioz literally doubles the dramatic impact of the scenes. This seems to be in line with his intention of impressing and even overwhelming his audience by going back to those elements of the sublime that lie at the heart of his own fascination with a specific literary tableau.[26] The significance of Berlioz's choice of quotation only becomes apparent from listening to and reading the new musical work itself.[27] This belief in the power of music to take an active part in co-producing the work within the minds of the audience justifies Berlioz's apparent surrender in the melologue *Le retour à la vie* to the new Romantic vogue of name-dropping.

The habit of combining different sources within a single work seems to be linked to another of Berlioz's idiosyncrasies: his borrowing from compositions of his own, which can change the programs considerably.[28] Does Berlioz effectively declare all his programs null and void if he recycles several pieces in a different context? Earlier scholarship tried to clear Berlioz of this charge. It has been argued that vagueness of meaning in music allows for changes in its semantics. Another argument is that Berlioz's programs were only concessions to the French audiences of his time whom Schumann believed to be devoid of any imagination.[29] The first argument ignores Berlioz's initial intention to ascribe a precise meaning, however provisional, to his musical compositions. He does this by supplying programs, by literary allusions in titles, or by the addition of epigraphs. His aesthetic concept of overwhelming his audience with a specific dramatic effect allows for no vagueness in semantics. His music is always meant either as an expression of a poetic idea[30] or as a bringing together of contrasting features to provoke his listeners and make them take an active part in the musical drama.

If we look at the text of the *Huit scènes,* a certain vagueness of meaning is initially apparent. This, however, is not so much a vagueness in the music, but in the quotations, whose semantic certainties seem to give way to new and complex meanings. The scenes invoked by the quotations do not negate each other; instead they complement each other by hinting at certain aspects of the other source text. The issues of context and source are therefore extremely important, and I would argue for an interpretation that looks at the images evoked by the literary allusions, and that takes into account the different meanings formerly ascribed by the composer to a musical phrase: in short, an interpretation that reads the semantic multiplicity of this music as poetry.

The juxtaposition of different layers of meaning perhaps reaches its apogee in the melologue *Le retour à la vie,* where music and language are combined in similar and yet quite different ways. Berlioz seems constantly to strive for new ways to express the spirit-realm of music — the subject of Hoffmann's stories — and to make the space created by the musical scenery audible and even visible. Like Hoffmann in *Der Dichter und der Komponist, Ritter Gluck* (Chevalier Gluck, 1809), or *Seltsame Leiden eines Theater-Direktors* (Strange Sorrows of a Theater Director, 1819), where the problems of writing, composing, performing and staging opera, music, and drama are vividly and controversially discussed, Berlioz's *oeuvre* seems to give an interpretation of the Janus-faced nature of his musical drama. The term "Janus-faced" is used here intentionally. Its mixture of language and music will inevitably create some problems if music is defined, as Hoffmann's narrators or personae define it, as the pure language of the spirits, void of any contrast. The language that is spoken or sung by the personae on stage — purified, even, by versification — belongs to this world. The function of music in this unholy alliance is to elevate its very plot (as well as the audience's minds) by artificial means to the upper regions of Art; this can only be achieved with the help of the audience's imagination. This "elevation" is evident in both versions of *Lélio.* The members of the audience, which in Berlioz's case is often denied the scenery of opera, are meant to discover instead the advantages of the inner stages of their imagination. The melologue, which was popularly believed to represent Berlioz's unhappy love affair with Harriet Smithson, is in fact staging the power of imagination itself.

The dramatic quality of Beethoven's instrumental music also seems to pave the way for the composer of the *Symphonie fantastique,* subtitled

"Episode de la vie d'un artiste" (Episode in the Life of an Artist). Its five movements show Berlioz's indebtedness to Beethoven's Sixth Symphony ("Pastoral"), albeit often by reversing the original features. Thus the first movement of Beethoven's symphony is recognizable as one of the sources for the daydreams of the first movement of the *Symphonie fantastique,* "Rêveries, passions."[31] Its third movement forms the thematic backdrop for Berlioz's second movement. Berlioz's description in an article of 1838 of the end of Beethoven's third movement recalls the second movement of the *Symphonie fantastique* and its parody in the fifth movement, and also the sound of the footsteps on the way to the scaffold in the fourth movement.[32] The third movement, "Scène aux champs" (Scene in the Fields), takes up motifs from the first, fourth, and fifth movements of the "Pastoral" in the storm and playfulness of the shepherds. The execution scene of Berlioz's fourth movement follows on from the storm hinted at towards the end of the third movement: a reversal of the joyous feelings evoked in Beethoven's fifth movement. The last movement of the *Symphonie fantastique* is in effect a musical parody on all the previous movements, as well as of those in the "Pastoral." A well-known example of this is the motif from the second movement, the *idée fixe,* which reappears in distorted form in the "ronde du sabbat"; another one is the superimposed "Dies Irae," which can be interpreted as a dark response to the scene of rejoicing after the storm.

Lélio (1855) is a sequel to the *Symphonie fantastique.*[33] The beginning of the monodrama reinterprets all five movements of the symphony as an opium-dream of the artist who has unsuccessfully tried to poison himself. (In earlier programs of the *Symphonie fantastique* the poisoning served only as a motivation for the sinister character of its last two movements.)[34] The artist-hero now comes to his senses. He passes through several stages, each marked by a piece of music that reflects his own changing moods. Each piece belongs to a different genre and corresponds both musically and semantically to the *Symphonie fantastique.* The musicians on stage are hidden behind the curtain, as the music is understood to exist only in the artist's mind. Each of the six pieces of music is preceded by a monologue from the artist who, standing in front of the curtain, slips into different roles, among them Hamlet, Faust, Byron's heroes, Orpheus, and Prospero. These monologues function as literary preludes and illustrate the power of literature to invoke the composer's inspiration. As in Hoffmann's novellas, it is the music that goes beyond the power of language to express the artist's inner visions. The following example illustrates this.

In the second monologue, the mention of Shakespeare and of the numinous world evoked by the ghost of Hamlet's father prepares the listener for the music in the following "Choeur d'ombres" (Choir of Ghosts). Lélio's description of the musical inspiration awakened by the speech of the royal ghost is made audible in various stages (*Lélio,* 234).

At the beginning the orchestra plays on its own; before the "Largo miste-rioso" of the ghost choir Berlioz writes in the score that the orchestra should start at Lélio's words of confirmation: "Oui, je l'entends!" (*Lélio*, 8). Only at the point when Lélio starts to read his book — presumably Shakespeare's *Hamlet* — is the choral singing to be heard. In the mon-odrama the exclusiveness of his imagination is accentuated: "cette faculté singulière qui subsistue ainsi l'imagination à la réalité" (*Lélio*, 234). The imagination does not just penetrate reality — it replaces it; in place of a real orchestra on the stage there is the ideal orchestra in the mind of the composer: "Quel est cet orchestre idéal qui chante en dedans de moi?" (*Lélio*, 234). The description of the singing of a sinister unison ghost choir (*Lélio*, 234) calls to mind Berlioz's musical and literary antecedents: the historical and the poetic Chevalier Gluck. The choice of vocabulary and figurative language are reminiscent of the comparable descriptions of the spirit-realm of music in Hoffmann's musical novellas and the spirit choir from *Orfeo ed Euridice* (1762), the opera composed by the real-life composer Christoph Willibald Gluck.

The monologue preceding the fifth piece of music also refers to Orpheus as another role model for the artist: "La Harpe éolienne — Souvenirs" (Aeolian Harp — Memories). The sublime, depicted by Hoffmann's narrator in Gluck's unison and in the *Kreislerianum* "Beethovens Instrumental-Musik," appears to find resonance in the music of the ghost choir in *Lélio:* here it is death, night, chaos, and the passing of time that dispel all hope. The music of this piece is familiar, coming from Berlioz's cantata, *La mort de Cléopâtre*. The first stanza of the final part, "Méditation," portrays Cleopatra's evocation of the spirits of the Pharaohs in the pyramids. She fears the wrath of those spirits living in the numinous world, as she is responsible for driving the gods out of Alexandria and for destroying the cult at Isis. Before the scene in the cantata Berlioz places Juliet's words from Act IV, scene iii: " 'How if I'm laid out into the tomb . . .' — Shakespeare." Two quite different scenes thus come together, where approaching death is evoked by images of tombs and pyramids blending in to one another. The magnitude of death, whose proximity Juliet senses more than actually fears, is thus visually enhanced, as it were, by the exalted size of the pyramids. Although both scenes are no longer present in the fifth piece, the threatening presence of the Pharaohs — a threat felt only by Berlioz and a few initiated listeners — is repeated in the ghost choir associated with Hamlet's father. Related to this somber tableau are not only the bright and dark dream sequences of the earlier *Symphonie fantastique,* but also the musical spirit world round-ing off the sixth and final musical piece, the "Fantaisie sur la tempête de Shakespeare" (Fantasy on Shakespeare's Tempest) where Miranda is released by the choir of the spirits of the ether and permitted to join Ferdinand in the real world.

The curtain opens on this final scene, the culmination of the drama. The composer's new creation marks his successful return to life and art, where all the previous pieces were little more than stages on the way to his masterpiece — though in his eyes it is imperfect. The uncovering of the stage hints at similar scenes of religious initiation. This expresses the realm of music of which one gets the rarest of glimpses, and it points to the place where the composer's art in this life belongs: the stage, where music and all arts combine to reflect the artist's inner vision. This final scene, where the imagined work of art becomes at once both audible and visible, is an artistic utopia.

Berlioz's final version does not end on this optimistic note, however. Having dismissed the musicians and singers of the "Fantaisie," the artist Lélio "hears" once again the *idée fixe,* the theme from the *Symphonie fantastique* symbolizing his beloved. Lélio's words: "Encore . . .? Encore et pour toujours! . . ." remind one of the artist at the opening of the monodrama. The pieces of music that follow on from each other are like role-plays of the composer, while his return to life is portrayed as a process, at the end of which he replaces his love for a woman with his love for art. His decision to live for sublime art (*Lélio,* 239), his hymn of praise to music — music apostrophized as his lover, whose assistance he seeks before the performance of the "Fantaisie," — shows him to be free from all ties, free to live for his art. He pauses at the moment when the *idée fixe* reminds him of his previous love. This suggests the painfulness of the liberation. A look at closing scenes of this nature in Hoffmann's artist novellas such as *Die Brautwahl* (The Choice of the Bride, 1820), *Der Artushof* (The Artus Courtyard, 1817) or *Die Jesuiterkirche in G.* (The Jesuit Church at G., 1817) reveals a similarity between Berlioz's *artiste* and Hoffmann's artist-figures — they all buy their masterpieces at the price of personal happiness. That pain, however, is the price Berlioz's artist has to pay in order to leave his compositional dreams and return to the real world. The world on the stage and the imaginary scenes that take place there are only ever a provisional halting-point, a helping-hand on the journey to self-knowledge. The words from the pact scene with the devil at the start of *Huit scènes* are ultimately an implicit warning against the absolutist demands of art: art, understood as the irrevocable pact between artist and art, can transform its liberating knowledge into a threat to life itself.

Translated by Siobhán Donovan and Andrew Johnstone

Notes

1 E. T. A. Hoffmann, *Späte Werke,* ed. Walter Müller-Seidel and Wulf Segebrecht (Munich: Winkler, 1979), 276.

2 For example, the set of the *Zauberflöte* at the end of *Der goldne Topf;* see Heide Eilert, *Theater in der Erzählkunst: Eine Studie zum Werk E. T. A. Hoffmanns* (Tübingen: Niemeyer, 1977), 5.

[3] For the reception of Hoffmann's works (particularly his musical novellas) in French Romanticism see Pierre-Georges Castex, *Le Conte fantastique en France de Nodier à Maupassant* (Paris: Corti, 1951); Elizabeth Teichmann, *La Fortune d'Hoffmann en France* (Geneva: Droz, 1961); Matthias Brzoska, *Die Idee des Gesamtkunstwerks in der Musiknovellistik der Julimonarchie* (Laaber: Laaber, 1995). Berlioz mentions Hoffmann very seldom in his correspondence, thus showing little evidence of knowing his works in any great detail. See Hector Berlioz, *Correspondance générale*, vol. 1, ed. Pierre Citron (Paris: Flammarion, 1972), 293: letter of 28 December 1829 to his sister Nancy: "Hoffmann, ses *Contes fantastiques* m'ont beaucoup plu," and 301: letter of 2 January 1830 to his friend Humbert Ferrand: "Avez-vous les *Contes fantastiques* d'Hoffmann. C'est fort curieux!" Prior to the publication of the French translation, Hoffmann was introduced into France by various channels; it is possible that Berlioz got to know some of his works through a friend of his, Richard, who, together with Toussenel, translated Hoffmann's works for the second Lefèbvre edition published from February 1830 onwards. My paper will focus largely on Berlioz's works, but will also highlight some of the aspects common to the works of both Berlioz and Hoffmann. Exactly how Berlioz became acquainted with Hoffmann's works is an another issue that cannot be considered here. Berlioz's *oeuvre* is itself (as much as Hoffmann's) striking proof of those mutual influences between art and artists that cannot be regarded in purely causal terms.

[4] For further connections between Hoffmann and Berlioz in the context of the French reception of Hoffmann (which goes beyond literature and music) see Andrea Hübener, "Kreisler in Frankreich: Die Rezeption E. T. A. Hoffmanns bei den Künstlern der französischen Romantik" (Ph.D. diss.: Technische Universität Berlin, 2000), forthcoming with Winter of Heidelberg in 2004.

[5] "Beethovens Musik bewegt die Hebel der Furcht, des Schauders, des Entsetzens, des Schmerzes, und erweckt eben jene unendliche Sehnsucht, welche das Wesen der Romantik ist." E. T. A. Hoffmann, *Fantasie- und Nachtstücke,* ed. Walter Müller-Seidel and Wolfgang Kron (Munich: Hanser, 1976), 43.

[6] Ibid., 44.

[7] From the wealth of studies on the interrelationship between language and music in symphony, opera, and sacred music in the works of Hoffmann, the following is a representative selection of titles that critically engage with the link between the sentimental and the Romantic concepts of music in his *oeuvre:* Norbert Miller, "E. T. A. Hoffmann und die Musik: Zum Verhältnis von Oper und Instrumentalmusik in seinen Werken und Schriften," in *Kaleidoskop: Eine Festschrift für Fritz Baumgart zum 75. Geburtstag,* ed. Friedrich Mielke (Berlin: Mann, 1977), 267–303; Carl Dahlhaus, *Die Idee der absoluten Musik* (Kassel: dtv, 1978) and " 'Geheimnisvolle Sprache eines fernen Geisterreiches' — Kirchenmusik und Oper in der Ästhetik E. T. A. Hoffmanns," in *Akademische Gedenkfeier des Musikwissenschaftlichen Instituts der Universität zu Köln für Prof. Dr. phil. Dr. h.c. Karl Gustav Fellerer,* vol. 63 of Kölner Universitätsreden (Cologne: Cologne UP, 1984), 23–35; Judith Rohr, *E. T. A. Hoffmanns Theorie des musikalischen Dramas* (Baden-Baden: Koerner, 1985); and Christine Lubkoll, " 'Absolute Musik' und 'romantische Poetik': E. T. A. Hoffmanns *Kreisleriana,*" in Lubkoll, *Mythos Musik: Poetische Entwürfe des Musikalischen in der Literatur um 1800* (Freiburg: Rombach, 1995), 225–81.

[8] Miller, "E. T. A. Hoffmann und die Musik," 274.

[9] E. T. A. Hoffmann, *Die Serapionsbrüder,* ed. Walter Müller-Seidel and Wulf Segebrecht (Munich: Winkler, 1976), 83.

[10] "[. . .] und nun bewegt in tollen Einbildungen, in allerlei seltsamen Sprüngen und abenteuerlichen Grimassen sich alles durcheinander." *Serapionsbrüder,* 90.

[11] The many biographical interpretations of Berlioz's works prove the effectiveness of this Romantic technique of staging the self.

[12] See *Correspondance générale* 1: 457.

[13] The translation was published in December 1827, with the year of publication given as 1828. See Gérard de Nerval, *Les Deux Faust de Goethe,* ed. Fernand Baldensperger (Paris: Champion, 1932), 1–214 (*Oeuvres complètes,* ed. Aristide Marie, Jules Marsan, and Edouard Champion, 7 vols. [Paris: Champion, 1926–32]). Subsequent references to this translation are given in the text using the abbreviation "Nerval" and the page number.

[14] See Hector Berlioz, *Mémoires,* ed. Pierre Citron (Paris: Flammarion, 1991), 148.

[15] For a detailed discussion of Berlioz's motivation for combining music and literature against the backdrop of contemporary music theory see the informative study by Brzoska, *Die Idee des Gesamtkunstwerks,* esp. 87–133.

[16] See Jacques Barzun, *Berlioz and the Romantic Century,* 2 vols. (Boston: Little Brown, 1950), 1:84.

[17] See Hugo's foreword to *Cromwell.* For significant aesthetic differences between Hugo and Berlioz see Brzoska, *Die Idee des Gesamtkunstwerks,* 126–30.

[18] *Huit scènes de Faust,* ed. Julian Rushton, vol. 5 of *New Edition of the Complete Works of Hector Berlioz* (Kassel: Bärenreiter, 1970), ix. Subsequent references to this work are given in the text using the abbreviation *HS* and the page number.

[19] "[. . .] les nombreux et énormes défauts de cette oeuvre [. . .] qui [. . .] était incomplète et fort mal écrite," *Mémoires,* 148.

[20] See Johann Wolfgang von Goethe, *Faust: Eine Tragödie,* ed. Erich Trunz, vol. 3 of Goethe, *Werke,* 14 vols. (Hamburg: dtv, 1998), 7–145 (lines 1766–67). Subsequent references to this work are given in the text using the abbreviation "Goethe" and the line number.

[21] For a similar connection, this time between Shakespeare and Moore, see the soliloquy preceding the second piece of music, "Choeur d'ombres irritées," in *Le retour à la vie* (1831). Here Berlioz has his artist say: "Shakespeare a opéré en moi une revolution qui a bouleversé tout mon être. Moore, avec ses douloureuses mélodies, est venu achever l'ouvrage de l'auteur d'Hamlet." "The Libretto of 1832," in *Lélio, ou Le retour à la vie,* ed. Peter Bloom, vol. 7 of *New Edition of the Complete Works of Hector Berlioz* (Kassel: Bärenreiter, 1992), *Appendix II,* 232–40 (here, 234). Subsequent references to this work are given in the text using the abbreviation *Lélio* and the page number.

[22] See *Mémoires,* 112: "L'effet de son [Harriet's] prodigieux talent, ou plutôt de son génie dramatique, sur mon imagination et sur mon coeur, n'est comparable qu'au bouleversement qui me fit subir le poète dont elle était la digne interprète."

²³ William Shakespeare, *The Complete Works,* ed. Peter Alexander (London: Collins, 1992). All subsequent references to Shakespeare will just give act, scene, and verse in the text.

²⁴ "[. . .] il faut que ton art soit divertissant." Goethe, 1435; Nerval, 66.

²⁵ *Mémoires,* 145. For a different version of this conversation see *Correspondance générale* 1:265–66: letter of 2 August 1829.

²⁶ See Klaus Heinrich Kohrs, "Berlioz' *coup rude de tam-tam.* Autobiographische Konstruktion als Kunstentwurf," *Deutsche Vierteljahresschrift für Literaturwissenschaft und Geistesgeschichte* 63 (1989): 120–53.

²⁷ For the pre-eminence of music over the other arts see Hector Berlioz, "Sur l'imitation musicale," in *Cauchemars et passions,* ed. Gérard Condé (Paris: Lattès, 1981), 98–109 (here, 105).

²⁸ See Hugh Macdonald, "Berlioz's Self-Borrowings," *Proceedings of the Royal Music Association* 92 (1965/66): 27–44.

²⁹ Robert Schumann, "Symphonie von H. Berlioz," *Gesammelte Schriften über Musik und Musiker* (Wiesbaden: Breitkopf & Härtel, 1985), vol. 1/2 (reprint, Leipzig: Wigand, 1854), 118–51 (here, 142): "Ich kann sie mir denken, mit dem Zettel in der Hand nachlesend und ihrem Landsmann applaudirend, der Alles so gut getroffen; an der Musik allein liegt ihnen nichts."

³⁰ See Hector Berlioz, "Sur la musique classique et la musique romantique," in *Cauchemars et passions,* 92–98 (here, 98), where, with reference to Beethoven and Weber, he defines the subject of Romantic music as "une pensée poétique qui se manifeste partout," "la vie sublime rêvée par les poètes."

³¹ See Berlioz's article on Beethoven's "Pastoral" Symphony in the *Gazette Musicale* of 4 February 1838, cited here in Hector Berlioz, *A travers chants,* ed. Léon Guichard (Paris: Gründ, 1971), 55–59 (see also 444–49 for the variants).

³² Berlioz, *A travers chants,* 57.

³³ Cf. *Lélio,* 232: "Cet ouvrage doit être entendu immédiatement après la Symphonie Fantastique, dont il est la fin et le complément."

³⁴ For the considerable changes of program of the *Symphonie fantastique* see vol. 16 of *New Edition of the Complete Works of Hector Berlioz,* ed. Nicholas Temperley (Kassel: Bärenreiter, 1972), "The Programme," 167–70. Its most important change with regard to both versions of *Lélio* was the poisoning with opium: in 1855 its position has moved from the beginning of the fourth movement to the start of the whole symphony. Now all five movements (not only the last two) are supposed to represent the opium-dream of the artist.

The Voice from the Hereafter:
E. T. A. Hoffmann's Ideal of Sound
and Its Realization in Early
Twentieth-Century Electronic Music

Werner Keil

Artificiality

Sobald nur unsere Betrachtung zur Idee der Natur als eines Ganzen sich emporhebt, verschwindet der Gegensatz zwischen Mechanismus und Organismus.

THUS WROTE FRIEDRICH WILHELM SCHELLING in his philosophical tract *Von der Weltseele* (Of the World Soul, 1798).[1] This "idea of nature as a whole" is for Schelling the "absolute," with the work of art as an authentic expression of the absolute. It resolves all conflict between the mechanical and the organic, and by authentically portraying the absolute it takes on a multiplicity of meanings. Schelling's juxtaposition of the mechanical and the organic has its origins in Immanuel Kant's *Kritik der Urteilskraft* (Critique of Judgment, 1790) where, in paragraphs 64–65, Kant uses the image of a wheel or cog as a metaphor for the one, and that of a tree for the other.[2] The cog is, of course, the prime component in clockwork — the very mechanism lying at the heart of late eighteenth-century automata. These mechanical puppets are exemplified in E. T. A. Hoffmann's tale *Die Automate* (1814), and by the doll Olimpia in his nocturne *Der Sandmann* (1816).

Before penning these stories Hoffmann had left his career in the Prussian administration in 1808 and moved to Bamberg to take up the post of *Kapellmeister*. Bamberg was a town intimately linked with Romanticism, having been home to Schelling and his experiments in natural philosophy and animal magnetism. Once Hoffmann was in Bamberg, his interest in such matters was quickly awakened, and he was soon reading (amongst other things) Gotthilf Heinrich Schubert's *Ansichten von der Nachtseite der Naturwissenschaften* (Views from the Dark Side of the Natural Sciences, 1808). A closer look at Hoffmann's conception of the mechanical is very revealing: just as the organic belongs to the natural world, the mechanical forms part of the artificial world.

Also in the year of his departure from Berlin, Hoffmann jotted down on a few (now missing) scraps of paper some ideas for an essay he was writing on sonatas. One year after Hoffmann's death, Julius Eduard Hitzig published from these scraps the following note:

> Vollkommenheit des Fortepianos. — Nur Schönheit der Harmonie, nicht des Tons. — Es muß anscheinende Willkür herrschen, und je mehr sich die höchste Künstlichkeit dahinter versteckt, desto vollkommener. — Größe des Theoretikers, Haydn. — Freude des gebildeten Menschen am Künstlichen u.s.w.[3]

Thus, "supreme artificiality" is the yardstick for perfection, and the "educated person's delight in the artificial" is enhanced when the artificial is masked by "apparent arbitrariness." Counterpoint was held to be musically "artificial" in Hoffmann's time, yet contrapuntal writing forms an integral part of his own compositions and is a frequent topic in his music reviews. In his famous piano sonata in F minor (AV 27), for example, the first and third movements are a fugue — actually the same fugue, which is "interrupted," so to speak, by the slow movement.[4] The introductory opening, the bipartite fugue, and the slow movement all have close motivic links, and contrapuntal writing dominates. Hoffmann knew that such a sonata was unconventional, and told the music publisher Ambrosius Kühnel and the music editor Friedrich Rochlitz that he was writing it in the "old style,"[5] working out everything thematically.[6] Elsewhere in his compositions Hoffmann shows his predilection for concise one- or two-measure motifs, which he combines simultaneously in invertible counterpoint. This ingenious arrangement of phrases is nonetheless presented as if it were a chance occurrence: "anscheinende Willkür."

Hoffmann's theoretical thinking is influenced by the aesthetic and philosophical thinking of the early Romantics — most importantly Wilhelm Heinrich Wackenroder, Ludwig Tieck, Novalis, Jean Paul, and the Schlegel brothers — whose views on music he had critically addressed. By and large the early Romantics understand "artificial" from a historical-philosophical point of view as the hallmark of the modern age. They saw instrumental music with its complex and motivically linked formulations as a corollary of the novel — the paradigm of Romantic art.[7]

According to Friedrich Schlegel, the "greatness" of music lies in its mechanical nature: for example, the device of fugue in sacred music can be compared to a screw or lever, or a similar device.[8] Similarly, in the *Phantasien über die Kunst* (Fantasies on Art, 1799), Wackenroder and Tieck emphasize that the instrumental music of their age is "modern" because of its colorfulness, garishness, and grotesqueness, its autonomy, and its freedom — in short, its wondrous confusion ("wunderbare Verworrenheit").[9] In Friedrich Schlegel we find all sorts of paradoxical expressions for confusion, contradiction, symmetry, chaos, and arbitrariness: "künstlich geordnete

Verwirrung,"[10] "reizende Symmetrie von Widersprüchen,"[11] "Symmetrie und Chaos,"[12] and "gebildete Willkür."[13] These lines of thought go back, as Ulrike Brütting has convincingly shown, to Alexander Gottlieb Baumgarten.[14]

Jean Paul, Wackenroder, and Tieck are particularly aware of the "apparent arbitrariness" — the exterior disorderliness — of instrumental music. Hoffmann, in contrast, tries in his reviews to expose the artifice (as opposed to *artificiality*) in compositional structure. He is concerned with the level-headedness ("Besonnenheit") and the stylistic expertise of the composer, with the *spirit* that manifests itself in the structure of each composition. For Hoffmann, the artificial (as opposed to *artifice*) in music reveals itself in another arena: in the invention of new instruments and mechanical musical dolls.

In the space of a few days in January 1814, Hoffmann wrote his tale *Die Automate*.[15] A month later, a much abridged version appeared in the *Allgemeine Musikalische Zeitung* (The General Musical Newspaper), with the complete text appearing the following April in the *Elegante Zeitung* (The Elegant Newspaper). In 1819 Hoffmann included the tale in his second volume of *Serapionsbrüder* collection (Serapion-Brethren, 1819–21). Having featured in the essay *Der Dichter und der Komponist* (The Poet and the Composer, 1813) only a few weeks earlier, Ferdinand and Ludwig, the chief characters in *Die Automate,* would have been known to readers of the *Allgemeine Musikalische Zeitung*. The two are fascinated and irritated by a talking mechanical doll that can apparently read people's thoughts. When they find out that its creator is a certain Professor X, a hermit-like figure shrouded in mystery, they pay him a visit. He leads them into a cabinet full of musical instruments and performing automata — a grand piano, a flute, an instrument that sounds like a glass harmonica, a large drum, a triangle, an orchestrion, and several musical clocks. The professor plays the piano, and the other instruments are played by the mechanical dolls. He touches them lightly, plays a march-like Andante, and they all join in a tutti that ends as abruptly as it began.[16] The tale goes on to describe the advanced form of mechanical action by which the figures produce their sounds: it seems they are bewitched by some kind of organon that obeys the human mind. Ludwig, himself a musician, is fascinated by the unusual way in which the sounds are produced from the most disparate of instruments:

Alle Versuche, aus metallenen, gläsernen Zylindern, Glasfäden, Glas, ja Marmorstreifen Töne zu ziehen oder Saiten auf ganz andere als die gewöhnliche Weise vibrieren und ertönen zu lassen, scheinen mir daher im höchsten Grade beachtenswert. (*Sb,* 348)

In *Die Automate* the musical dolls strike fear into Ludwig and Ferdinand. The musical Ludwig compares them to dead human figures; they have something uncanny about them, and this would be even more uncanny if, for example, a wooden puppet were to dance with a human dancer.[17] One year later, Hoffmann would make a dancing mechanical doll, Olimpia, the subject of his most uncanny nocturne of all, *Der Sandmann*.

Musico-mechanical dolls thus both fascinate and terrify Hoffmann, and so does "artificial" music. In the tale *Die Fermate* (The Fermata, 1815), like the *Kreisler*-novel a partly autobiographical work, Bach's music — then, as now, recognized as the apogee of contrapuntal art — is compared to a ghost story whose listeners are gripped with fear:

> [. . .] mancher Satz vorzüglich von dem alten Sebastian Bach glich beinahe einer geisterhaften graulichen Erzählung und mich erfaßten die Schauer, denen man sich so gern hingibt in der fantastischen Jugendzeit (*Sb*, 59).[18]

This is the fear to which one readily submits during one's "fantastical youth." Hoffmann extends his "artificial" interpretation to the music of Beethoven; the notorious review of his Fifth Symphony speaks of the music as setting in motion the levers of fear and pain.[19]

The gruesome, artificial world of musical automata and mechanical instruments is, however, juxtaposed with another type of music in *Die Automate*. Here, Ferdinand is in love with an unknown female singer whom he hears singing one sleepless night:

> [. . .] wie wurde mir, als die herrliche göttliche Stimme eines Weibes in einer herzergreifenden Melodie die Worte sang: "Mio ben ricordati [. . .]." Wie soll ich es denn anfangen, dir das nie gekannte, nie geahnete Gefühl nur anzudeuten, welches die langen — bald anschwellenden — bald verhallenden Töne in mir aufregten. Wenn die ganz eigentümliche, nie gehörte Melodie [. . .] in einfachen Melismen bald in die Höhe führte [. . .], bald in die Tiefe hinabsenkte [. . .], dann fühlte ich, [. . .] wie mein Selbst unterging in namenloser, himmlischer Wollust. (*Sb*, 335–36)

The description of the melody as comprising "simple melismas" is incompatible with artificiality. The effect on Ferdinand is rather one of celestial sensuality; the voice he hears belongs to a higher realm.

In *Ombra adorata!* (Adored Shadow, 1814) the narrator sits at a concert with his eyes closed and undergoes the synesthetic and religious experience of a female voice: "[. . .] wie ein himmlisches Licht die glockenhelle Stimme eines Frauenzimmers aus dem Orchester empor[strahlt]" (*FN*, 34). A further Italian aria, this time by Girolamo Crescentini, is performed, filling the narrator with melancholic longing, "wehmütige Sehnsucht" (*FN*, 34). "Artificial" music also comes into this tale, as the narrator wonders what would have happened to him if Beethoven's powerful ghost had transported him to the vast and terrifying realm opened up by his music.[20]

For Hoffmann the musician, the educated person's "delight in the artificial" is a delight in the very music that unleashes horror, terror, and fear.

But what of that other music, the music Hoffman experiences in the female singing voice? Could some link exist between the "artificial" world of instrumental music and this other music? This possibility will be explored in the following sections.

Sound

In the 1970s and 1980s the revered musicologist Carl Dahlhaus tried to show that Romantic music aesthetics is primarily based on instrumental music. He famously described Hoffmann's review of Beethoven's Fifth Symphony as the "founding document of Romantic music aesthetics."[21] But is this not a rather one-sided view? Other reviews by Hoffmann, such as his essay on *Alte und neue Kirchenmusik* (Ancient and Modern Church Music, 1814) or his *Nachträgliche Bemerkungen über Spontinis Oper "Olympia"* (Afterthoughts on Spontini's Opera "Olympia," 1821) testify to other approaches. Whatever his subject, Hoffmann comes across as a vehement proselytizer, praising to the heights the genre in question: with Beethoven this is instrumental music, with Palestrina it is ancient church music, while with Spontini, it is opera.

In order to understand properly these reviews — which seem mutually exclusive, bearing in mind Hoffmann's various partisan stances on genres and composers — it is important to recognize that in all three cases Hoffmann is speaking not as music aesthetician, but as legal advisor. Being the good lawyer he is, he defends first Beethoven, then Palestrina, then Spontini. His three clients have one thing in common — all have fallen on hard times. Beethoven is accustomed to rather harsh criticism in contemporary reviews, polyphony is sinking into oblivion, and Spontini, having been appointed and brought to Berlin by the king, is not popular with many Berliners. As a skilled lawyer, Hoffmann is concerned not so much with the truth as with winning his clients' cases, and he achieves this by means of forensic rhetoric. Just as it would be absurd to claim that Hoffmann was an early supporter of the keep-fit movement because he defended Jahn, the father of German gymnastics, so it has been erroneous to predicate a new aesthetics of instrumental music on his defense of Beethoven.

From the compositional point of view, the "most sophisticated artificiality" has no clearly defined purpose other than "the educated person's delight in the artificial." In Hoffmann's novels, fairy-tales, and stories, however, it is not just a question of musical structures; often music is reported, but the piece in question is not identified. What is important here is the *artificial production of sound:* sounds that disturb us, for example, because we hear voices without seeing any singers, or we hear strange or unusual instruments — be they old violins, Aeolian harps, a glass harmonica, or the mysterious euphone in *Ritter Gluck* (Chevalier Gluck, 1809). Could it be that a definite Romantic idea of sound lurks behind these artificially created sounds? As a composer, Hoffmann had a heightened sensibility for unusual sound effects, and his reviews give much consideration to issues of instrumentation. And, as we shall see, the artificial production of sound, and its metaphysical intent, do indeed form the kernel of his aesthetics.

Theremin

The Russian engineer Lev Sergeyevich Termen (1896–1993) might justly be described as one of the twentieth century's most enigmatic figures.[22] Of noble Huguenot stock, he was a regular commuter between East and West, adroitly combining the roles of scientist, technician, musician, and secret agent. At a private audience in the Kremlin in 1922, he performed for Vladimir Ilyich Lenin on an instrument he had invented, enchanting him with such melodies as the famous cello solo *Le cygne* (The Swan) from Camille Saint-Saëns's *Le carnaval des animaux* (The Carnival of Animals, 1886), and "Zhavoronok" (The Skylark, 1840), a song by Mikhail Glinka.

Termen's instrument produced notes by means of two frequency oscillators housed in a wooden chest. Extending from this chest were two antennae. No fingerboard or keys, nor indeed any playing device in any shape or form, was visible. The notes, ranging in duration, intensity, and pitch, were mysteriously produced by hand movements made in the air above the chest, or, to be precise, in the proximity of the antennae. Samuel Hoffman, one of the first virtuosi of the instrument, used to say ironically: "Technically speaking, you hypnotize it by waving your hands in front of it, and out comes the music."[23] The resulting impression that notes were conjured up by hand movements in mid-air gave the instrument its name: "etherovox" or "etherophone" — the voice from the air. Later on the instrument would be called "termenvox" after its inventor, or simply "theremin," after its inventor's name as he spelled it during his stay in the United States.

The fantastic nature of the theremin or etherophone has an uncanny pre-echo in the Romantic period. One evening in 1816 Hoffmann found himself at his desk, devoid of inspiration. He set about writing a letter of apology to Baron Friedrich de la Motte-Fouqué, editor of the ladies' almanac to whom he had promised a story. But just as he finished the letter, something strange happened that made him reach for his quill and add a postscript. He wrote that night was falling when, suddenly, what seemed to be a sound emanating from a female breast echoed gently through the room. This "wunderbare Laut" seemed to be addressing his spirit, yet he couldn't be sure whether it was real or he was dreaming.[24] The "wondrous" sound must have been produced by a draught acting on an instrument in the room, but it resembled the voice of a well-known female singer, and inspired Hoffmann to give it the name "Antonie." Thus was born the story of the female singer, forbidden to sing at the risk of death.

More than a century later, Termen's etherophone impressed Lenin greatly and prompted Stalin to send the engineer and his invention abroad to promulgate the technical superiority of the socialist Soviet Union. At the same time, Termen was to act as a secret agent with the task of spying on the West's technical innovations.[25] In 1928 Termen — who was now calling himself by the name his instrument would come to be called, Theremin — obtained patents in both Germany and the United States. The American broadcasting corporation RCA marketed the theremin under license, and in the 1920s and 1930s five hundred such instruments were manufactured. The inventor remained in the United States until the outbreak of the Second World War. He, and more especially, his pupil Clara Rockmore, a former violinist, appeared as virtuosi in a series of sensational concerts. Rockmore (1911–98), née Reisenberg, from Lithuania, became the most famous thereminist of the twentieth century. She used to perform together with her older sister Nadia, a pianist. It was her specialty to perform on the theremin difficult music for violin or cello, and in 1937 Termen built her an instrument that improved technically on the RCA model. Audiences were enthralled by the sight of a female performer who, while retaining complete bodily composure and with only minimal hand movements, could produce such beguiling sound effects.

Termen's United States début on 24 January 1934 took place in the large ballroom of the Hotel Plaza, New York, before a small, invited audience that included Sergey Rachmaninoff, Fritz Kreisler, and Arturo Toscanini. Praise quickly followed:

> It was as close to a miracle as anything we have ever witnessed [. . .]. There were tones produced last night [. . .] that were of so mysterious and otherworldly a beauty, a musical quality so alembicated and enchanting, that one's imagination leaped wildly in contemplating their possibilities.[26]

Clara Rockmore's first concert, on 30 October 1934 in New York's Town Hall, drew encomiums from the New York newspapers. In addition to works by Tchaikovsky, Rachmaninoff, and Glazunov, she performed the *Andante* from Édouard Lalo's *Symphonie espagnole,* op. 21 (Spanish Symphony, 1873) and *Berceuse* (Cradle Song) from Stravinsky's *L'Oiseau de feu* (Firebird Suite, 1911):

> From her deft and dainty fingers over the ghostly box, came dulcet and lovely sounds, shaded, diminished and swelled with musical intention and result [. . .] which was more than Mr. Theremin achieved [. . .]. She gave evident pleasure to a large audience and received numerous rounds of warm applause.[27]

> Miss Rockmore's success with it [the theremin] gave a prophetic indication of a future not too distant. No violin or human voice ever was made to give forth such smooth and delicate legati nor was capable of such evenly graduated portamenti.[28]

Clara Rockmore favored transcriptions of music originally composed for strings, playing works such Henryk Wieniawski's *Romance* (1852), Tchaikovsky's *Sérénade mélancolique* (1875), or the piece often played by Termen himself, "The Swan" by Saint-Saëns. Other works that Termen liked to play were transcriptions of Lieder, especially Schubert's.

The theremin is strikingly similar in sound to the violin or the human voice. Shown on an oscilloscope, its frequency curves are like those of a violin.[29] As with the violin or the human voice, it can produce a portamento, a crescendo or decrescendo, and vibrato. During its playing it is not possible to fix a mechanical basis for pitch, and in this respect it resembles the singing voice. Because its sounds are manipulated by hand movements, however, its effect is closer to that of the violin. Yet with respect to tonal range and duration, it surpasses both.

Surprisingly, this early electronic music instrument was by and large used to play popular classics, despite the extreme difficulty of obtaining pure, tonal melodic sequences from it. In a 1937 lecture on the future of music, John Cage lamented that the avant-garde potential of the theremin was not being recognized by its followers:

> Thereministes did their utmost to make the instrument sound like some old instrument [. . .]. Although the instrument is capable of a wide variety of sound qualities [. . .] thereministes act as censors, giving the public those sounds they think the public will like.[30]

Hollywood

In the early 1930s Soviet composers such as Shostakovitch (1931) and Gavriel Popov (1934) saw how well the instrument was suited to film, and capitalized on its unusual tonal color in uncanny, macabre, or gruesome scenes. Max Steiner deployed it in his score for *King Kong* (1933), as did Franz Waxman for *The Bride of Frankenstein* (1935). Hollywood followed suit a few years later: "With Robert E. Dolan's 1944 score for *Lady in the Dark,* the theremin arrived in Hollywood and began to inch closer to the psychological foreground in motion picture soundtracks."[31] It reached new heights of fame in the Alfred Hitchcock film *Spellbound* (1945) with Ingrid Bergman and Gregory Peck in the lead roles. Miklós Rósza, who wrote the music for *Spellbound,* had been told about the theremin and needed to sign an accomplished performer on the instrument who was also a good sight-reader. Clara Rockmore, dubious about the possible effect on her artistic reputation, declined the offer. Undeterred, Rósza discovered Samuel Hoffman, a doctor (1904–67). This accomplished violinist was living a double life, running a podiatry practice by day and performing as a theremin-soloist in dance bars and clubs by night. In Hitchcock's psychothriller, the theremin is always heard when Gregory Peck, who plays the part of a likeable but mentally-confused doctor, goes from a normal to an abnormal state of consciousness and claims to hear voices from another world. The sound of the theremin in combination with the classic Hollywood orchestra brings about a subtle disquietude — an unnerving effect of alienation. The admirable tension created by this film is achieved predominantly through its music.

The *Spellbound* score won an Oscar, enabling Hoffman to give up his medical job. Performing on the theremin he featured in more than twenty Hollywood films. He successfully marketed his best-selling music and made a number of records. His LP sleevenotes describe the hypnotic beauty of the music, its atmospheric, even disquieting nature, and its purpose of encouraging relaxation at the end of long and strenuous day at work:

> In every life there are times when [. . .] business and health, life and love, dovetail into a pleasant pattern that results in "peace of mind." Our troubled and complex world today offers all too few periods when we can relax in this happy mood. [. . .] The music in this album is dedicated to such moments. [. . .] simple relaxed harmonies . . . gentle rhythms . . . the warm, vibrant tones of a flute in the low register, and themes on the exotic Theremin. Turn down the lights, relax in an easy chair, and listen.[32]

The pieces are typified by such evocative titles as *Lunar Rhapsody, Radar Blues, Celestial Nocturne,* and *Your Soft Hand on My Brow.*

Towards the end of the 1950s, general interest in the theremin started to wane; and until his death in 1967 Hoffman once again practiced medicine. Termen, meanwhile, was arrested by the secret police on returning to the Soviet Union, and for fifty years the Western world heard precious little of him. He was taken to secret locations and made responsible for the development of electronic tracking and surveillance equipment during the Cold War. It is to him that we owe the first bugging device.

In the United States, however, a small group of enthusiasts remained loyal to his instrument. One of these was Robert Moog, who had made a business for himself building theremins, and who in 1964 invented the synthesizer. In 1989 Moog organized an international conference on electronic music in Bourges. Mikhail Gorbachev's "glasnost" made it possible for Termen — now over ninety years old — to leave the Soviet Union and attend the conference.[33] He was greeted with universal enthusiasm, and the interest in his musical invention acquired a new momentum. Fresh recordings were made and Termen gave countless interviews.[34] By the time he died in 1993, at the ripe old age of ninety-seven, an updated version of the theremin had been successfully launched by Moog. In place of the old radio technology, this new theremin — the "Etherwave" — used digital sound processors. There was, however, no change in the method of playing, with the electrical field surrounding the two antennae being controlled by the processors as before. Much of today's pop music would be scarcely conceivable without this digital theremin.

Over the last few years, composers of the new generation have been turning their attention to Termen's instrument. One is Lydia Kavina (b. 1967), a cousin twice removed of the inventor, and his last pupil, who is recognized today as the best thereminist in the world. A recent work is *Voice of Theremin*[35] by Vladimir Komarov, which was composed in 1996 to celebrate the centenary of Termen's birth. It merges the sound of the theremin (played by Lydia Kavina) with recordings of the speaking voice of its inventor from 1991. These sounds are processed by computer and at times modified beyond recognition. The work consists of three sections. In the first, sounds produced by the theremin are modified by the computer to produce an effect reminiscent of bird-song. In the second, Termen's voice is adapted digitally. In the third, both instrument and voice sound together, and Termen's words are distorted, the result being a waltz-like instrumental texture. The theremin meanwhile has the melody of Glinka's song "The Skylark" — the very song that Termen performed for Lenin in 1922. Perversely, the functions of voice and instrument here are switched, with the instrument singing the song and the human voice becoming the accompaniment. This reversal of roles is reflected in the ambiguity of the work's title: *Voice of Theremin* can refer either to Termen's own voice or to the voice of the instrument he created — both interpretations are valid.

Krespel

It is, of course, pure chance that one of the leading figures in the history of theremin music had the same surname as the creator of the singer Antonie; but the coincidence now returns us from the Hoffman of Hollywood to the earlier bearer of that surname, Ernst Theodor Amadeus. Samuel Hoffman — by day a doctor and by night a performer, who once said of himself: "I am a Dr. Jekyll and Mr. Hyde"[36] — has certain similarities with the Prussian magistrate who spent his nights imbibing in pubs and assuming the role of Kapellmeister Kreisler. The detective stories and horror films of Hitchcock, which always end in death and destruction, likewise resonate with E. T. A. Hoffmann's ghost and horror stories, where female singers die and artists lose their sanity, where vampires, *Doppelgänger*, and murderers are up to no good.

The postscript to Hoffmann's 1816 letter rapidly took on a life of its own, and Fouqué soon published what had become the fascinating story of Antonie and her violin-playing father, Rat Krespel (Councillor Krespel). Krespel is a violinmaker, driven by a desire for tonal perfection. He buys every old violin he can lay his hands on and saws it open, in the hope of discovering its inner secret. He is an eccentric and cantankerous man; the narrator finds him horrifying and awkward (*Sb*, 51–52), and his tone of voice is often incongruous. While he does not mince his words in his condemnation of a particular contemporary composer, his tone softens and becomes ecstatic in his praise of the tonal perfection he finds in Antonie's voice: "— Dann fuhr er heftig und wild heraus: "Sie ist ein Engel des Himmels, nichts als reiner Gott geweihter Klang und Ton! — Licht und Sternbild alles Gesanges!" (*Sb*, 34). For Krespel, Antonie belongs to the celestial realm.

Krespel embodies the world of the artistic. He is a literary relative of Professor X, the character in the story *Die Automate* whose collection of musical puppets has already been described. Krespel is the architect of his own extravagant house. The narrator first encounters him at a lunch where, with the help of a small lathe and much to the joy of their host's children, he is busy turning or sculpting a miniature toy from the smooth bones of roast rabbit. At Antonie's request, Krespel leaves one of his violins — a particularly splendid one — untouched. Having forbidden her to sing, he plays to her on this violin which has the strange capacity to reproduce the sound of her own voice:

> Kaum hatte er die ersten Töne angestrichen, als Antonie laut und freudig rief: "Ach, das bin ich ja — ich singe ja wieder." Wirklich hatten die silberhellen Glockentöne des Instruments etwas ganz eigenes Wundervolles, sie schienen in der menschlichen Brust erzeugt. Krespel wurde bis in das Innerste gerührt, er spielte wohl herrlicher als jemals, [. . .] Antonie schlug die Hände zusammen und rief entzückt: "Ach, das habe ich gut gemacht! das habe ich gut gemacht!" (*Sb*, 50)

This quotation describes Antonie's ecstasy at the mysterious affinity between her voice and the violin.

Though debarred from singing on medical grounds, Antonie has the most glorious voice:

> Der Klang von Antonies Stimme war ganz eigentümlich und seltsam, oft dem Hauch der Äolsharfe, oft dem Schmettern der Nachtigall gleichend. Die Töne schienen nicht Raum haben zu können in der menschlichen Brust. (*Sb*, 48)

> Nie hatte ich eine Ahnung von diesen lang ausgehaltenen Tönen, von diesen Nachtigallwirbeln, von diesem Auf- und Abwogen, von diesem Steigen bis zur Stärke des Orgellautes, von diesem Sinken bis zum leisesten Hauch. (*Sb*, 36)

These descriptions of Antonie's voice emphasize its naturalness, comparing it to a nightingale while alluding to its instrumental quality in terms of the organ and the Aeolian harp.[37]

Professor X too has a daughter with a beautiful and unusual voice. One evening, standing beside a garden, the two friends Ludwig and Ferdinand hear her. At once the mysterious sound fills them with terror.[38] Soon they see Professor X and witness his reaction to the "wunderbare

Klänge" of his daughter's singing. As with Antonie's voice, the "wondrous sounds" seem to come from another, higher world. On hearing them, the professor is transfigured.[39]

Rat Krespel has a similar theme to the story of the mad Baron von B. from the third volume of the *Serapionsbrüder*. Not only does the baron consider himself to be the most important living violinist: he believes that he alone knows how the perfect violin should sound. He maintains he is the last pupil of Tartini, and that he has taught all famous contemporary violinists. He allows his musical friends to play the old violins he has collected. Occasionally he demonstrates to a pupil the essence of violin playing, that is: the production of the perfect and pure sound with a single stroke of the bow. While this is to the baron the incarnation of the perfect sonority, to the ears of his listeners it is nothing more than a scratchy, squeaky noise. For in truth, the baron is quite incapable of playing the violin.

Voice

Owing to her mysterious illness, Antonie, the figure who originated in Hoffmann's letter to Fouqué, must not sing. One day, however, she rebels, sings for a young musician with whom she is in love, and dies. Krespel recounts to the narrator the circumstances that attended her death:

> [. . .] als sie starb, zerbrach mit dröhnendem Krachen der Stimmstock in jener Geige, und der Resonanzboden riß sich auseinander. Die Getreue konnte nur mit ihr, in ihr leben; sie liegt bei ihr im Sarge, sie ist mit ihr beerdigt worden. (*Sb*, 42)

Unable to exist without Antonie, the sound-post ("Stimmstock") inside the violin (controlling the tension between the soundboard and the back and transmitting vibrations from the bridge to the resonating body) collapses, and the violin explodes. In German terminology the sound-post contains the word for "voice" ("Stimme"). This enables Hoffmann to achieve an interchange of instrument and voice that nicely presages the achievement of Komarov in *Voice of Theremin*.

Antonie associates herself and her voice with the sound of the violin, and the violin self-destructs, just as a singer, on losing his or her voice, is a singer no longer. Reciprocally, Antonie's voice is instrumental in quality, sounding like the Aeolian harp and the organ. The violin resembles the voice, and the voice resembles an instrument. In general, however, Krespel, the male violinist and violinmaker, stands for an instrumental world that connotes the grotesque and the uncanny, while Antonie, the female singer, stands for a vocal world that is pure and dedicated to God.

From Hoffmann's postscript to Fouqué we learned how the figures of Antonie and Krespel came into being. The female name Antonie occurred to Hoffmann when he heard a sound made by the air, and is presumably an amalgam of the note *a* and the word "Ton." Hoffmann then imagined a mocking figure seated next to him, a devil-like creature. This gaunt man in a gray coat stood up and approached the door, his gesture and gait suggesting to Hoffmann the fictitious Krespel: "Wie sollte ich denn nicht gleich auf den ersten Blick den Rath Krespel erkannt haben?" (*Sb*, 1041). Thus Antonie, the female singer, was inspired by an incorporeal note, and Krespel, the instrumentalist, by a mocking, devil-like figure. Such dualism is characteristic of Hoffmann, and is fundamentally no different from Schelling's dualism of the artificial versus the natural, or of the mechanical versus the organic. The "male" instrumental music of Beethoven, for example, is the force behind the "Hebel des Schauers, der Furcht, des Entsetzens, des Schmerzes" — this is the message of Hoffmann's essay on Beethoven's instrumental music (*FN*, 43). In this context, it is appropriate to quote again, this time more fully, from *Ombra adorata*. Here, the narrator describes his reaction to the singing of an aria by a female voice, a voice that, like Antonie's, has an otherworldly sound:

> Wer vermag die Empfindung zu beschreiben, die mich durchdrang! — Wie löste sich der Schmerz, der in meinem Innern nagte, auf in wehmütige Sehnsucht, die himmlischen Balsam in alle Wunden goß. — Alles war vergessen und ich horchte nur entzückt auf die Töne, die wie aus einer andern Welt niedersteigend mich tröstend umfingen. [. . .] was soll ich von dir sagen, du herrliche Sängerin! [. . .] Wie holde Geister haben mich deine Töne umfangen, und jeder sprach: "Richte dein Haupt auf, du Gebeugter! Ziehe mit uns, ziehe mit uns in das ferne Land, wo der Schmerz keine blutende Wunde mehr schlägt, sondern die Brust, wie im höchsten Entzücken mit unnennbarer Sehnsucht erfüllt!" (*Sb*, 34–35)

The celestial tones become spirits that address the narrator, begging him to join them on their journey.

The narrator's "inexpressible longing" lies at the heart of Romanticism. It is a longing for far-off lands, for that other world whence soprano voices beckon. It turns out, however, that there is nothing female about these particular soprano voices: *Ombra adorata* is, of course, a composition by the castrato Girolamo Crescentini, whom Napoleon had called to Paris in 1805 to assume the post of royal singing teacher. This aria — an interpolation in the opera *Giulietta e Romeo* (1796) by Niccolò Antonio Zingarelli — became a hit for Crescentini. Much to the annoyance of Zingarelli, its popular fame soon overtook that of the opera itself. In 1804 the Leipzig *Allgemeine Musikalische Zeitung*, one of whose keenest readers and contributors was Hoffmann, described in some detail a new production of the opera and the incomparably delightful and malleable voice of the castrato.[40] In *Ombra adorata* Hoffmann hides the fact that a castrato voice is singing. At the beginning of the tale he has the protagonist withdraw to the "furthermost corner of the room" (*FN*, 33), and a few moments later has him shut his eyes. On hearing an otherworldly voice the protagonist assumes it to be a female soprano. But in reality the sound is no such thing.

The Voice from the Hereafter

Termen's etherophone exemplifies Hoffmann's ideal of sound. The theremin or etherophone is an artificial instrument, like Krespel's violin, but it sounds like a human voice. Its notes, made without physical contact with any sort of apparatus, seem to emerge from thin air. And in physical terms the instrument produces the purest form of sound possible: sine tones.

Early twentieth-century musicians and music lovers were so steeped in Romantic music aesthetics that they willingly surrendered to the spell of the theremin. But the pure sound, the otherworldly voice, cannot survive in this world. Thus Antonie dies, and both the singer Donna Anna in the story *Don Juan* (1812) and Julia, the converted Moorish girl in the nocturne *Das Sanctus* (1816), meet similar ends: all of them must die. And Baron von B., who has his own concept of the perfect sound, is unable to realize this on any violin, despite having a large collection of the most ancient and valuable instruments.

Voices from the hereafter, from another world, make us shudder. They terrify us just as Hitchcock's thrillers with their theremin-accompaniment terrify us. Our everyday lives are interrupted by a strange and distant world, be it Hitchcock's films, Hoffmann's ghost stories, Beethoven's instrumental music (which awakens in us an inexpressible longing for another world), or the pure voice of a soprano.

The composers of the nineteenth century tried in vain to realize the Romantic ideal of sound, to synthesize the vocal and the instrumental, the male and the female. Such a sound, androgynous and transcending earthly dualism, would be quite literally the "absolute" music of which the Romantics dreamt, the music that Gotthilf Heinrich Schubert spoke of in his in *Ansichten von der Nachtseite der Naturwissenschaft* as belonging to an earlier, golden age. In *Die Automate* Hoffmann cited Schubert and the discovery of the most perfect sound in the legendary music of the spheres:

> In jener Urzeit des menschlichen Geschlechts, als es, um mich ganz der Worte eines geistreichen Schriftstellers zu bedienen (Schubert in den Ansichten von der Nachtseite der Naturwissenschaften) in der ersten heiligen Harmonie mit der Natur lebte [. . .], da umfing sie den Menschen wie im Wehen einer ewigen Begeisterung mit heiliger Musik, und wundervolle Laute verkündeten die Geheimnisse ihres ewigen Treibens. Ein Nachhall aus der geheimnisvollen Tiefe dieser Urzeit ist die herrliche Sage von der Sphärenmusik. (*Sb*, 348–49)

When Carl Dahlhaus one-sidedly drew on Hoffmann's review of Beethoven's Fifth Symphony to illustrate his own idea of Romantic music aesthetics, he perpetrated an error with serious implications. As we have seen, Krespel has no time for the music of contemporary composers.[41] Dahlhaus's assumption that a new aesthetics of music could be derived from Hoffmann's literary writings — an aesthetics of instrumental music leading to an "idea of absolute music" — quite overlooked the status of vocal music in his *oeuvre* as a whole: was he not, amongst other things, a composer of opera? With Hoffmann, instrumental music always has something one-sided about it, something of the "Krespel," something that evokes terror and fear, something artificial and mechanical. While Beethoven's Fifth Symphony awakens the longing for the eternal, an Italian aria, sung perhaps by an Antonie, can be the means whereby "holde Geister" ("propitious spirits") of that other world speak directly to us (*FN*, 34–35).

If we want to keep hold of the idea of absolute music, we must have music that breaks down the barriers between voices and instruments, between male and female — music that unites Krespel and Antonie, as it were. For the whole of the nineteenth century this was an unattainable ideal. Some composers — Beethoven and Wagner, for instance — extended the tonal spectrum of the orchestra, while others — such as Rossini and Verdi — did the same with the voice. But only with the twentieth-century invention of the theremin — the voice from the air, the instrument with a sonority akin to the human voice — was the Romantic ideal of sound finally attained. United in this ideal of sound are Krespel and Antonie, the male violinist and the female singer, terror and longing.

If the theremin has realized the Romantic ideal of sound, then that very ideal can no longer exist, for a realized ideal is a contradiction in terms. If longing is what lies at the heart of Romanticism, then the satisfaction of that longing deprives Romanticism of its *raison d'être*. Thus Romanticism dies with the advent of the theremin, just as Antonie has to die when she sings. Romanticism reaches its end in the theremin; Hoffmann's hopes are fulfilled and thus annulled. To paraphrase Walter Benjamin, the theremin is the death mask of Romanticism.[42] And a favorite solo of Lev Termen's, Saint-Saëns's "The Swan," prompts the conclusion that the song of the theremin is nothing less than the swan song of Romanticism, a swan song in which the conflict between the mechanical and the organic finds its ultimate resolution.

Translated by Siobhán Donovan and Andrew Johnstone

Notes

[1] Friedrich Wilhelm Schelling, preface to the first edition of *Von der Weltseele,* vol. 1 of *Schellings Werke,* ed. Manfred Schröter (Munich: Beck, 1927), 416.

[2] Immanuel Kant, *Kritik der Urteilskraft,* vol. 8 of *Werke in zehn Bänden,* ed. Wilhelm Weischedel (Darmstadt: Wissenschaftliche Buchgesellschaft, 1983), 480–88.

[3] E. T. A. Hoffmann, *Schriften zur Musik*, ed. Friedrich Schnapp, 2nd ed. (Munich: Winkler, 1977), 16.

[4] E. T. A. Hoffmann, *Sonate f-moll*, AV 27, ed. Werner Keil (Wiesbaden: Breitkopf & Härtel, 1984).

[5] "[. . .] nach der älteren Art gesetzt." *Der Musiker E. T. A. Hoffmann: Ein Dokumentenband*, ed. Friedrich Schnapp (Hildesheim: Gerstenberg, 1981), 66.

[6] Ibid., 74.

[7] Klaus-Dieter Dobat, "Zwischen Genie und Handwerk: Magier oder Mechaniker? Metamorphosen der Musikergestalt bei E. T. A. Hoffmann," in *E. T. A. Hoffmann et la musique: Actes du Colloque International de Clermont-Ferrand*, ed. Alain Montandon (Bern: Lang, 1987), 239–57 (here, 243).

[8] Friedrich Schlegel, *Literary Notebooks, 1797–1801*, ed. and with an introduction and commentary by Hans Eichner (London: U of London, Athlone P, 1957), no.1990 (German first edition: *Literarische Notizen, 1797–1801* [Frankfurt a. M.: Ullstein, 1980]).

[9] Wilhelm Heinrich Wackenroder, *Sämtliche Werke und Briefe: Historisch-kritische Ausgabe*, ed. Silvio Vietta and Richard Littlejohns (Heidelberg: Winter, 1991), 1:240–46.

[10] Friedrich Schlegel, *Rede über die Mythologie*, in Schlegel, *Charakteristiken und Kritiken 1 (1796–1801)*, ed. Hans Eichner, vol. 2 of *Kritische Friedrich-Schlegel-Ausgabe* (Paderborn: Schoeningh, 1966), 318–19.

[11] Ibid.

[12] Schlegel, *Literary Notebooks*, no.1961.

[13] Friedrich Schlegel, *Über Goethes Meister*, in *Charakteristiken und Kritiken 1 (1796–1801)*, 134. I am grateful to Prof. Steven Paul Scher, Dartmouth College, New Hampshire, USA, for drawing my attention to these Schlegel references.

[14] Ulrike Brütting, "Konturen eines Bach-Bildes in der Kunstkonzeption E. T. A. Hoffmanns" (M.A. diss.: University of Paderborn, 2002). Besides his *Aesthetica acrodinatica*, also of particular importance are his *Meditationes philosophicae de nonnullis ad poema pertinentibus: Philosophische Betrachtungen über einige Bedingungen des Gedichts*, 1735, trans. and ed. Heinz Petzold (Hamburg: Meiner, 1983). My thanks to Ulrike Brütting for pointing out these parallels to Enlightenment aesthetics.

[15] Hoffmann's own plural of *das Automat*.

[16] "Der Professor ging nur flüchtig an dem Orchestrion und den Spieluhren vorüber, und berührte kaum merklich die Automate; dann setzte er sich aber an den Flügel und fing pianissimo ein marschmäßiges Andante an; bei der Reprise setzte der Flötenbläser die Flöte an den Mund und spielte das Thema, nun paukte der Knabe richtig im Takte ganz leise auf der Trommel, indem der andere einen Triangel kaum hörbar berührte. Bald darauf fiel das Frauenzimmer mit vollgriffigen Akkorden ein, indem sie durch das Niederdrücken der Tasten einen harmonikaähnlichen Ton hervorbrachte! Aber nun wurde es immer reger und lebendiger im ganzen Saal, die Spieluhren fielen nacheinander mit der größten rhythmischen Genauigkeit ein, der Knabe schlug immer stärker seine Trommel, der

Triangel gellte durch das Zimmer und zuletzt trompetete und paukte das Orchestrion im Fortissimo dazu, daß alles zitterte und bebte, bis der Professor mit seinen Maschinen auf einen Schlag im Schlußakkord endete." *Die Automate,* in *Die Serapionsbrüder,* ed. Walter Müller-Seidel and Wulf Segebrecht (Munich: Winkler, 1963), 345–46. Subsequent references to this edition of the *Serapionsbrüder* are hereafter given using the abbreviation *Sb.*

[17] "Schon die Verbindung des Menschen mit toten, das Menschliche in Bildung und Bewegung nachäffenden Figuren [. . .] hat für mich etwas Drückendes, Unheimliches, ja Entsetzliches. Ich kann mir es denken, daß es möglich sein müßte, Figuren vermöge eines im Innern verborgenen Getriebes gar künstlich und behende tanzen zu lassen, auch müßten diese mit Menschen gemeinschaftlich einen Tanz aufführen [. . .], so daß der lebendige Tänzer die tote hölzerne Tänzerin faßte und sich mit ihr schwenkte, würdest du den Anblick ohne inneres Grauen eine Minute lang ertragen?" (*Sb,* 346).

[18] Cf. a similar passage in the *Fantasiestück,* "Höchste zerstreute Gedanken": "Es gibt Augenblicke — vorzüglich wenn ich viel in des großen Sebastian Bachs Werken gelesen — in denen mir die musikalischen Zahlenverhältnisse, ja die mystischen Regeln des Kontrapunkts ein inneres Grauen erwecken. — Musik! — mit geheimnisvollem Schauer, ja mit Grausen nenne ich dich." *Fantasie- und Nachtstücke,* ed. Walter Müller-Seidel und Wolfgang Kron (Munich: Winkler, 1960), 50. Subsequent references to this edition of the *Fantasie- und Nachtstücke* are hereafter given in the text using the abbreviation *FN.*

[19] "[. . .] die Hebel des Schauers, der Furcht, des Entsetzens, des Schmerzes." Hoffmann, *Schriften zur Musik,* 36.

[20] "Was wäre aus mir geworden, wenn, beinahe erdrückt von all dem irdischen Elend, das rastlos auf mich einstürmte seit kurzer Zeit, nun Beethovens gewaltiger Geist auf mich zugeschritten wäre, und mich wie mit metallnen, glühenden Armen umfaßt und fortgerissen hätte in das Reich des Ungeheuern, des Unermeßlichen, das sich seinen donnernden Tönen erschließt —" (*FN,* 33–34).

[21] Carl Dahlhaus, *Die Idee der absoluten Musik* (Kassel: Bärenreiter, 1978), 47.

[22] During his stay in the United States, Termen used the French spelling of his name (Theremin), reflecting his original French ancestry. In this paper, for purposes of clarity, I refer to the man as Termen throughout, and call the instrument he invented the theremin.

[23] Cited in Albert Glinsky, "Portrait of the Doctor Jekyll and Mister Hyde of the Ether Waves," booklet to the CD recording: *Dr Samuel J. Hoffman and the Theremin,* BASTA Audio/Visuals 30-9093-2 (Netherlands, 1999), 9.

[24] "Glauben Sie wohl, Baron! daß ich, [. . .] nachdem ich in der miserabelsten philistermäßigsten Stimmung Ihnen brieflich den gewünschten Beitrag abgesagt hatte, glauben Sie wohl, daß ich dann an Lauretta und Teresina denkend, Ihr Taschenbuch [. . .] zur Hand nahm [. . .]? [. . .] Es war tiefe Abenddämmerung geworden, und mochte es sein, daß der durch das Fenster hineinströmende Abendwind über den offenstehenden Flügel hineingestreift, oder daß ein flatternder Sommervogel die Saiten berührt hatte — genug, ein klarer Ton, wie aus weiblicher Brust hervorgehaucht, ging lang und leise verhallend durch das Zimmer. Ich hielt den Athem an, um das Verschweben des wunderbaren Lautes recht deutlich

zu vernehmen, und da war es mir, als sei es die Stimme einer mir wohlbekannten Sängerin, die zu meinem Geist spräche, und doch wußt' ich nicht, hatt' ich sie einst wirklich oder nur im Traum gehört" (*Sb*, 1040–41).

25 For detailed information on Termen's double life as engineer und spy see Albert Glinsky, *Theremin: Ether Music and Espionage* (Urbana und Chicago: U of Illinois P, 2000).

26 *New York Herald Tribune,* cited in ibid., 78.

27 *New York American,* ibid., 160.

28 *World Telegram,* ibid.

29 Rockmore's extraordinary expertise with the instrument is impressively documented on an LP from 1975 produced by Robert Moog and re-released on CD in 1987: *The Art of the Theremin* (Delos DE 1014). I recommend listening to this recording for a fuller understanding of my article.

30 "The Future of Music," in Cage, *Silence* (London: Calder & Boyars, 1968), 3.

31 Glinsky, *Theremin,* 253.

32 *Music for Peace of Mind* (1950), Capitol CC-221. This, along with Hoffman's two other LPs, *Perfume Set to Music* (1948), RCA Victor P-231, and *Music out of the Moon* (1947), Capitol CC-47, can be heard on the CD recording produced by the Netherlands Label of BASTA Audio/Visuals in 1999 listed in note 23.

33 The so-called *synclavier,* the invention of Jon Appleton, Professor of Music und Electroacoustics at Dartmouth College, Hanover, New Hampshire, USA, was also presented at this conference. Afterwards, Appleton visited Termen a few times in Moscow; today one can visit there (in the Conservatoire) a museum devoted to Termen's inventions. I am very grateful to Jon Appleton for the stimulating conversation, and also for his valuable advice during my guest lectureship at Dartmouth College in October 2001.

34 Particularly impressive (as well as being of great significance) is the documentary film *Theremin: An Electronic Odyssey* made by Steven M. Martin in 1993. It contains a film sequence from 1928 that shows Termen as a young engineer playing Saint-Saëns's "The Swan," and also has many interviews with him as a nonagenarian, with Clara Rockmore, and with eye-witnesses (available as VHS-Video from *MGM Home Entertainment,* Santa Monica 2000 [ISBN 0-7928-4602-8]).

35 A recording is available on the CD: *Music from the Ether: Original Works for Theremin,* Mode records 76 (New York, 1999).

36 Glinsky, "Portrait of the Doctor Jekyll and Mister Hyde," 3.

37 The latter is a wind harp, an instrument which, like the organ, needs air to make it sound.

38 "Plötzlich wehte ein seltsamer Klang durch die Luft, der im stärkern Anschwellen dem Ton einer Harmonika ähnlich wurde. Die Freunde blieben von innerm Schauer ergriffen, wie an den Boden festgebannt, stehen; da wurde der Ton zur tiefklagenden Melodie einer weiblichen Stimme" (*Sb*, 351).

39 "Aber welch ein Erstaunen, ja welch ein inneres Grausen durchdrang sie, als sie den Professor X. erblickten, der mitten im Garten unter einer hohen Esche stand. Statt des zurückschreckenden ironischen Lächelns [. . .] ruhte ein tiefer

melancholischer Ernst auf seinem Gesicht, und sein himmelwärts gerichteter Blick schien wie in seliger Verklärung das geahnete Jenseits zu schauen, was hinter den Wolken verborgen, und von dem die wunderbaren Klänge Kunde gaben, welche wie ein Hauch des Windes durch die Luft bebten" (*Sb*, 351).

[40] *Allgemeine Musikalische Zeitung* 8 (February 1806), 301.

[41] "Wollt ich doch, daß der schwarzgefiederte Satan den verruchten Tonverdreher zehntausend Millionen Klafter tief in den Abgrund der Hölle schlüge!" (*Sb*, 34).

[42] Walter Benjamin, *Einbahnstraße* (Frankfurt a. M.: Suhrkamp, 1955), 49: "Das Werk ist die Totenmaske der Konzeption."

Lieder

"My song the midnight raven has outwing'd": Schubert's "Der Wanderer," D. 649

James Parsons

A S ANYONE WHO HAS PONDERED the German Lied can attest, the attempt to uncover what a composer has made of a poet's text is generally thought to be the first step toward understanding a song's mediation of words. Indeed, the first sentence of Richard Kramer's recent *Distant Cycles: Schubert and the Conceiving of Song* asks: "What does Schubert want from poetry?"[1] Susan Youens makes the point even more emphatically: "Lieder begin with words," she insists. "They are born when a composer encounters poetry."[2] Pursuing the same question from a perspective now including the performer, listener, or critic, Kristina Muxfeldt warns "how profoundly our reading [of a Lied's poem] in fact affects the way we account for the musical events."[3]

Although each of these statements conveys a subtly varied viewpoint, they nevertheless are united by a common thread: the belief that if one can come to terms with a poet's verse one also will succeed in apperceiving the song composed in response to it. Doing so, I maintain, is not always as easy as it seems, especially if the poem possesses the enigmatic density of Friedrich Schlegel's "Der Wanderer" (The Wanderer/Wayfarer, 1802), set to music by Schubert in 1819 (D. 649). A Lied clearly comes into being when a composer encounters poetry, yet the way we read a poem influences our interpretation of the song in ways not altogether adequately acknowledged. If each reader is capable of multiple readings of a poem, does it not follow that an equally endless number of interpretations of the resulting Lied likewise are possible? How do we know when our reading of a poem and interpretation of a song are valid?

I begin with Schlegel's poem:

> Wie deutlich des Mondes Licht
> Zu mir spricht,
> Mich beseelend zu der Reise:
> "Folge treu dem alten Gleise,
> Wähle keine Heimat nicht.

5

Ew'ge Plage
Bringen sonst die schweren Tage;
Fort zu andern
Sollst du wechseln, sollst du wandern,
Leicht entfliehend jeder Klage."   10

Sanfte Ebb' und hohe Flut
Tief im Mut,
Wandr' ich so im Dunkeln weiter,
Steige mutig, singe heiter,
Und die Welt erscheint mir gut.   15
Alles reine
Seh' ich mild im Widerscheine,
Nichts verworren
In des Tages Glut verdorren:
Froh umgeben, doch alleine.[4]   20

Schlegel's poem is given over to an arresting inversion of a topos long-favored by eighteenth-century literature: the trek of a lone wanderer toward a clearly defined yet distant destination.[5] The journey, while arduous, is carried out by and large with optimism, given that it takes ignorance and darkness as its starting-point and moves toward self-understanding and light. Retold time and again, the story, while popular throughout Europe, was mined with notable acclaim in German-speaking lands. Goethe's Bildungsroman *Wilhelm Meisters Lehrjahre* (Wilhelm Meister's Apprenticeship Years, 1796) is a telling case in point. As the central character avers in Book V, chapter 3, his life's ambition is the "harmonious development" of his personality ("harmonische Ausbildung meiner Natur"), in short: Enlightenment.[6] Drawing on themes from earlier sources, this self-cultivation or *Bildung* found a ready outlet in the image of the solitary pilgrim. Representing all humanity, the solitary seeker's journey is emblematic of life's journey, for the *Bildungsweg* on which the wayfarer is embarked is premised on regaining the unity thought to have been lost when a once organic world split into rationalized and unrationalized pieces.[7] The story of Adam and Eve is a prime example. A primordial paradise provides sanctuary to an originary couple who live in concord with each other and the land that is their home. Driven from this utopia, Adam and Eve's exile becomes the quest of all humankind to regain that lost Elysium.[8] Closer in time to Schlegel, Georg Wilhelm Friedrich Hegel reinterprets this paradigmatic story in his *Phänomenologie des Geistes* (Phenomenology of Spirit, 1807). The guiding force within us all, Hegel states, has a long and difficult journey ahead of it if it is to attain real knowledge. Such a voyage — precisely the quest on which Schlegel's wanderer has embarked — is not accomplished in an instant, but requires time and effort. Both the effort and the length of journey have to be endured, because the whole can only be pieced together gradually.[9]

Schlegel's wanderer, while related to this tradition, deviates from the norms of the *Bildungsweg* in significant ways. Revealing neither where he has been nor where he is going, he begins: "Wie deutlich des Mondes Licht / Zu mir spricht." If this is where the song begins, as Youens would have it, the obvious question is, what will Schubert make of such a beginning and how will he transform its utter vagueness in terms of music? Schlegel renders these questions more complex still, given that his poem is part of a larger whole entitled *Abendröte* (Sunset).[10] The titles of all twenty-two poems are provided in the table:

Table 1. Friedrich Schlegel's "Der Wanderer" in the context of his poem-cycle *Abendröte* and Schubert's settings of the same[11]

Abendröte, **Part I**	
"Tiefer sinket schon die Sonne" [untitled by Schubert] (The sun is setting fast)	D. 690, as *Abendröte.* March 1823
"Die Berge" (The Mountains)	D. 634. March 1820?
"Die Vögel" (The Birds)	D. 691. March 1820
"Der Knabe" (The Youth)	D. 692. March 1820
"Der Fluß" (The River)	D. 693. March 1820
"Der Hirt" (The Shepherd)	—
"Die Rose" (The Rose)	D. 745. 1822 (published 1827 as op. 73)
"Der Schmetterling" (The Butterfly)	D. 633. March 1820?
"Die Sonne" (The Sun)	—
"Die Lüfte" (The Skies)	—
"Der Dichter" (The Poet)	—

Abendröte, **Part II**	
"Als die Sonne nun versunken" [untitled by Schubert] (Now that the sun has set)	—
"Der Wanderer" (The Wanderer)	D. 649. February 1819
"Der Mond" (The Moon)	—
"Zwei Nachtigallen" (Two Nightingales)	—
"Das Mädchen" (The Girl)	D. 652. February 1819
"Der Wasserfall" (The Waterfall)	—
"Die Blumen" (The Flowers)	—
"Der Sänger" (The Singer)	—
"Die Sterne" (The Stars)	D. 684. 1820
"Die Gebüsche" (The Shrubs)	D. 646. January 1819
"Der Dichter" (The Poet)	—

Over a period of some four years, Schubert set to music half the poems from Schlegel's cycle. The question as to whether or not Schubert intended these eleven songs as a cycle is taken up by Richard Kramer (among others) in his previously mentioned study. Here, I am concerned only with how "Der Wanderer" is part of a larger whole and how that cycle influenced the , way in which Schubert musically depicts Schlegel's poem.

Predictably enough for a poet-philosopher who takes equal delight in the process of introspection as well as its ultimate goal of self-cultivation, reading the single poem against the backdrop of its companions does not lead to lucidity — at least, not at first. What emerges is that Schlegel's cycle divides into two halves.[12] The first half treats the charms of twilight, the second those of nightfall. "Der Wanderer" is the second poem within the cycle's second section and is the first therein to treat the concerns of an (ostensibly) human being in the realm of night. The interplay of human characters and nature is striking, a move presumably calculated to blur the division between humans and the world around them. Although extended exegesis of how this works is beyond the scope of this essay, a brief overview is in order, especially since doing so promotes greater under-standing of the interrelationships between the poems in the cycle. In the process, clarity is shed on "Der Wanderer." Most important, such contex-tual consideration reminds us that the Romantic era effected a fundamen-tal reversal as to how twilight and nighttime were regarded. Edward Young's *The Complaint, or Night Thoughts* (1751) prefigures that about face by more than forty years. The last page of Young's exuberantly lengthy work anticipates with amazing prescience what the Romantics found so alluring in twilight's lengthening shadows. Darkness aids intellectual light, Young declares: "And sacred Silence whisp'ring truth divine, And truths divine converting pain and peace, My song the midnight raven has outwing'd, And shot, ambitious of unbounded scenes."[13] The bright sun of Enlightenment guides the intellect, while night inspires the unham-pered imagination.

Schlegel's contemporaries evidently agreed, as is attested by John Field and Frédéric Chopin's nocturnes for solo piano, a great many of Caspar David Friedrich's paintings (for example, his "Mondaufgang am Meer" [Moonrise over the Sea, 1822]), Novalis's *Hymnen an die Nacht* (Hymns to the Night, 1801), or Gotthilf Heinrich von Schubert's *Ansichten von der Nachtseite der Naturwissenschaft* (Views from the Dark Side of the Natural Sciences, 1808). Thus when Schlegel, in the opening poem of his *Abendröte* cycle, announces the calmness that comes with the setting sun: "Tiefer sinket schon die Sonne, / Und es atmet alles Ruhe," it is not sim-ply a reflection of his era's affinity for nighttime, but rather because it is at twilight that the earth seems more verdant ("Grüner glänzt die grüne Erde"), given that at dusk the sun's light possesses a special glow. In the second poem Schlegel's mountains inspire the desire to soar above the clouds and the mundanely rooted reality that is human existence. In the fourth poem, "Der Knabe" (The Youth), he treats of a boy who dreams he is a bird whose flight far excels that of all other birds, a reference that underscores two important things. First, in the inspired province of twilight, anything is possible, and second, all creatures at sunset speak to the poet in a way not possible during the light of day. As Schlegel asserts, the already verdant earth becomes even more so at dusk, a reality that sets the stage for a more momentous turn of events. When the opposing dominion of day unites with night, everything seems to speak to the poet ("Alles scheint dem Dichter redend"). What is heard then? It is nothing less than the sounding union of Enlightenment — the "harmonious development of personality" — multiplied by and conjoined with those of all creation: "Denn er hat den Sinn gefunden; / Und das All ein einzig Chor, / Manches Lied aus einem Munde."[14]

It is in the cycle's second half that night instructs the imagination. This said, the reader of Schlegel's "Der Wanderer" is still not fully prepared for the startlingly abrupt manner in which the poem begins. Although the reader has little recourse but to accept that moonlight *is* clearly speaking, it is just as evident that *nothing* is clear. In the non-poetic real world moonlight is not empowered to speak. Moreover, a person who admits to hearing moon speech is commonly said to be loony. (The word, as any dictionary reveals, relates to "lunatic," a person affected with recurring mental instability set in motion by the phases of the moon.) Is Schlegel's wanderer such a person, a forerunner of the unhinged protagonist to be sketched more than a century later by Arnold Schönberg in his *Pierrot Lunaire* (Moonstruck Pierrot, 1912)? For the moment, one is left wondering; the only thing possible to say with any assurance is that moonlight is *the* archetypal emblem of things hidden. From the poem's start, then, the one thing that is clear is that nothing is clear. Nonetheless, from uncertainty clarity may emerge. Given the Romantic perspective on nighttime, it is possible at this point to conclude at least two things. First, understanding does not necessarily stem from the brightly-lit certainty of Enlightenment but sometimes from darkness, and second, Schlegel's wanderer is open to the subjective swerve of the imagination and toleration for ambiguity. What follows tests the way-farer's capacity for both, for it is the speech of an oracle. Although Schlegel never spells this out, the narrative content of the poem's first three lines and the quotation marks starting in line 4 and continuing until line 10 make it reasonably evident that the moonlight is speaking. Schlegel's crescendo of calculated confusion at length yields a purpose. Carolyn Abbate declares that utterance by "an unseen presence" is like "the sound of an Aeolian harp," with the utterance seeming "to have complete authority since we sense an ultimate speaker [. . .] who is mysterious and omniscient."[15]

Before considering this oracular speech, a look at the poem's formal design will prove instructive.

Table 2. Rhyme scheme and structure of Schlegel's "Der Wanderer"

Line and scan (– unstressed) (/ stressed)	Rhyme	No. of syllables	Poetic meter
– / – – / – / Wie deutlich des Mondes Licht	a	7	Two amphibrachic feet in triple poetic meter terminated by a single stress
– – / Zu mir spricht,	a	3	One anapaestic foot in triple meter
/ – / – / – / – Mich beseelend zu der Reise:	b	8	Iambic duple meter begins, and continues until end of poem (shift in meter occurs one line before start of moon's speech)
"Folge treu dem alten Gleise,	b	8	
Wähle keine Heimat nicht.	a	7	
Ew'ge Plage	c	4	
Bringen sonst die schweren Tage.	c	8	
Fort zu andern	d	4	
Sollst du wechseln, sollst du wandern,	d	8	
Leicht entfliehend jeder Klage."	c	8	
Sanfte Ebb' und hohe Fluth	a	7	
Tief im Muth,	a	3	
Wandr' ich so im Dunkeln weiter,	b	8	
Steige mutig, singe heiter,	b	8	
Und die Welt erscheint mir gut.	a	7	
Alles reine	c	4	
Seh' ich mild im Widerscheine,	c	8	
Nichts verworren	d	4	
In des Tages Glut verdorren:	d	8	
Froh umgeben, doch alleine.	c	8	

On first inspection the design gives the impression of consisting of two symmetrical, ten-line strophes each with an identical rhyme scheme. The apparent symmetry is lent additional support, as in each strophe the corresponding line contains the same number of syllables. That initial insight turns out to be only half the story, for structure and content are at odds with each other: strophe 1 concerns in the main a speaking character, strophe 2 the wayfarer's introspective musings. Although both first lines contain seven syllables, the difference in content is paralleled in their respective accent patterns, a strategy that results in what might be called a similar-dissimilar relationship. Something of the same process is at work in lines 6 and 7 and in the corresponding place in strophe 2 (lines 16 and 17). Both of these lines are *c* lines, but line 6 has four syllables while line 7 has eight. The two *d* lines in each strophe have a comparable similar-dissimilar relationship. All of this presents the reader with one of the oldest of riddles: an indisputable *one* that is simultaneously an incontestable *two*.

What do these brushes with the uncanny accomplish? As Schlegel explains elsewhere, a poet ought to create a medium capable of overcoming the gap "between the absolute and the relative."[16] As will be seen, such formulations may have influenced some of the more noteworthy compositional strategies in Schubert's song. For the moment, Schlegel's reader is left to ponder an additional question. How does a single self fuse with other selves? The larger cycle from which the poem derives provides one answer. Schlegel already has suggested precisely this in the continuously blurred division between humankind and nature. This indistinctness, we recall, culminates in the poetical divination that when day and night come together "the universe becomes a single choir, singing many a song with one voice."[17] What has gone unnoticed is that such a union allows Schlegel to update a conviction widely held during the Age of Reason, that Enlightenment is attained only when a person combines variously head and heart, this life and the life to come — or some other synthesis of extremes. As Immanuel Kant notes in the second edition of his *Kritik der reinen Vernunft* (Critique of Pure Reason, 1787), the quest for reason entails a joining together, a *Vereinigung,* of all that makes up a person.[18] From this, it may be said that Schlegel, like the Goethe of *Wilhelm Meisters Lehrjahre,* is still pursuing "the harmonious development of the personality." Confirmation for this as well as an additional explanation as to why Schlegel blurs the distinction between humanity and nature is to be had in his wholly original concept of Romantic irony. As he writes in his *Gespräch über die Poesie* (Dialogue on Poetry, 1800), Romantic poetry only manifests itself in the structure of the whole, wherein one perceives an "artfully ordered confusion" governed by "a charming symmetry of contradictions."[19] This species of Romantic poetry, as Schlegel makes known in his *Athenäums-Fragment* 116, brings together extremes: poetry, prose, philosophy, criticism, and so on. Furthermore, this is not chaos for the sake of chaos — it all leads to a point. Such poetry holds up a mirror to the universe and hovers selflessly between the "portrayed and the portrayer," intensifying the "poetic reflection."[20]

What, if anything, did Schubert make of all this? At first glance, his Lied, like Schlegel's poem, divides into two evenly balanced halves, as may be seen below in example 1, and is so constructed as to facilitate comparison of the similar-dissimilar strophes.

Example 1: Schubert's Der Wanderer, D. 649: measure-by-measure comparison of similar-dissimilar strophes.

Example 1: (continued)

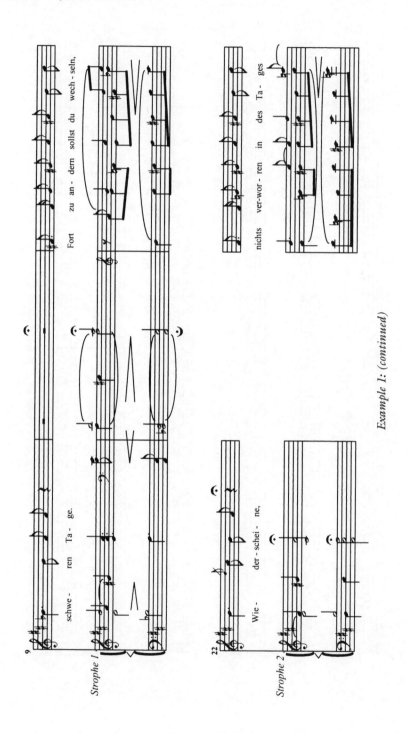

Example 1: (continued)

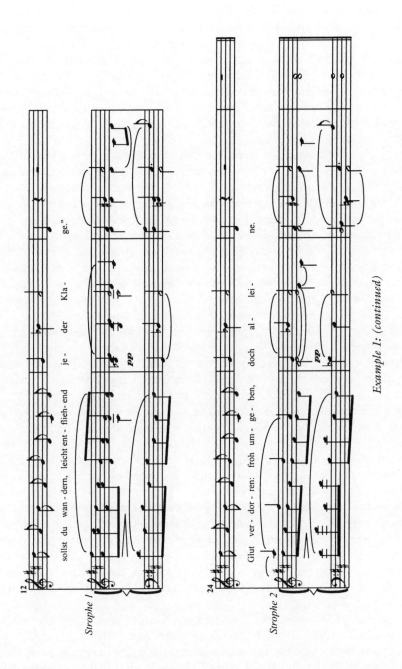

Example 1: (continued)

Mirroring the poem once more, each musical strophe is subdivided into two smaller units. Again, that first glance tells only part of the story. In much the same way that Schlegel arrives at a means of satisfying his requirement that a poem possess a "charming symmetry of contradictions," Schubert's Lied likewise is similar-dissimilar. The result of this is that he finds a way of reproducing Schlegel's call for a "wondrous" alternation of enthusiasm and irony within the sum of its parts.[21] In thus skillfully portraying the oppositions at the heart of Schlegel's poem, Schubert presents the listener with the same riddle of contradiction, an irrefutable two that is at once an undeniable one.

An understanding of how this is accomplished necessitates one last look at Schlegel's poem. It appears that the moonlight is speaking, and the addressee is a protagonist whose identity — save for the poem's title — is unstated. From this Schlegel impels the reader to negotiate a synthesis out of conflicting ideas: "eine absolute Synthesis absoluter Antithesen, der stets sich selbst erzeugende Wechsel zwei streitender Gedanken."[22] Thus, we must accept that the moonlight *is* and *is not* speaking to a person who *is* and *is not* present. The poem itself lends support for this contention. First, there is the truncated repetition of rhymed *a* lines in lines 1 and 2. What is more, from the standpoint of poetic meter, the opening two lines lie outside the rest of the poem. Whereas beginning in line 3 the poem adheres strictly to iambic duple meter, the first two lines hem and haw in a near riot of shifting metrical gears, a ploy that arguably countermands the moon's speech. Line 1 includes two amphibrachic poetic feet while line 2 is made up of one anapaestic foot. Interestingly, the poetic meter changes to iambs in line 3, one line *before* the moon begins to talk. The result is that Schlegel succeeds in blurring the boundaries between the wanderer and moonlight. The abridged repetition of lines identical in rhyme yet unequal in length yields a gap in which something is left unstated, the effect of which is to direct the drama of Schlegel's poem *between the lines*. Thus the reader supplies a question mark at the end of line 2, one that casts doubt not only on the clarity of the moon's speech but also on the number of personae populating the poem. Schubert hits upon a musical means of duplicating this "charming confusion" by engaging in a varied repetition of measure 3 in measure 4. In keeping with Schlegel, the repetition is similar-dissimilar. While it is exact in the piano, in the voice it is subtly different. In the first two lines of strophe 2, then, the concern is not only with what has been said and left unsaid, but with the question of who has said it or not.

Schlegel and Schubert's contemporary Samuel Taylor Coleridge offers a possible answer to such questions when he describes "a species of ventriloquism where two are represented as talking, while in truth one man only speaks."[23] In a notebook entry Coleridge writes that ventriloquism is nothing less than "Thought and Reality, two distinct corresponding Sounds, of which no man can say positively which is the voice and which the Echo."[24] Jonathan Culler amplifies the point in a recent study: "Writing," he suggests, "becomes truly writing only when it prevents one from answering the question 'who is speaking?' "[25] In this way, "Der Wanderer" satisfies Schlegel's aim that a poem unite the finite with the infinite. Schlegel says as much when, through the prophetic voice of the moon, he discloses that the wayfarer's journey is to be always onward to other lands (line 8). While such open-endedness provides Schlegel the means to join a single self with all others, we would do well to question whether this goal is Schubert's. As Barbara Herrnstein Smith notes: an "open-ended conclusion will [. . .] affirm its own irresolution and compel the reader to participate in it."[26] In just this way, Schlegel's "Der Wanderer" attains the otherwise impossible "interchange between two conflicting thoughts."[27] Smith further remarks that the participatory outcome of an open-ended poem may imply questions that transcend the concerns of a single poem. Open-ended poems therefore ask: "What do we know? How can we be sure we know it?" Such questions cause one to distrust "the validity and even the possibility of unassailable [. . .] final words."[28]

Whereas Schlegel's poem lacks closure, given that the wanderer is enjoined to choose no homeland (line 5), Schubert's setting does achieve closure. Whereas throughout much of its twenty-seven measures it abounds in harmonic ambiguities — the cadence on the major mediant in measure 7 at the words "Wähle keine Heimat nicht" and the chromatic mutations in measure 11 at the words "Fort zu andern / Sollst du wechseln" provide two compelling examples — the song ends with the most tried and true means of harmonic closure: a V–I cadence. Or does it? The listener is left to wonder. The way Schubert accomplishes this is as subtle as it is skillful. The song's conclusion literally falls back on its beginning, the penultimate measure being a modified repeat of the first. In much the same way that Schlegel's poem calls attention to its start with those mixed poetic meters, Schubert's Lied attains a similar effect. From the standpoint of harmonic vocabulary, the beginning is a succession of starts — four to be exact — each moving from the tonic to a half cadence in measures 2, 3, 4, and 6. In the second strophe the comparable measures are 17, 18, 19, and 21, only now the outcome is veiled given the fuller texture and passing tones in the piano's inner lines. From this Schubert conditions the listener to expect that when the tonic is sounded it will be followed by its dominant. In the second to last measure, when the piano moves once more from tonic to dominant, it is heard as another start instead of the end it professes to be. In the most paradoxical of ways, the dominant-tonic relationship is subverted; it is heard not as a resolution of harmonic tension but as a tension of opposites, for the final tonic points to the possibility of another start. In this way, the Lied lacks conclusive closure; it compels the listener to ask both what is known and how it is known.

This is not the first time Schubert eschews musical closure as a means by which to illumine Schlegel's text. Beginning with line 5, the poem admonishes: "Wähle keine Heimat nicht. / Ew'ge Plage / Bringen sonst die schweren Tage." Starting on beat 4 of measure 6, the harmony moves from the dominant of A major, touching down in measure 9 on an augmented sixth chord at the words "schweren Tage." In measure 10, this time in the piano alone, the augmented sixth returns with telling effect. Anticipating the next line, where the wanderer is exhorted to roam onward, the augmented sixth chord is left hanging on the dominant. In measure 11, instead of moving to the tonic, the chord that begins measure 11 only *implies* the tonic. Its lack of the one note that would make it a tonic chord, namely D, masterfully mirrors the text's injunction to "Wähle keine Heimat nicht." The parallel spot in the second strophe is no less effective. Starting on beat 4 of measure 20, at the words "Alles reine / Seh' ich mild im Widerscheine," the harmony touches down first on D major and then moves to B minor before moving to V/V and then a half cadence on the dominant of D major in measure 22. It is intriguing that in both spots Schubert winds up on the dominant, but the difference in approach, given the context of the Lied's scant twenty-seven measures, is almost cosmic. Having heard the augmented sixth chord in the first strophe we expect it again, and even though it is not provided, our memory nonetheless provides it *and* does not. In this way, the straightforwardness of the moon's reflection, even though the harmonic motion in the second strophe is now less complex and clarified, is called into question. What key is the music in here: D major, or the parallel key of B minor? The sense of harmonic home base further is called into question as the music moves chromatically thereafter in measures 23 and 24. Undermining the primacy of D major, Schubert may be said to ask: "What do we know? How can we be sure we know it?" At length, questions of this sort reveal themselves to relate to the question that began this study: how do we know when our reading of a poem and ensuing interpretation of a song are valid? Such questions lead to others. Is Schubert merely rephrasing by means of music the queries that Schlegel poses in his poem, or is he replacing them with those of his own?

Answers prove difficult. One reply might be that Schubert does provide a musical analog to Schlegel's concept of Romantic irony, just as another might be that he does not. A further response might be that Schubert is aware that Schlegel's "charming symmetry of contradictions" had implications not only for literature but for all of life. From here it is a small step to say that Schubert saw in Schlegel's poem the means to artic-ulate concerns relating to his own life. Having arrived at this juncture, it would be tempting to push on, tackling what such "contradictions" might mean for a composer such as Schubert. This especially would appear to be the case since he is widely regarded as *the* Romantic composer who employed music to reflect "a new form of western social organization in the first years of the nineteenth century."[29] That organization has everything to do with Romantic subjectivity — a program well suited to Schubert's conception of song. The latter, with its characteristic union of music and words, does not merely reflect an expanded view of self, but, in the opinion of some, actively participates in the construction of such. To be sure, I could imagine the reading of "Der Wanderer" advanced here pressed into service in support of the ongoing debate as to whether or not Schubert left clues about his own subjectivity in his music. For the moment, I will resist that temptation to pursue this matter if for no other reason than it surely cannot be argued on the basis of a single Lied. That said, I think it only fair to make clear how the type of interpretation put forward here might figure in future discussions of Schubert, his music, and whether or not his music reflects his attitudes about life. Even though I likely have succeeded in further complicating the question that launched this study — how one knows when one's reading of a poem and ensuing interpretation of a song are valid — I trust I have succeeded at least in showing that Schlegel's "Der Wanderer" takes its cue from Edward Young's meditation on the powers of night. Like Young, Schlegel sought new modes of artistic expression in order to explore not only new concerns but old ones, too. Fundamentally, it seems, he was interested in opening windows and doors of all kinds. If Schubert responded to the enlarged view of self at the heart of Schlegel's "Der Wanderer" — and I believe he did — then it will be seen that Schubert likewise was interested in Young's "sacred Silence whisp'ring truth divine," of song that might outwing the midnight raven, soaring upwards "ambitious of unbounded scenes." Like Schlegel, Schubert constructs a song premised, as Herrnstein Smith would have it, on its own open-endedness and irresolution, traits that push to the forefront the questions: "What do we know? How can we be sure we know it?" If this is so, then it will be seen that Schubert's "Der Wanderer" forces us to ask a great deal more. If such a song can impel one to ask: "How can we be sure we know it?" then it also mandates the converse, insisting that we ask as well: "How can we be sure we do *not* know it?"

Notes

[1] Richard Kramer, *Distant Cycles: Schubert and the Conceiving of Song* (Chicago and London: U of Chicago P, 1994), 3.

[2] Susan Youens, "Schubert and His Poets; Issues and Conundrums," in *The Cambridge Companion to Schubert,* ed. Christopher H. Gibbs (Cambridge: Cambridge UP, 1997), 99.

[3] Kristina Muxfeldt, "Schubert, Platen, and the Myth of Narcissus," *Journal of the American Musicological Society* 49/3 (fall 1996): 495.

[4] Friedrich Schlegel, *Dichtungen,* ed. Hans Eichner, vol. 5 of *Kritische Friedrich-Schlegel-Ausgabe* [hereafter *KA*] (Munich: Ferdinand Schöningh Verlag; Zurich: Thomas-Verlag, 1962), 186. The following translation is my own:

> How clearly the light of the moon
> Speaks to me,
> Inspiring me on my journey:
> "Follow faithfully the old track,
> Choose no place as your home,
> Lest difficult times
> Bring endless miseries.
> To other places
> Should you roam, should you go on,
> Lightly casting off every care."
>
> With gentle ebb and high tide
> Deep in my spirit,
> I walk on in darkness,
> Climbing courageously, singing merrily,
> And the world seems good to me.
> I see everything clearly
> In the [moon's] gentle reflection,
> Nothing is blurred
> Nor wilted in the heat of day:
> Surrounded by joy, yet alone.

[5] For a study of the wanderer and the importance of the topic for Schubert and his songs see David Gramit, "Schubert's Wanderers and the Autonomous Lied," *The Journal of Musicological Research* 14/3–4 (1995): 147–68. Gramit's approach to the subject, together with the conclusions he draws, differs from mine considerably.

[6] Johann Wolfgang Goethe, *Briefe und Gespräche,* ed. Ernst Beutler, vol. 7 of *Gedenkausgabe der Werke* (Zurich: Artemis Verlag, 1949), 7:313.

[7] Ibid., 311: "Daß ich dir's mit einem Worte sage, mich selbst, ganz wie ich da bin, auszubilden, das war dunkel von Jugend auf mein Wunsch und meine Absicht." Goethe remarks that the general education of the self demands that one stake out one's "own path" (ibid., 312: "so muß ich einen eigenen Weg nehmen"), a remark that supports my contention that the journey of the solitary wanderer is symbolic of the quest for Enlightenment on the part of everyone.

[8] "Of all the serious games in Romanticism, the most earnest and at the same time the most light-hearted is the quest for Paradise Lost. It concentrates the Romantic essence for us, as in a burning glass. It is the longing for something lost; it is the sorrowful remembrance of [. . .] the unity, harmony, happiness and contentment that were present in a distant past but can now be evoked only in imagination [. . .]. In a state of longing, the imagination recreates a lost Whole out of the fragments of past happiness." Peter-Klaus Schuster, "In Search of Paradise Lost: Runge, Marc, Beuys," *The Romantic Spirit in German Art: 1790–1990,* ed. Keith Hartley et al. (London: South Bank Centre, 1994), 62. The classic treatment of this topic remains that by M. H. Abrams, *Natural Supernaturalism: Tradition and Revolution in*

Romantic Literature (New York: W. W. Norton, 1971), esp. chapters 3, 4, and 5. For more on this topic and its place within western philosophy and literature see Franco Moretti, *The Way of the World: The Bildungsroman in European Culture,* trans. Albert J. Spragia (London: Verso, 1987, 2000). For a detailed examination of the same subject within German literature see Michael Beddow, *The Fiction of Humanity: Studies in the Bildungsroman from Wieland to Thomas Mann,* Anglica Germanica Series 2 (Cambridge: Cambridge UP, 1982).

[9] "Dies Werden der *Wissenschaft überhaupt* oder des *Wissens* ist es, was diese *Phänomenologie* des Geistes darstellt [. . .]. Um zum eigentlichen Wissen zu werden oder das Element der Wissenschaft, das ihr reiner Begriff selbst ist, zu erzeugen, hat es sich durch einen langen Weg hindurchzuarbeiten. — Dieses Werden [. . .] wird [. . .] auch etwas anderes als die Begründung der Wissenschaft, — so ohnehin als die Begeisterung, die wie aus der Pistole mit dem absoluten Wissen unmittelbar anfängt [. . .]. Der Einzelne muß auch dem Inhalte nach die Bildungsstufen des allgemeinen Geistes durchlaufen, aber als vom Geiste schon abgelegte Gestalten, als Stufen eines Wegs, der ausgearbeitet und geebnet ist [. . .]. Einesteils ist die *Länge* dieses Wegs zu ertragen, denn jedes Moment ist notwendig [. . .]." Georg Wilhelm Friedrich Hegel, *Phänomenologie des Geistes,* vol. 3 of Hegel, *Werke* (Frankfurt a. M.: Suhrkamp, 1986), 31–33. A good English translation is the one by A. V. Miller (Oxford: Oxford UP, 1977), 15–16.

[10] Schlegel's cycle was first published in the *Musen-Almanach für das Jahr 1802,* ed. A. W. Schlegel and L. Tieck (Tübingen: Cotta'sche Buchhandlung, 1802; facsimile reprint, Heidelberg: L. Schneider, 1967), 133–57. For a modern edition see *KA*5:178–91.

[11] This table is a simplified conflation of tables to be found in Kramer, *Distant Cycles,* 197, and in Graham Johnson's program notes accompanying his recording of Schubert settings of the poetry of August and Friedrich Schlegel (*The Hyperion Schubert Edition,* vol. 27, Matthias Görne, baritone, Graham Johnson, piano. Hyperion CD J33027, 30).

[12] The cycle's division into two parts appears only in the Berlin 1809 and Vienna 1816 publications of Schlegel's poems (Berlin: Julius Eduard Hitzig, 1809; Vienna: Ph. Bauer, 1816).

[13] Edward Young, *The Complaint, or Night Thoughts, on Life, Death, and Immortality* (New-Bedford: A. Shearman, 1808 [1st ed. 1758]), 264. In 1759 Young brought out his *Conjectures on Original Composition.* Both works were widely read and highly influential in Germany: see John Louis Kind, *Edward Young in Germany: Historical Surveys, Influence upon German Literature, Bibliography* (New York: Columbia UP; London: Macmillan, 1906) and Martin William Steinke, *Edward Young's Conjectures on Original Composition, in England and Germany* (Folcroft: Folcroft Press, 1970 [1st ed. 1917]).

[14] Here I quote respectively from "Der Knabe" (*KA*5:180–81) and the opening unnamed poem of the cycle (*KA*5:179).

[15] Carolyn Abbate, *Unsung Voices: Opera and Music Narrative in the Nineteenth Century* (Princeton: Princeton UP, 1991), 214.

[16] "[. . .] enthält und erregt ein Gefühl von dem unauflöslichen Widerstreit des Unbedingten und des Bedingten, der Notwendigkeit und Unmöglichkeit einer vollständigen Mitteilung." Schlegel, *Lyceums-Fragment* 108, *KA*2:368.

[17] *KA*5:179.

[18] Immanuel Kant, *Werke: Akademie-Textausgabe,* vol. 3 (Berlin: Walter de Gruyter, 1968), 520. I have examined the implications of this particular type of union on music of the latter eighteenth and early nineteenth centuries in greater detail in James Parsons, "Ode to the Ninth: The Poetic and Musical Tradition Behind the Finale of Beethoven's Choral Symphony" (Ph.D. diss.: University of North Texas, 1992); see also Parsons, " *'Deine Zauber binden wieder':* Beethoven, Schiller, and the Joyous Reconciliation of Opposites," *Beethoven Forum* 9:1 (2002): 1–53.

[19] *KA*2:318–19: "[. . .] der romantischen Poesie, der nicht in einzelnen Einfällen, sondern in der Konstruktion des Ganzen sich zeigt [. . .]. Ja diese künstlich geord-nete Verwirrung, diese reizende Symmetrie von Widersprüchen [. . .]." The English translation is from Schlegel, *Dialogue on Poetry and Literary Aphorisms,* trans. Ernst Behler and Roman Struc (University Park: Pennsylvania State UP), 86.

[20] "Die romantische Poesie ist eine progressive Universalpoesie. Ihre Bestimmung ist nicht bloß, alle getrennten Gattungen der Poesie zu vereinigen und die Poesie mit der Philosophie und Rhetorik in Berührung zu setzen. Sie will und soll auch Poesie und Prosa, Genialität und Kritik, Kunstpoesie und Naturpoesie bald mis-chen, bald verschmelzen [. . .]. Nur sie kann gleich dem Epos ein Spiegel der ganzen umgebenden Welt, ein Bild des Zeitalters werden. Und doch kann auch sie am meisten zwischen dem Dargestellten und dem Darstellenden, frei von allem realen und idealen Interesse auf den Flügeln der poetischen Reflexion in der Mitte schweben, diese Reflexion immer wieder potenzieren und wie in einer endlosen Reihe von Spiegeln vervielfachen." *KA*2:182–83. (The English translation is from Schlegel, *Philosophical Fragments,* trans. Peter Firchow [Minneapolis: U of Minnesota P, 1991], 31–32.)

[21] "[. . .] dieser wunderbare ewige Wechsel von Enthusiasmus und Ironie, der selbst in den kleinsten Gliedern des Ganzen lebt." Schlegel, *Gespräch über die Poesie,* *KA*2:319.

[22] Schlegel, *Athenäums-Fragment* 121, *KA*2:184.

[23] Samuel Taylor Coleridge, *Biographia Literaria,* ed. J. Shawcross, 2 vols. (Oxford: Clarendon P, 1895), 2:109.

[24] *The Notebooks of Samuel Taylor Coleridge,* ed. Kathleen Coburn (London: Routledge, 1961), no. 2557.

[25] Jonathan Culler, *Structuralist Poetics: Structuralism, Linguistics, and the Study of Literature* (London: Routledge, 1975), 200.

[26] Barbara Herrnstein Smith, *Poetic Closure: A Study of How Poems End* (Chicago: U of Chicago P, 1968), 233.

[27] See note 22 above.

[28] Smith, *Poetic Closure,* 233–34.

[29] Lawrence Kramer, *Franz Schubert: Sexuality, Subjectivity, Song* (Cambridge: Cambridge UP, 1998), 1.

The Notion of Personae in Brahms's "Bitteres zu sagen denkst du," op. 32, no. 7: A Literary Key to Musical Performance?

Natasha Loges

B RAHMS'S SONGS PRESENT a provocative front to the scholar-performer. While the academic community does not dispute Brahms's significance as a song-writer, this esteem is not reflected by the performance community, which restricts itself to the same handful of songs for which Brahms became famous during his lifetime.[1] How can this contradiction be resolved? Certainly, Brahms himself gives no clues. Although the legacy of Brahms's teasingly cryptic comments about song *composition* has been thoroughly documented,[2] there is no single successful and specific study of song *interpretation*. The occasional ungrateful vocal line and virtuosic accompaniment could perhaps be responsible for pushing the performer into more immediately rewarding directions, but a principal deterrent is Brahms's bewilderingly variable choice of poetry, which resists all attempts to be pummeled into the neat categories so beloved of both scholar and diligent concert programmer.[3] However, this should by no means render individual songs inaccessible or difficult to characterize (often the obstacle to successful performance).[4] Brahms's criteria for potential settings echo those of many poetry-based Lieder scholars; as one writer challengingly asserts:

> The fact of the matter is that a song-lyric has a melody of its own, to which the art of the composer can only superadd. Often he clogs the sense in so doing, and sometimes he finds it necessary to wrench the rhythm about. So it is the lighter and slighter song-lyrics that tend to be set to music successfully.[5]

Although innumerable Lieder could be cited to refute this statement, Brahms's attitude to viable poetry resonates with it. A notion of *incompleteness* as central to Brahms's poetic choice is reflected in his statement:

> das Gedicht darf als Kunstwerk nicht zu vollkommen sein, es muß dem Komponisten Spielraum lassen, die Musik muß es gleichsam "veredeln" können.[6]

Fig. 1: Brahms's op. 32, no. 7: "Bitteres zu sagen denkst du".

Furthermore, the musical setting should "ennoble" the original poem. Hence, an interpretative method grounded in poetic analysis may only reinforce the predominant opinion regarding Brahms's poor taste; in fact, exactly the opposite approach is required — the poetry cannot be treated as a complete work of art.[7] This paper attempts to demonstrate a methodology whereby the text of a single song, op. 32, no. 7: "Bitteres zu sagen

Fig. 1: (continued)

denkst du" (You mean to say something bitter, 1864), is explored from several viewpoints within its musical context. An analysis of Brahms's "completion" illustrates the practicality of his poetic criteria; more essentially, it provides a key to performance. It becomes apparent that the slightly facile poem — one of Georg Friedrich Daumer's (1800–75) many free interpretations of the works of the Persian poet Hafis (ca. 1327–90) — has undergone a critique within the accompaniment, resulting in a rich dialectic between singer and piano.

The notion of non-verbal viewpoints in song stems from Edward Cone's study, *The Composer's Voice,* in which he proposes an interpretative model based on the assumption of different personae within a single setting. Cone stresses that the composer is actually generating a unique performance of the poem, thereby appropriating it into his creation and replacing the original with his own overarching perspective, which Cone calls the view of the "implicit persona" (or "composer's persona"). He subdivides this as follows: the "virtual persona" who provides a commentary through the accompaniment, and the "vocal persona" who sings. The latter can usefully be divided into the "speaking persona" for the purely textual aspect, and the "melodic persona" who presents the pure line. The melodic persona is uniquely the composer's creation, and thus presents another aspect of the implicit persona, even though it exists through the singer. As Cone puts it:

> The art of song thus exploits a dual form of utterance, related to but not to be confused with the dual medium of voice and instrument. It combines the explicit language of words with a medium that depends on the movements implied by non-verbal sounds and therefore might best be described as a continuum of symbolic gesture.[8]

One form of utterance is restricted to the words being sung, while the other communicates solely through accompaniment and melody. Of the two, Cone places special emphasis on the latter, since, regardless of the melodic shape, the protagonist is engaged in poetic action; only the accompaniment is free to play commentator (see fig. 2a).

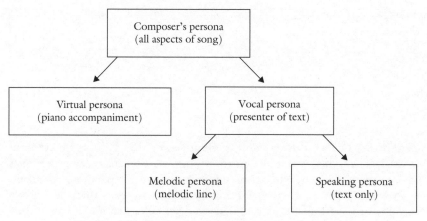

Fig. 2a: A diagrammatic presentation of Cone's personae.

Hence, the embedding of the speaking voice in the melody generates an analytical springboard on three levels: i) the poetic (strictly verbal), ii) the poetic-melodic (text conjoined with melodic line), iii) the vocal-instrumental (line embedded in the complete texture).

Through textual and melodic manipulation, Brahms can alter the speaking persona's position; he is also empowered to create the crucial virtual persona. Two disparate threads of thought emerge, simultaneously conspiring with and gently undermining the speaking persona. Thus my analysis attempts to go beyond Cone's work, which has been criticized for its assumption that the implicit persona presents a single viewpoint equivalent to the composer's own.[9] A setting can take an ambiguous stance towards a poem, and it is in this equivocation that the richness of the song lies (see fig. 2b).

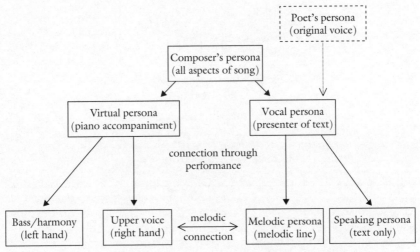

Fig. 2b: The relationship between musical and non-musical personae in op. 32, no. 7: "Bitteres zu sagen denkst du".

Analysis

Poetic Analysis

At the outset it must be stated that the declamation of poetry is a subjective practice; hence, the metric and quantitative analyses presented here are freely open to modification in terms of extent; however, the basic stresses remain consistent.

A comparison between Daumer's text and Brahms's rendition (see fig. 3b) yields the impression that central to the Brahmsian speaking persona is the overwhelming obsession with the beloved, to the extent that all evidences of her cruelty are overridden, and all praises of her emphasized.[10]

Brahms's treatment considerably smoothes the texture with constantly extended syllables, thereby creating a lulling emphasis on the trochaic foot that deliberately defies natural declamation (for example, the last syllable of "Bitteres"). Also, the brief pause created by the semicolon at the end of the first line encourages a momentary dwelling on the cruel actions of the beloved — but it is ignored. The natural emphasis of words like "kränkst du,"

> Bitteres zu sagen denkst du;
> aber nun und nimmer kränkst du,
> ob du noch so böse bist.
> Deine herben Redetaten
> scheitern an korallner Klippe;
> werden all zu reinen Gnaden,
> denn sie müssen, um zu schaden,
> schiffen über eine Lippe,
> die die Süße selber ist.

Fig. 3a: The text of the poem.[11]

Fig. 3b: Analysis on poetic level, comparing Brahms's and Daumer's rhythmic and quantitative stresses (with Brahms's text repetitions in parentheses).

Long —	largest emphasis /	small emphasis \
Medium –	medium emphasis ^	unemphasized ∪
Short -		

Brahms quantity	—	–	–	-	—	-	-	-
Daumer quantity	-	-	-	-	—	-	-	—
Brahms rhythm	/	∪	∪	\	/	∪	^	∪
Daumer rhythm	/	∪	∪	∪	/	∪	^	∪
Text	Bit-	te-	res	zu	sa-	gen	denkst	du,

Brahms quantity	—	—	–	–	—	-	-	-
Daumer quantity	—	-	-	-	-	-	-	—
Brahms rhythm	\	∪	/	∪	/	∪	/	∪
Daumer rhythm	\	∪	^	∪	^	∪	^	∪
Text	a-	ber	nun	und	nim-	mer	kränkst	du,

Brahms quantity	–	–	-	–	—	-	-	
Daumer quantity	-	—	-	—	—	-	-	
Brahms rhythm	∪	^	\	∪	/	∪	\	∪
Daumer rhythm	\	∪	^	∪	/	∪	\	
Text	ob	du	noch	so	bö-	se	bist.	

	Dei-	ne	her-	ben	Re-	de-	ta-	ten
Brahms quantity	—	-	—	-	—	-	—	-
Daumer quantity	–	-	—	-	–	-	—	-
Brahms rhythm	/	U	∧	U	/	U	\	U>
Daumer rhythm	∧	U	/	U	/	U	\	U>

	schei-	tern	an	ko-	rall-	ner	Klip-	pe;
Brahms quantity	—	-	-	—	—	-	—	-
Daumer quantity	–	-	-	—	–	-	—	-
Brahms rhythm	/	U	∧	U	/	U	\	U
Daumer rhythm	/	U	\	U	/	U	/	U

	(schei-	tern	an	ko-	rall-	ner	Klip-	pe;)
Brahms quantity	—	-	—	—	—	-	—	-
Brahms rhythm	/	U	/	U	/	U	∧	U

	wer-	den	all	zu	rei-	nen	Gna-	den,
Brahms quantity	–	-	-	-	—	-	—	-
Daumer quantity	–	-	-	-	—	-	—	-
Brahms rhythm	∧	U	U	\	/	U	∧	U
Daumer rhythm	∧	U	/	U	/	U	/	U

	denn	sie	müs-	sen,	um	zu	scha-	den,
Brahms quantity	–	–	-	-	—	-	—	-
Daumer quantity	-	-	-	-	—	-	—	-
Brahms rhythm	∧	U	/	U	∧	U	/	U>
Daumer rhythm	\	U	/	U	U	U	/	U>

	schif-	fen	ü-	ber	ei-	ne	Lip-	pe,
Brahms quantity	-	-	—	-	—	-	-	-
Daumer quantity	-	-	—	—	—	-	-	-
Brahms rhythm	/	\	/	U	\	U	/	U
Daumer rhythm	/	U	\	U	\	U	/	U

	die	die	Sü-	ße	sel-	ber	ist.	
Brahms quantity	–	–	–	-	—	-	-	
Daumer quantity	—	—	–	-	-	-	-	
Brahms rhythm	\	U	/	U	/	U	\>	
Daumer rhythm	U	U	/	U	/	U	U	

	(die	die	Sü-	ße	sel-	ber	ist.)	
Brahms quantity	—	-	—	—	—	-	—	
Brahms rhythm	∧	U	/	U	/	U	∧	

"herben Redetaten," "scheitern," and "schaden" is gently blunted. Only the two repeated lines interrupt the rhythmic motion: one reaffirms that the cruel words of the beloved founder on the coral of her lips, while the other restates that those same lips — and by inference, the beloved — are sweetness itself.

Looking at the natural divisions, it is clear that Brahms's nearly equal phrase structure is based on emotional content rather than poetic form,

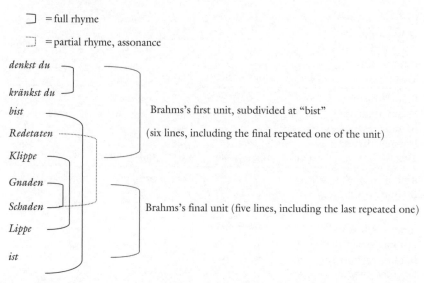

Fig. 4: Daumer's rhyming patterns and divisions compared with Brahms's.

since he disregards the somewhat unusual rhyming pattern of the poem. The strongest internal division is at the word "bist" (line 3), but the striking spondee is neutralized by the extension of the word over two notes, thus sustaining the trochaic pattern and the more passive feminine ending.

Poetic-Melodic Analysis

A melodic analysis affirms the sense of Brahms conspiring with Daumer in order to neutralize the ache of the beloved's stinging words, partly through the sensuousness of line. A comparison of the natural declamatory emphasis with melodic high points reveals that Brahms has deliberately avoided highlighting any articulation of the beloved's cruelty; both the speaking persona and the melodic persona are determined to focus only on the beloved as the object of love. A more obvious setting would have been to word-paint emotive words such as "Bitteres" or "kränkst." The word "böse" (line 3) is the only significant word that is not also the high-point of the vocal line.

Fig. 5 reveals Brahms's choice of structural division to be dictated by the poem's shift in focus: in his first section, which refers to the beloved's cruelty, his melodic focus-points differ from Daumer's. In the second, however, poet's and composer's thoughts converge, especially in the last three lines. Brahms's ascending motion highlights the words "Lippe," "selber," and "Süße," hammering home the equation of the beloved with sweetness.

Daumer	Brahms
Bitteres zu sagen denkst du;	Bitteres zu **sagen** denkst du;
aber nun und nimmer **kränkst** du,	aber **nun** und **nim**mer kränkst du,
ob du noch so **böse** bist.	ob du noch so böse bist.
Deine **herben** Redetaten	Deine herben Redetaten
scheitern an korallner **Klippe;**	scheitern an ko**rall**ner Klippe; (x2)
werden all zu **reinen Gnaden,**	werden all zu **rein**en Gnaden,
denn sie **müssen,** um zu schaden,	denn sie **müssen,** um zu **scha**den,
schiffen über eine **Lippe,**	schiffen über eine **Lippe,**
die die **Süße selber** ist.	die die Süße **sel**ber ist. (x2)

Fig. 5: A comparison between Daumer's naturally significant words and those highlighted by Brahms.

Fig. 6 deals exclusively with melodic peaks. Clearly, the impression of overall expansion is actually confined to the piano part, since the melodic high-points trace an inexorable, self-entangling pattern of opposing pairs of seconds, despite the wider intervals towards the end (compare the opening seconds and thirds with the sixths and sevenths in the final measures). The dropping semitone is the universal musical symbol depicting the sigh, and it extends the word "bist" (m. 8) effectively. However, Brahms expands and inverts the motif, creating a line that is in effect one extended sigh, simultaneously evoking nostalgia, suffering, and perverse contentment by virtue of constancy. At the climax, this motion is divided between two unfolding melodic lines, one tracing G-F-C, the other B♭-A-G-E-F. So, despite the expanded intervals, the sighing motion is not abandoned, but composed into a deeper level.

Another significant point regarding parallel settings should be noted: within the modified strophic form, a comparison reveals that the line "Bitteres zu sagen denkst du" is set identically to "werden all zu reinen

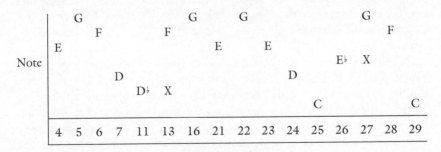

Fig. 6: Brahms's Höhepunkte.

Gnaden" (m. 20); in other words, the neutralization of her cruel words is effected on the melodic level. The setting of "eine Lippe, die die Süße" (mm. 25–26) echoes the motivic formation of "Deine herben Redetaten scheitern an korallner Klippe" (mm. 10–13), but concentrates the opposing seconds motion, sublimating the dotted rhythm of the earlier lines into a dogged ascent to the word "selber" (m. 27); the repetition of this central thought is so eager that the breath must be snatched in measure 28.

Vocal-Instrumental Analysis

The relationship between the two aspects of the song described above and the piano accompaniment is one of extraordinary complexity. Additionally, the accompaniment merits a division, because the upper part allies itself to the melodic persona by shadowing its line. Thus the setting of "aber nun und nimmer kränkst du" (mm. 5–6) is of particular note, because this motion is altered; had the line been set according to the piano, the word "kränkst" would have fallen on a vocal high point — precisely what the vocal-melodic persona is striving to ignore (see fig. 7).[12] The unswerving sympathy of the upper part is attested to by its otherwise faithful mirroring of the melody; at times, it even reinforces it by adding momentum (see approach to first climax, mm. 14–17), hence, its ambivalence is demonstrated in this single measure.

As supportive onlooker, the virtual persona agrees with the singer's plaintive "so böse bist" (m. 9); but it also anticipates the song's outcome (compare mm. 18–19 and 28–30). However, both repetitions are selective. The piano avoids the melodic persona's qualifier: "ob du noch (so böse bist)"; similarly, in measures 18–19 the re-entry of the voice provides necessary affirmation through a perfect cadence. The nature of the two-measure prelude and the four-measure postlude is symptomatic of the whole song, in that the tonic as melody-note is constantly avoided. The absence of a perfect cadence with a melodic tonic (the final one is overshadowed by the third in the piano part) imbues the song with a sense of endlessness; even the final cadence is imperfect, relegating actual closure to the weaker half of the measure. One imagines that the vocal persona will never escape this ungratifying situation of constant abuse.

Brahms's attitude to the bass line in itself merits a separate study. When playing through students' compositions, he would cover up the middle parts and play only the outer two voices, so significant did he consider the bass in terms of formal construction, harmonic direction, and counterpoint. How much more significant then, that Brahms consistently avoids writing a bass note on the downbeat! Taken in conjunction with the metric strictness of the upper voices, it suggests to us that there is yet another attitude to be considered. The bass delays its support, but is

Fig. 7a: Brahms's alteration of the vocal line in mm. 5–6.

Fig. 7b: The same text, but following the piano line.
(This setting places "kränkst" on a vocal high-point.)

nevertheless essential, because its arrival on the second eighth-note of the measure defines each harmonic event. It clarifies the D minor harmony in measure 6; without it, one could surmise a prolongation of F major. Additionally, the ubiquitous falling second motion (which lent such pathos to the upper voices) serves here only to obscure harmonic events through appoggiaturas in the tenor line (for example, evoking the relative minor, albeit briefly, in the opening measure). Interestingly, no appoggiatura coincides with the arrival of the minor sixth harmony in measure 6, suggesting that the song would be more comfortable in the minor mode. Most important, the bass line instigates the interrupted cadence of measure 28, necessitating the reiteration of the final line; closure in the form of an F would have affirmed the lover's rather fatuous equation of the beloved's lips with sweetness itself.

The predominant minor inflection also controls the harmony on a larger scale: D minor, F minor (with its relative A-flat major), and C minor are never distant. It becomes clear that, rather than word-painting specific moments, an entire mood has been sublimated into the harmony. Thus the persona of the bass (as controller of the harmony) can be viewed either as the speaking persona's subconscious articulating his suffering, or as the implicit persona's darker commentary on the beloved herself in all her unreliability and downright nastiness. Both interpretations are supported by the lurking chromatic unease, surfacing at moments such as measure 8 ("böse bist"), and the afore-mentioned interrupted cadence at the first statement of "die die Süße selber ist" (m. 28).

Hafis-Daumer-Brahms?

Brahms set Daumer more than any other poet. This argues a sympathy between the creative personae of both men; hence it is useful to explore Daumer's background and motivations. A theologian, translator, and poet, Georg Friedrich Daumer is a historically significant and immensely prolific author, whose absence from lexicons of German poetry is misleading, even though the bulk of his writing was non-fiction in prose form. His creative years spanned the period 1836 to 1855, with the Hafis phase occupying the center of this period.

Daumer's initial claim to fame was his association with the mysterious figure of Kaspar Hauser; however his religious ideals also excited a range of emotions from outrage to admiration. During the cholera epidemic of 1834 (to which Hegel also succumbed), Daumer published a pamphlet attacking the popular belief that the sins of the people were responsible for the plague; the pamphlet was duly confiscated. To be merely anti-establishment would have been forgiven; Daumer, however, retracted his antireligious stand (causing the break in his friendship with Ludwig Feuerbach), dabbled in both Judaism and Islam, attempted to found his own religion,[13] and ultimately converted to Catholicism. However, the Catholic Church in Mainz withdrew its support, so he had to recon-vert to Protestantism in order to retain publication opportunities. In old age, he occupied himself with phenomenology and theories of the supernatural. By then, his reputation was in decline; however, his *Hafis-Sammlungen* (Collections of Hafis poems, 1846, 1852 [second edition]) remained popular well into the following century, outliving many a similar work.

The *Hafis-Sammlungen* belong firmly to the west-to-east movement in literature that reached its pinnacle in the early nineteenth century. Owing to the general unfamiliarity with the original languages, it is to the Austrian oriental and linguistic scholar Josef von Hammer-Purgstall that the movement is indebted. His *Fundgruben des Orients* (Treasures of the Orient, 1809–18) were a veritable treasure-trove, providing fodder for all, including Goethe. The lack of authenticity disturbed no-one; Rückert's *Ghaselen nach Dschelalladin Rumi* (Ghasels after Jelalludin Rumi, 1820), his *Östliche Rosen* (Eastern Roses, 1821), and Platen's *Spiegel des Hafis* (Mirror of Hafis, 1822) were successes despite the fact that none were first-hand translations. For the poets involved, the Orient itself was immaterial (none of them traveled there); central was their conception of what the Orient signified.[14] Together with the interest in the Middle Ages and nature-worship, orientalism took its place within the gallery of Romantic topics.

Hence the lack of authenticity of the poems was felt to be irrelevant to their genuine effectiveness.[15] "Hafis" was essential as a persona through which Daumer could conceal and reveal his own nature as he chose. He may have felt a genuine affinity with Hafis because of the latter's well-known unorthodox mysticism. Kluncker comments:

> Hafis war nach Daumers eigener Aussage seine dichterische Maske. [. . .] Mit seiner Identifikation geht Daumer einen entscheidenden Schritt weiter als Goethe, der Hafis als Zwillingsbruder neben sich stellt und Gedichte *auf* Hafis schreibt. Daumer spricht stets *als* Hafis und tauscht mit ihm sein lyrisches Ich. Neben Daumers sprödem und humorfreiem Prosawerk nimmt sich der Hafis-Ton mit seiner sorglosen Libertinage und ihren rauschhaften Höhepunkten in der Tat wie das Werk *eines anderen Menschen* aus.[16]

Kluncker explains here how much Daumer identified with Hafis: where Goethe addresses poems to Hafis, Daumer dons his Hafis-mask and thus takes on a new persona. This assertion is remarkable. Following Cone's line of reasoning, there emerges a complex psychological game: the performers "speak" in the voices of Brahms, who speaks through Daumer's poetry — however, Daumer in turn is using the Hafis-mask.

Hafis's works belong in a courtly context, in which the beloved is often taken as a metaphor for God.[17] Daumer revels purely in the sensuality of the topics, concretizing and directly addressing the beloved. In Brahms's setting, however, the poem simultaneously acquires its most intimate and most universal guise; the poet is soliloquizing, with only an accompaniment to comment on the situation. Although the *text* is in the second person, the equivocations of the piano part render the *song* a private plaint. Thus, it becomes a universal incarnation of lovesickness, another offering in Brahms's lifelong homage to unrequited love.

Daumer's personal life also provides an insight into his poetic choices — and, incidentally, Brahms's. Although married, Daumer complained that his wife plagued him with her spiritual superiority; in any case, his relationship with women was always problematic. Chronically shy and naturally prudish, he formed his closest female relationships with women who were in some way inaccessible. Simultaneously, however, the idea of womanhood was central to his religious beliefs, and he idealized the notion of femininity. This conception of women as simultaneously exalted, untouchable, and yet deeply desirable repeatedly finds expression in his poetry, and the resonance with Brahms's own experience cannot be denied; this perhaps explains his fidelity to poetry that was generally considered to be scandalous.[18]

Hence, it is not entirely self-indulgent to hypothesize that this reading of the song may resonate with Brahms's own. He may have tried to infuse an element of realism, even irony, into the poem.[19] However, this leaning towards the equation of composer's persona with the composer himself is fraught with difficulty; it is clear that Cone endorses this position, since he seems to use the terms "composer" and "composer's persona" interchangeably — where the terms "narrator" or "authorial voice" are clearly distinct from the author.[20] One could well argue that when the notion is transferred to song, there are even stronger grounds for maintaining a clear distinction between the two — principally because, regardless of the particular slant the setting imparts, it cannot obliterate the mark of the poet's own creative persona. However, this is a question of tendency, the varying extent of which is revealed by even a superficial glance at other songs: for example, in op. 95, no. 2: "Bei dir sind meine Gedanken" (My thoughts are with you, ca. 1883), the lyric is entirely affirmed by the accompaniment. Conversely, another Daumer setting, op. 57, no. 2: "Wenn du mir zuweilen lächelst" (Those times you smile at me, ca. 1867) also displays a disjunction between the virtual and speaking persona. In any case, as Cone himself puts it, "categorical generalization, whether of fact or opinion, is always false";[21] analytical or interpretative methods tend to collapse unless they are infinitely adaptable to their material, rather than vice versa. The three-tiered method I have used would be applicable to all of Brahms's songs,[22] but is particularly apposite to his love songs, since the presence of the beloved as protagonist (albeit on a subconscious level) guarantees the dramatic identification so essential to the singer and pianist.

An academic inroad into performance has oxymoronic undertones; in practice, however, the nature of the insights, being grounded in characterization, renders them communicable on stage. In addition, one understanding of how Brahms completes a poem has been detailed, thereby illuminating his unique criteria: he occupies the strange position in which the greatest poetry is inappropriate, therefore deliberately shunned. In the case of op. 32, no. 7, Brahms rescues Daumer's poem from its own sentimentality by providing a gently questioning musical subtext. Where an attempt to gain a general critical overview of Brahms's Lied oeuvre would necessarily be laden with emendations and qualifications, a flexible interpretative method opens a vista of endless possibilities for scholar and performer alike.

Notes

[1] For Stockhausen's own account of the Brahms songs he performed see Julia Wirth, *Julius Stockhausen: Der Sänger des deutschen Lieds* (Frankfurt a. M.: Englert & Schlösser, 1927), 164–65, 210–15, 310–25. Individual songs are not always mentioned, but those referred to remain favorites today. A similar tendency is noticeable throughout Max Kalbeck's biography: *Johannes Brahms,* 4 vols. (1908; reprint, Tutzing: Hans Schneider, 1976).

[2] See Christiane Jacobsen, *Das Verhältnis von Sprache und Musik in ausgewählten Liedern von Johannes Brahms, dargestellt an Parallelvertonungen* (Hamburg: Karl Dieter Wagner, 1975), 22–79; see also Ludwig Finscher, "Brahms' Early Songs: Poetry versus Music," in *Brahms Studies: Analytical and Historical Perspectives,* ed. George Bozarth (Oxford: Clarendon P, 1990), 331–44 (here, 331–32).

[3] See Jacobsen, *Das Verhältnis von Sprache und Musik,* 80–96, for her categorization of Brahms's song texts.

[4] August Gerstmeier, in discussing the quality of Daumer's poetry, maintains that with Lieder it is "irrelevant" to consider the literary quality of the poem: the issue for the composer is rather whether or not the poem is suitable for setting to music: "Ist das Gedicht für eine Vertonung geeignet"? Gerstmeier, "Brahms und Daumer," in *Brahms als Liedkomponist,* ed. Peter Jost (Stuttgart: Franz Steiner, 1992), 116–36 (here, 117).

[5] Philip Hosbaum, *Metre, Rhythm and Verse Form* (London: Routledge, 1996), 39–40.

[6] Jacobsen, *Das Verhältnis von Sprache und Musik,* 45. When Brahms was confronted with his reluctance to set Goethe, he replied, "Die [Gedichte] sind alle so fertig, da kann man mit Musik nicht an." Kalbeck, *Johannes Brahms,* 3:87.

[7] Brahms, like Schubert, set certain poems for reasons that have more to do with the poet than the poetry; for example, he set poems by Felix Schumann as a birthday gift to Felix's mother Clara. His concept of *Liedersträuße* as opposed to traditional song-cycles presents related problems; the connections between the songs in a given opus are tenuous. See Imogen Fellinger, "Cyclic Tendencies in Brahms' Song Collections," in *Brahms Studies,* ed. Bozarth, 379–88.

[8] Edward T. Cone, *The Composer's Voice* (Berkeley: U of California P, 1974), 17.

[9] See Ann Clark Feyn and Jürgen Thym, "Who is speaking? Edward T. Cone's Concept of Persona and Wolfgang von Schweinitz's Settings of Poems by Sarah Kirsch," *Journal of Musicological Research* 11 (1991): 1–31.

[10] Although for simplicity's sake, the beloved is referred to as a woman, in fact neither Hafis, nor Daumer, nor indeed Brahms, assigns gender to the beloved in the songs. This is in keeping with the original tradition of the poetry, written in praise of God; a beautiful woman and a youth were both commonly used metaphors.

[11] The poem comes from Georg Friedrich Daumer, *Hafis: Eine Sammlung persischer Gedichte: Nebst poetischen Zugaben aus verschiedenen Völkern und Ländern* (Hamburg: Hoffmann & Campe, 1846), poem XXXV, 21. For a brief discussion of the *west-östliche Literaturbewegung* ("west-to-east movement in literature") see

Karlhans Kluncker, *Georg Friedrich Daumer: Leben und Werk 1800–1875* (Bonn: Bouvier Verlag, 1984), 104–8.
The following translation is my own:

> You mean to say something bitter;
> But neither now nor ever will you insult (me),
> Although you are so annoyed.
> Your harsh speeches
> Founder on coral reefs;
> Becoming pure favors,
> For in order to cause harm,
> They have to sail over a pair of lips,
> Which is sweetness itself.

[12] A more famous example of this technique is found in Robert Schumann's op. 48, no. 7: "Ich grolle nicht." In measures 27–29, the piano extends the motif to D-A-G, while the voice transfers to the inner alto line in the accompaniment. Although many singers opt to sing the higher version — the option being given in later editions by Schumann — the original seems to be similar to our example. The content of the poem is related, in that Heine's subject says (in summary): "I am not angry [that we have parted], even though my heart breaks, because you are cruel." Although this is openly bitter compared with Daumer's poem, Brahms's setting enables the two songs to share the sense that the subject denies the extent of his distress. Similarly, the commentator in the accompaniment takes over the "true" melodic line. Opinions on this are divided, especially since the preferred option is more vocally flamboyant, and is also motivically justified. The tendency for the vocal and upper instrumental line to shadow one another in Schumann's settings is also notable — however, this in itself seems to draw attention to the fact that in the original version Schumann deliberately avoided the direct mirroring, suggesting a division in the viewpoints of the personae involved. See Eric Sams, *The Songs of Robert Schumann,* 2nd ed. (London: Eulenberg, 1975), 114.

[13] In 1850 he published his three-volume *Die Religion des neuen Weltalters,* which earned heavy criticism.

[14] Kluncker quotes an aphorism from Friedrich Schlegel's journal *Athenäum* (1800): "Das höchste Romantische müssen wir im Orient suchen." Kluncker, *Georg Friedrich Daumer,* 107.

[15] A study by Hans Effelberger concludes that Daumer translated the poems not only into the German language, but also into the German spirit. "Georg-Friedrich Daumer und die west-östliche Dichtung," *Mittheilungen für die Geschichte der Stadt Nürnberg* 42 (1951): 236–88 (here, 258, 263–65).

[16] Kluncker, *Georg Friedrich Daumer,* 110 (my italics for emphasis). Daumer styled himself as "einen hageren, ascetisch lebenden Mann," which contrasts oddly with Hafis's praise of sensuous pleasures (117).

[17] See Mulla Dinshan Furdunji, *Translation with Explanation of the Seventy-Five Odes of Hafiz* (Bombay: Education Society's Steam Press, 1891), ix.

[18] Elisabeth von Herzogenberg (close friend of Brahms in Vienna, and informal critic of his works) wrote ruefully on one occasion to Brahms complaining that she constantly had to defend his Daumer settings. Kalbeck, *Johannes Brahms,* 1:137.

[19] See also Finscher, "Brahms' Early Songs," 336–37, in which he discusses the impact of Brahms's metric manipulation, and his rejection of a stanza in op. 6, no. 4: "Juchhe!," possibly because of its excessive sentimentality.

[20] The presence of the author in a literary work as narrator or commentator cannot be so easily resolved. Fred Maus, in his discussion of Cone's work, cites the example of Huckleberry Finn, who is used by Samuel Clemens to voice his own views, including those that differ from the character's views: Fred Everett Maus, "Agency in Instrumental Music and Song," *College Music Symposium* 29 (1989): 31–43 (here, 32).

[21] Edward T. Cone, *A View from Delft: Selected Essays,* ed. Robert P. Morgan (Chicago: U of Chicago P, 1989), 3.

[22] Cone's original thesis was designed to be all embracing; he cites applications for instrumental music, hymns, and national anthems. See *College Music Symposium* 29 (1989) for various responses to Cone's work, including a study involving film music.

Romantic Overtones in
Contemporary German Literature

Robert Schneider's *Schlafes Bruder* — A Neo-Romantic *Musikernovelle?*

Jürgen Barkhoff

ICH WEIß NICHT, irgend jemand hat geschrieben, das sei Biedermeier. [. . .] Gut, kann man schreiben. Ich würde sagen, Romantik und nicht Biedermeier. Es ist in viel höherem Maße ein romantisches Buch." The book in question, which none other than Marcel Reich-Ranicki labels a Romantic book in his "Literarisches Quartett," was one of the rare literary successes of the 1990s in German-language literature, and the fact that it was given the full treatment on television is certainly indicative of the dimensions of this success.[1] *Schlafes Bruder* (Brother of Sleep, 1992), the first novel of the Austrian writer and musician from the region of Voralberg, Robert Schneider, was first rejected by twenty-three publishing houses, before being finally published by Reclam Leipzig in 1992. It became an immediate and overwhelming success with the reading public and the majority of critics alike.[2] To date it has sold over 1.4 million copies in the German-speaking world and has been translated into more than twenty-four languages.

What was it that gripped the imagination of its readers to such an extraordinary extent? *Schlafes Bruder* tells the story of the musical genius Elias Alder, who is born into the remote hamlet of Eschberg in deepest Voralberg in the early nineteenth century. In a sublime, but also deeply terrifying experience, he is initiated into the music of nature and, through this, endowed with a unique musical talent. But in the village, far away from any civilizing influence and inhabited by just two family clans, constantly threatened by hostility and incestual deformation, and surrounded by ignorance, brutality, insanity, and intolerance, he is given little room to capitalize on his talents. Suffering under the insensitivity and open hostility of his environment, he is consumed throughout his life by his largely unfulfilled passion for music and his futile love for Elsbeth, a girl from the village, whose heartbeat he heard during his initiation into the sounds of nature while she was still in her mother's womb. After his one musical triumph at an improvisation competition on the organ in the nearby town of Feldberg, he does not choose the musical career that all of a sudden opens up for him after many years of frustration, but decides to sacrifice himself to his unrequited love. Remembering that once a traveling preacher had told the congregation in Eschberg "Wer schläft, liebt nicht" ("He who sleeps, does not love"),[3] the impressionable and melancholic young man decides in the end to prove his love by refusing to sleep until first insanity comes, and then death; thus he chooses to be a moribund genius desperately in love rather than celebrate this love in music.

Strong stuff, the impact of which is greatly enhanced by the style of narration. An omniscient narrator, alternating between emotional sympathy for and intellectual distance from his main character, tells the story of his hero's life from birth to death in a fairly straightforward and linear fashion and, for the most part, in the tone of a nineteenth-century chronicle. The language he employs is, however, anything but simple. It oscillates between an archaic and sensual directness full of regionalisms and an almost biblical, highly rhetorical pathos, which, however, on occasion shows that its author is as well versed in today's psycho-speak as he is in musicological terminology. This dazzling and masterfully handled array of styles, coupled with the rather conventional mode of narration, makes the book eminently readable and enjoyable.

The book's dense web of intertextual references adds further complexity to the reading experience, and this attracted the attention of critics right from the start.[4] The parallel to Patrick Süsskind's bestseller *Das Parfüm* (Perfume, 1985) is the most obvious, Süsskind's hero being a genius at smelling just as Schneider's is at hearing — both times with fatal consequences. The factual manner in which the supernatural elements of the story are presented and the focus on one small village have prompted comparisons with Gabriel Garcia Marquez's *One Hundred Years of Solitude* (1967) and its literary technique of "magic realism." But Elias has also been compared with Oskar Matzerath, Günter Grass's hero in *Die Blechtrommel* (The Tin Drum, 1959), on account of his disfiguration and physical transformation at the age of five when his body goes through puberty in an instant; with Thomas Mann's tragic composer Adrian Leverkühn in *Doktor Faustus* (1947); and with Hans Castorp in the *Zauberberg* (The Magic Mountain, 1924), as Elias's metaphysical experience also takes place in the snow. Moving closer to the Romantic epoch, Elias was seen to have in common with Goethe's Werther the choosing of self-destructive love over its sublimation in art. The Romantic overtones of *Schlafes Bruder* did, of course, not go unnoticed, but received little more than a mention in passing (from, for example, Reich-Ranicki). The most observant comment was from Beatrice von Matt, who called Elias "a sort of peasant Novalis" who experiences the universe acoustically.[5]

In following this lead I intend to investigate in this paper the extent to which the novel in general, its musician of genius, and particularly his music are grounded in and modify Romantic concepts of music and their relationship to literature. In doing this, I want to ask whether the success of the book can perhaps be linked to its neo-Romantic quality.

The most obvious pointer is the narrated time of the novel: Elias Alder's life span from 1803 to 1825. It coincides almost exactly not only with the heyday of literary Romanticism in Germany, but also with the period in which Beethoven and Schubert composed most of their masterpieces: cultural movements of which the yokel in his hamlet in the back of the woods has, of course, no knowledge.

But even the title of the book has Romantic overtones. While overtly referring to the Bach chorale "Kömm, o Tod, Du Schlafes Bruder,"[6] on which Elias has to base his improvisation at the organ competition, it also evokes the Romantic fascination with the nocturnal side of human existence: Romantic anthropology's belief in the deep affinity between sleep, trance, madness, artistic inspiration, and death.[7] And indeed: Elias's potent and dangerous mix of unappreciated musical talent, unfulfilled love, and melancholic infatuation with self-destruction makes him a brother of the dark protagonists of almost all important *Musikernovellen* of German Romanticism. With Wackenroder's Berglinger and Hoffmann's Kreisler he shares the role of misfit and outsider in uncomprehending and unsympathetic social surroundings, as well as the closeness of inspiration and madness that such limiting circumstances almost inevitably produce.[8] Like Grillparzer's Jakob in *Der arme Spielmann* (The Poor Fiddler, 1847) he demonstrates, as Osman Durrani notes, "the great gap between imagination and reality," and like the protagonist in Mörike's *Mozart auf der Reise nach Prag* (Mozart on the Journey to Prague, 1855) he exemplifies "the propensity of great artists to burn themselves out."[9]

In establishing these parallels, however, let us not overlook the distinct differences. Elias is neither a culturally refined intellectual in a logocentric environment, nor an articulate and self-reflexive artist suffering under the narrow-mindedness of middle-class philistines or the false pretensions of courtly life. He is an uneducated peasant, chosen by nature or God to be different, although he does not understand the reasons for this, and the confines against which he is struggling are far more repressive and stifling than in the average German *Kleinstadt* or *Kleinstaat*. Thus his story is as much a *Musikernovelle* in the Romantic mould as it is a *Dorfgeschichte* or, rather, with its unsparing unmasking of the peasant idyll as barbaric primitiveness, a fairly malicious "Anti-Heimatroman" (as the author himself put it) in the Austrian tradition of Innerhofer, Jelinek, and Bernhard.[10] With this *caveat* in mind, let us examine its Romantic elements in more detail.

The basis for Elias's unrivaled musical talent is an experience he has on a huge stone in the bed of the local river, to which the young boy is magically attracted (*SB*, 33) — not unlike the attraction Chrysostomus feels towards a mysterious stone in Hoffmann's *Johannes Kreislers Lehrbrief* (Johannes Kreisler's Letter of Apprenticeship, 1815).[11] In response to the stone's calling, Elias is drawn towards the river, and it is then that the miracle occurs: "An diesem Nachmittag hörte der fünfjährige Elias das Universum tönen" — he hears the sounds of the universe (*SB*, 33–34). This central scene, spanning more than five pages, vividly conveys the highly expressive and evocative way in which Schneider turns the (imagined) experience of music into language. Elias's initiation into the sounds of nature first manifests itself as a heightened sensitivity for the acoustic sensations of the microcosm of his own body, but soon extends to the macrocosmic totality of nature:

> Und abermals vervielfältigte sich sein Gehörkreis, explodierte und stülpte sich gleichsam als ein riesenhaftes Ohr über den Flecken, auf dem er lag. Horchte hinunter in hundert Meilen tiefe Landschaften, horchte hinaus in hundert Meilen weite Gegenden. Über die Klangkulisse der eigenen Körpergeräusche zogen mit wachsender Geschwindigkeit um vieles gewaltigere Klangszenarien. Szenarien von unerhörter Pracht und Fürchterlichkeit. Klangwetter, Klangstürme, Klangmeere und Klangwüsten. [...] Und er sah noch tiefer und noch weiter. Sah das Getier des Meeres, den Gesang von Delphinen, den gigantischen Wehklang sterbender Wale, die Akkorde riesiger Fischschwärme, das Klicken des Planktons, [...] das Raunen, Krachen und Bersten gigantischer Wolkenchöre, den Klang des Lichtes... Was sind Worte! (*SB*, 36–38)

Familiar features of the Romantic literary discourse on music can be identified here.[12] There are the obvious synesthetic qualities of this acoustic sensation being equally described as a visual one, or the narrator's marker at the end about the paradoxical undertaking of transcending the limits of language through language. More noteworthy, however, are the origins of this scene in the Pythagorean concept of the spherical music of nature. In the baroque period, Athanasius Kircher further developed his concept when he wrote about those universal harmonies of the world that we would be able to hear, had God granted us an extraordinarily enhanced capacity of hearing.[13] In Schneider's work, the extraordinary enhancement of Elias's faculties is explicitly the work of a god. Elias's susceptibility towards this acoustic cosmos is seen as the basis for his ability to express it in art. This extension of the Pythagorean philosophy of music was conceptualized in German Romanticism *inter alia* by Schelling, who saw music as nothing less than the original rhythm of the universe manifesting itself in our world via this very art.[14]

But such a transformation of Elias's initially traumatic encounter into artistic creativity is far away at this stage. He emerges from this experience, which is as much bodily as spiritual, both gifted and disfigured, privileged and stigmatized. From this moment on the five-year-old possesses a beautiful deep bass singing voice, a unique talent for imitating voices, and the Orphean ability to communicate with animals at their

frequency (cf. *SB*, 56, 197). And there is a further perplexing and shock-
ing corporeal stigma of his otherness: the color of his pupils changes to
yellow, giving the village community a pretext for seeing him as a
monster and treating him as an outcast. For years his embarrassed parents
lock him up in total isolation, the other children fear him and taunt him,
and the village community excludes him with consistency and cruelty.
While his close rapport with nature enables him to grow up a mild-
mannered, sensitive, and kind person despite the trauma of this exclusion, he also becomes a shy *Sonderling* and social misfit who lives in the
fantasy world of his music rather than in the reality of everyday village life.
This is the outer, social side of his newly-found status as an exceptional
character. Its other features are equally familiar from the debates about
the nature of the genius during the *Sturm und Drang* (Storm and Stress)
and Romanticism.

Like a true genius he owes all his talents to nature.[15] The tension
between *ingenium* and *studium*, which was the focus of so many debates
on artistic talent, is almost suspended in his case, since all his achievements flow from his *ingenium*. He is a complete autodidact who never
learns to read music, let alone the rules of composition. The only music
to which he is exposed is the music at the local Sunday mass, played
badly on a deficient organ. But this is enough to inspire him and to give
him an intuitive understanding of the principles of composition for this
instrument. During his secret practices in the village church by night he
effortlessly achieves great mastery in his technical command of its keys
and stops. His intuitions even extend to the inner workings of the
instrument; so much so, that one night he is able to repair and tune the
neglected and out-of-tune organ in the village church without any previous knowledge of its mechanics. The only type of music he performs is
improvisation, and just like Kreisler's fantasies, and Mignon's songs in
Goethe's *Wilhelm Meisters Lehrjahre* (Wilhelm Meister's Apprenticeship
Years, 1796), these exist only in the one ephemeral moment of their
production; they are never written down, refusing to be fixed in the
language of signs that would take away from their spontaneous authenticity and intensity.

Elias's very first musical attempts are mimetic: a mimesis of nature
and its harmonies. Recalling the movements of two brimstone butterflies,
he imitates their playful interaction in his melodies: "Die Stimme in
seiner rechten Hand ließ er zuerst flattern. Dann folgte die linke. Wo aber
die rechte aufwärts ging, wogte die linke launig nieder, und dennoch
zogen beide Stimmen eine wohlklingende Bahn" (*SB*, 69–70). But when
later asked at the organ competition to play a traditional prelude and
fugue, he equally demonstrates his quick grasp of the tradition of church
music as well as his ability to transcend it — another typical feature of
the artistic genius. His playing is of a previously unheard complexity,

elevating the art of the fugue to hitherto unknown and seemingly impossible heights:

> Denn das Fugenthema war von einer so gigantischen Erfindungskunst und Länge, daß man glauben mußte, auf der Empore gehe es mit übernatürlichen Dingen zu. Das Thema bestand aus den Grundtönen des zu improvisierenden Chorals, hatte aber eine so filigran-träumerische Gestimmtheit, daß ein jüngeres Weib auf der Evangelienseite zu Recht ausrief: "Ich sehe den Himmel." (*SB*, 179)

This leads to the real test for Elias Alder's claim to genius: the transcendent effect his music has on his audience.

For the theoreticians of pre-Romantic *Ausdrucksästhetik* (the aesthetics of expression) the relation between nature and heart forms the foundation for the ability of a musician; because his heart is in tune with nature, he is able to imitate the sounds through which nature itself can express its feelings and passions. Similarly, Carl Philipp Emanuel Bach demanded that the performer play from the soul in order to create within the audience — preferably through free improvisation — the emotions moving the musician himself, so that such emotions might have a civilizing effect on the souls of the listeners.[16] And Elias's music fits this theory. The basis of all his improvisations is the rhythm of his loved one's heartbeat, which has been with him since his first initiation into the great rhythm of nature. His first public performance in the village church on an Easter Sunday has a moving effect:

> Und Elias jubilierte. Komponierte ein Adagio von so anrührender Zartheit, daß den Bauern die klammkalten Hände plötzlich warm wurden. [. . .] Die Bauern verließen das Kirchlein mit hochgestimmter Seele. Die Musik des Organisten machte ihre sturen Gemüter lammfromm, denn eigentümlicherweise verließ niemand die Kirche vor der Zeit. (*SB*, 115)

The congregation of farmers leaves the church exalted by Elias's playing. However, the naturalness and authenticity of the congregation's feelings is called into question by the narrator's observation of a certain artificiality and manneredness in their behavior, evident in their adopted French accent (*SB*, 115). In the long term, Elias's music does not seem to have the desired civilizing influence on their dulled hearts, and they soon start complaining about the undue length of time for which their new organist plays.

But the persuasiveness of Elias's music develops just like the aesthetics of music around that time, and its genuinely Romantic qualities can be detected at the organ festival in front of a more educated urban public:

> Allmählich begriffen die so erschrockenen Zuhörer die Botschaft des Organisten. Nein, der da oben machte nicht bloß Musik, er predigte. Und was er predigte, war von kalter, glasklarer Wahrheit. Für Augenblicke schien es dem Eschberger Bauern gelungen, die Geister dieser mannigfaltigen

Menschen in einem einzigen Geist zu verschmelzen. Denn es entstand im Dom eine derart unheimliche Stimmung, als ahnten das Kind und der Greis zu gleicher Zeit: Der Tod ist in diesen Mauern und der Schlaf, sein Gefährte, wird dich zudecken. In den Gesichtern der Menschen stand plötzlich Wahres zu lesen. Die Masken waren herabgeschmolzen und ein numinoses Stilles lag auf jedem Antlitz, [. . .]. (*SB*, 175)

This description of Elias's organ playing as a sermon evoking metaphysical truth in the minds of the congregation reminds us of Hoffmann's appreciation of church music as the true source of the impact of Romantic music,[17] as described in his essay *Alte und neue Kirchenmusik* (Ancient and Modern Church Music, 1814):

Die Ahnung des Höchsten und Heiligsten, der geistigen Macht, die den Lebensfunken in der ganzen Natur entzündet, spricht sich hörbar aus im Ton und so wird Musik, Gesang, der Ausdruck der höchsten Fülle des Daseins — Schöpferlob! — Ihrem innern eigentümlichen Wesen nach ist daher die Musik religiöser Kultus und ihr Ursprung einzig und allein in der Religion, in der Kirche zu suchen.[18]

However, many other statements by Hoffmann and other Romantics on the metaphysical dignity of music highlight a vital difference. The well-known passage from Hoffmann's *Gedanken über den hohen Wert der Musik* (Reflections on the High Value of Music, 1814), the third piece of his *Kreisleriana* (Kreisler Papers, 1812–20) professes music to be the most Romantic of all the arts:

[. . .] sie nennen sie die romantischste aller Künste, da ihr Vorwurf nur das Unendliche sei; die geheimnisvolle, in Tönen ausgesprochene Sanskritta der Natur, die die Brust des Menschen mit unendlicher Sehnsucht erfülle, und nur in ihr verstehe er das hohe Lied der — Bäume, der Blumen, der Tiere, der Steine, der Gewässer! (*FN*, 39)

This Romantic concept of what Dahlhaus calls absolute music[19] is initially freer of mimetic ambition than Schneider's philosophy of music, although the theme of Elias's music — the fear of death, and in a later passage, its final jubilant transcendence — fits the Romantic bill well. However, the contrast I wish to focus on here is one of form, not of content: namely, the narrative status of these two passages. Schneider's narrator speaks with the authority of an omniscient narrator who has access even to God's intentions, and who asserts his statements with ontological certainty. Hoffmann's narrative perspective, by contrast, is relativized in more than one sense: its first person narrator is the highly dubious Johannes Kreisler, and his statement can be found in a piece which despite — or perhaps because of — the elevated claim of its title worries the narrator that it might be taken ironically.[20] As if this were not enough, the above remark about music as the most Romantic of all art forms is attributed not to people with a godlike overview like theoreticians or omniscient narrators, but to artists who are seen as a greatly endangered borderline species (not unlike Elias), precisely because of their deep affinity for the ecstatic experiences that music can trigger.

These observations can be generalized. Romantic statements on the metaphysics of music are tentative and ambiguous. It is no coincidence that "Ahnungen" ("premonitions") and "Sehnsucht" ("longing") are Hoffmann's key-words in this context. And there is hardly a statement on the Romantic metaphysics of music that does not refer somehow either to music as a language with its complex relationship between signifier and signified and all its implications, or to its speculative or mythical element. Novalis, for example, clearly labels the following fragment from his *Allgemeines Brouillon* (General Sketch, 1798/99) describing music as an Aeolian harp, as a mere *"Ideenassociation"*: *"Wolkenspiel — Naturspiel* äußerst poetisch. Die Natur ist eine Aeolsharfe — Sie ist ein musikal[isches] Intrument — dessen Töne wieder Tasten höherer Sayten in uns sind."[21] And Hoffmann hardly ever talks about music without reflecting on the impossibility of direct mimesis of nature in music. A quotation from *Johannes Kreislers Lehrbrief* illustrates this:

> Die Musik bleibt allgemeine Sprache der Natur, in wunderbaren, geheimnisvollen Anklängen spricht sie zu uns, vergeblich ringen wir danach, diese in Zeichen festzubannen, und jenes künstliche Anreihen der Hieroglyphe erhält uns nur die Andeutung dessen, was wir erlauscht. (*FN*, 326)

Schneider pursues a different strategy. He simply says of Elias's mimetic efforts "Die Natur wurde Musik" (*SB*, 176), and then goes on to explain the spell Elias casts over his audience in physical rather than metaphysical terms: as a form of hypnosis that synchronizes the heartbeats of his audience with the frequency of his own heart. Schneider's explanation of this unique phenomenon cites the pre-Romantic aesthetics of music to show how Elias transcends its effects. The ordinary musician may be able to arouse in his audience emotions that are intensified — more or less consciously — by each individual listener. Elias, however, induces a trance-like state that captivates his whole audience. It, as a result, loses all self-control:

> Wenn er also musizierte, vermochte er den Menschen bis auf das Innerste seiner Seele zu erschüttern. Er brauchte nur die gefundenen Harmonien in größere, musikorganische Zusammenhänge zu stellen, und der Zuhörer konnte sich der Wirkung nicht mehr entziehen. Ohne seinen Willen traten ihm dann Tränen aus den Augen. Ohne seinen Willen durchlitt er Todesangst, Kindesfreuden, ja bisweilen gar erotische Empfindungen. Solches in der Musik geleistet zu haben, war das Verdienst des Johannes Elias Alder. (*SB*, 178–79)

The proximity between the magic of music and hypnosis — or, rather, its eighteenth-century precursor, animal magnetism — is, of course, a Romantic invention too, explored by Hoffmann in novellas like *Die Automate* (1814) or *Don Juan* (1814).[22] And this reinterpretation of the metaphysical as the physical and corporeal is a trend in contemporary neo-Romantic writing to be found elsewhere, for example in the poetry of Peter Rühmkorf or Durs Grünbein; a reinterpretation that simultaneously preserves and undermines Romantic intentions.[23] Something similar happens in *Schlafes Bruder*: on the one hand, rooting the ecstatic dimensions of music in the subconscious and corporeal strengthens its experiential base and thus its existential seriousness.[24] Highlighting the "fortschreitende Zerrüttung der Seele," its negative impact on the soul (*SB*, 179), as a precondition for the production of such revelatory music at the same time preserves its potentially pathogenic element. On the other hand, investing the full pathos of the body and all the rhetoric of the sublime in the description of the organ festival endangers the numinous qualities of Romantic music and threatens to eliminate the tentativeness so central to Romantic literary discourse on music. This element of ambiguity is, however, reintroduced at the level of form.

In a recent volume on the relevance of Romanticism for the present, Albert Meier reminds us how much an appropriate reading of Romantic texts depends on an appreciation of their self-reflexivity and Romantic irony.[25] This goes for neo-Romantic texts as well. Right from the start reviewers and scholars have been debating whether *Schlafes Bruder* possesses such qualities and should thus be labeled a postmodern novel.[26] Two aspects of the book received particular attention in this respect.

First, many critics commented on how the certainty of the authorial voice is undermined by its chameleon-like character. The tone and style of narration often change from one sentence to the next, giving it on occasion a parodistic quality. At one moment it is a self-assured and authoritative chronicle in Lutheran fashion, at another it suddenly erupts into truly biblical pathos, only to change again to a sentimental *Biedermeier*-style *Dorfgeschichte*. But sentimentality is also subverted by obvious catachresis in sentences that ironize the authenticity of sentiment; for example: "In der ungelenken Faust pulsierte ein empfindsames Herz" (*SB*, 114). In addition, the narration is shot through with calculated anachronisms like "Hypnose" or words like "mongoloid" and "masochistisch": modern analytic terms that indicate that this is a contemporary and thoroughly self-conscious narrator.[27] Overall, this produces a playful pastiche of styles and attitudes, of which the above-mentioned self-assuredness is just one — admittedly, the dominant one — but nevertheless a calculated gesture, and one that asks to be identified as such. However, the indicators for this are often subtle and ambiguous, and thus easily overlooked. When, for example, the narrator tells us about the revelatory effect of Elias's music on the woman who "mit Recht ausrief: 'Ich sehe den Himmel,'" we may or may not trip over the inappropriate certainty of the narrator's intervention "mit Recht" and may or may not read it as an overstatement, ripe with irony.

References to the tradition of the music of nature are not unaffected by such subversions. When the narrator time and again praises Elias as the greatest composer who ever lived, this hyperbole surely undercuts the very concept of genius that it seems to reaffirm. Or another example: when the narrator speculates about a possible happier ending to the tragic story of his hero, he falls into a parodistic fairy-tale tone that highlights the impossibility of a happy ending, and then in an aside mocks the Orphean myth that is taken so seriously and literally elsewhere in the book:

> Wie gern wollten wir davon erzählen, wie unser Held Abschied nimmt von seinem Vaterhaus [. . .]. Wie er zum letzten Mal Zwiesprache hält mit den Tieren der Emmer, mit Resi der Hirschkuh, Wunibald dem Dachs, Lips dem Rotfüchschen, Sebald dem Iltis und mit dem einstelzigen Dompfaff! Wie er nach Feldberg wandert, dort durch seinen wundervollen Baß das Musicalische Institut in helle Aufregung versetzt! (*SB*, 61)

Of course this is kitsch, but kitsch that asks to be read as such and plays with its own exaggerations.[28] Kitsch as the exaggerated, the homogenous and the affirmative, is the opposite of originality, and thus here playfully undermines the very concept it seeks to endorse. At the same time, kitsch — as well as an aversion to it — signals a strong affective involvement and often encodes, as in this book, a vague and very real, though often uncritical, utopian longing.[29]

The intertextual dimension of the book is, of course, relevant in this context too. By intertextually citing and evoking the whole spectrum of a literary discourse on music — which had its heyday in Romanticism, but which spans a much longer tradition from antiquity to Thomas Mann and beyond — Schneider demonstrates his indebtedness to that tradition. He also makes it clear that his own contribution to, and rewriting of, what Christine Lubkoll calls the *Mythos Musik,* is in itself a literary construct. Schneider consciously cites and exaggerates the Romantic myth of the musical genius to the extent of trivialization. This produces kitsch, but in so doing, it turns the myth and its history reflexively against itself. Historically, the emergence of kitsch as an aesthetic category is linked to the notions of authenticity and originality, which its affirmative attitude endangers.[30] Using it parodistically then, exposes the dangerous proximity of any evocation of authenticity. The double-coding by which Schneider's novel reestablishes and affirms, but also exaggerates and ironizes Romantic concepts of music, fully exploits the tension between the sublime and the trivial, the elusive and the entertaining in a postmodern fashion.[31] Its author knows very well that in (post-)modernity it is impossible to portray authenticity without questioning it. He knows equally well that an ascetic and purely intellectual discussion in the modernist vein does not address the deep emotional resonances of his theme. As a consequence, his text, not unlike its Romantic precursors, attempts a fine balance between a celebration and a critique of the affective and experiential dimensions of music — and of its myth.

Yet Albert Meier's title: "Ironie ist Pflicht. Wie romantische Dichtung zu lesen ist" shifts the emphasis away from the text and towards the reader, so that the final decision as to whether the text achieves and maintains this balance lies with its readers. In conclusion, I would like to argue that the literary success of *Schlafes Bruder* can indeed be attributed to its neo-Romantic character, but also that the text invites different readers to pick up different facets of this tradition. The textual signals that flag formal aspects of the Romantic tradition — playfulness, referentiality, self-reflexivity, and irony — serve to remind us that our Romantic longing for the intense emotions expressed and evoked by the text deserves to be taken seriously, but at the same time needs to be checked by our humor and our critical faculties. Yet their presence is subtle and often ambiguous; they form a textual signal system that is in danger of being drowned out by powerful Romantic themes, which are forcefully presented by an omniscient narrator and expressed in opulent language: the intensity of sensation, the totality of experience, the power of love, and the metaphysics of music. Not unlike E. T. A. Hoffmann's tales, which enjoyed enormous popularity in their own time, *Schlafes Bruder* presents itself to the reader as a complex postmodern artifice of styles, allusions, and attitudes, which employs Romantic irony to question its own sincerity, but which also shows the enormous attraction of taking its message seriously. Thus it lends itself to different readings: one that offers the promises and pleasures of Romantic sentiment without the pains and efforts of Romantic reflection, but another that complements the latter with the delights of postmodern playfulness.

Notes

[1] Marcel Reich-Ranicki et al., "Das Literarische Quartett: Diskussion über *Schlafes Bruder* vom 19.11.1992," quoted in Rainer Moritz, *Robert Schneider: "Schlafes Bruder": Erläuterungen und Dokumente* (Stuttgart: Reclam, 1999), 64–70 (here, 68–69). On this occasion Sigrid Löffler agreed with him: "Ja, [. . .] der Geniebegriff ist ein romantischer. [. . .] Ja, das Thema ist romantisch."

[2] For good selections of important reviews see Moritz, *Schneider: "Schlafes Bruder,"* 47–64, and also Rainer Moritz, ed., *Über "Schlafes Bruder": Materialien zu Robert Schneiders Roman* (Leipzig: Reclam, 1996), 139–74.

[3] Robert Schneider, *Schlafes Bruder* (Leipzig: Reclam, 1994), 103. All subsequent page references to this work are given in the text using the abbreviation *SB*.

[4] For a comprehensive list of intertextual references see Angelika Steedts, *Robert Schneiders "Schlafes Bruder"* (Munich: Oldenbourg, 1999), 84–90.

[5] Beatrice von Matt, "Föhnstürme und Klangwetter," in Moritz, ed., *Über "Schlafes Bruder,"* 154–57 (here, 156).

[6] The closing chorale of Johann Sebastian Bach's cantata "Ich will den Kreuzstab gerne tragen" (BWV 56).

[7] See, as a paradigmatic example, Gotthilf Heinrich Schubert, *Ansichten von der Nachtseite der Naturwissenschaft* (Dresden: Arnoldische Buchhandlung, 1808).

[8] Steedts, *Schneiders "Schlafes Bruder,"* 31–34, discusses intertextual links with both characters, but neglects the philosophical context. Similarly Nicholas Vazsonyi, "Of Genius and Epiphany: *Schlafes Bruder, Das Parfum* [*sic*], and *Babette's Feast,*" *Studies in Twentieth-Century Literature* 23 (1999): 331–51 (here, 340).

[9] Osman Durrani, "Non-verbal communication in Robert Schneider's novel *Schlafes Bruder,*" in *Contemporary German Writers, Their Aesthetics and Their Language,* ed. Arthur Williams, Stuart Parks, and Julian Preece (Bern and New York: Peter Lang, 1996), 223–36 (here, 234).

[10] "Interview mit Robert Schneider," *Der Deutschunterricht* 48/2 (1996): 93–101 (here, 93). Reprint in Moritz, *Robert Schneider: "Schlafes Bruder,"* 26–46. For a discussion of this see Klaus Zeyringer, "Felders Stiefbruder oder Der verkleidete Erzähler," in Moritz, ed., *Über "Schlafes Bruder,"* 55–78. For the wider context see Jürgen Koppensteiner, "Anti-Heimatliteratur in Österreich: Zur literarischen Heimatwelle der siebziger Jahre," *Modern Austrian Literature* 15/2 (1982): 1–10.

[11] E. T. A. Hoffmann, *Fantasie- und Nachtstücke,* ed. Walter Müller-Seidel (Munich: Winkler, 1960), 321–27, esp. 323. All subsequent page references to this work are given in the text using the abbreviation *FN*.

[12] For this complex see *inter alia* Christine Lubkoll, *Mythos Musik: Poetische Entwürfe des Musikalischen in der Literatur um 1800* (Freiburg: Rombach, 1995); Pia-Elisabeth Leuschner, *Orphic Song with Daedal Harmony: Die 'Musik' in Texten der englischen und deutschen Romantik* (Würzburg: Königshausen & Neumann, 2000); Walter Hinderer, "Literarisch-ästhetische Auftakte zur romantischen Musik," *Jahrbuch der Deutschen Schillergesellschaft* 41 (1997): 210–35; Walter Wiora, "Die Musik im Weltbild der deutschen Romantik," in *Beiträge zur Geschichte der Musikanschauung im 19. Jahrhundert,* ed. Walter Salmen (Regensburg: Gustav Bosse, 1965), 11–50.

[13] Athanasius Kircher, *Musurgia Universalis,* ed. Ulf Scharlkau (Rome: 1650; reprint, Hildesheim: Olms, 1970). On this see Jörg Zimmermann, "Wandlungen des philosophischen Musikbegriffs: Über den Gegensatz von mathematisch-harmonikaler und semantisch-ästhetischer Betrachtungsweise," in *Musik und Zahl: Interdisziplinäre Beiträge zum Grenzbereich zwischen Musik und Mathematik,* ed. Günter Schnitzler (Bonn-Bad Godesberg: Verlag für systematische Musikwissenschaft, 1976), 81–135 (here, 107). On the harmony of spheres see also Paul von Naredi-Rainer, "Harmonie," in *Die Musik in Geschichte und Gegenwart: Allgemeine Enzyklopädie der Musik,* 2nd rev. ed., ed. Friedrich Blume, Ludwig Finscher, 20 vols. (Kassel: Bärenreiter, 1994ff.), vol. 4 ("Sachteil"), 116–32.

[14] Cf. Wiora, "Die Musik," 27.

[15] See Hermann Schlösser, "'Wie kein Meister vor oder nach ihm. . .': Die Einzigartigkeit des Komponisten Elias Alder," in Moritz, ed., *Über Schneiders "Schlafes Bruder,"* 79–91.

[16] Carl Philipp Emanuel Bach, *Versuch über die wahre Art das Clavier zu spielen* (1759), cited in Lubkoll, *Mythos Musik,* 61.

[17] For the importance of sermons in German Romanticism see Nicholas Saul, *"Prediger aus der neuen romantischen Clique": Zur Interaktion von Romantik und Homiletik um 1800* (Würzburg: Königshausen & Neumann, 1999).

[18] E. T. A. Hoffmann, *Die Serapionsbrüder,* ed. Walter Müller-Seidel (Munich: Winkler, 1963), 401–15 (here, 409).

[19] See the seminal study by Carl Dahlhaus, *Die Idee der absoluten Musik* (Kassel: Bärenreiter, 1978).

[20] "[. . .] wohl gar als heillose Ironie" (*FN,* 41).

[21] Novalis, *Das philosophische Werk 2,* ed. Richard Samuel, vol. 3 of *Schriften Novalis: Die Werke Friedrich von Hardenbergs,* ed. Paul Kluckhohn, Richard Samuel, 6 vols., 2nd rev. ed. (Darmstadt: Wissenschaftliche Buchgesellschaft, 1968), 452.

[22] See Jürgen Barkhoff, *Magnetische Fiktionen: Literarisierung des Mesmerismus in der Romantik* (Stuttgart: Metzler, 1995), 204–21; also Barkhoff, "Töne und Ströme: Zur Technik und Ästhetik der Glasharmonika im Mesmerismus und bei E. T. A. Hoffmann," in *Ästhetische Erfindung der Moderne? Perspektiven und Modelle 1750–1850,* ed. Britta Herrmann and Barbara Thums (Würzburg: Königshausen & Neumann, 2003), 165–91.

[23] On Rühmkorf see Astrid Keiner and Günter Oesterle (eds.), *Ein Dichter mit und ohne Hut: Dr. h.c. Peter Rühmkorf* (Gießen: Ferber, 1991); and Hartmut Steinecke, "Der rote Romantiker," in Steinicke, *Gewandelte Wirklichkeit — verändertes Schreiben: Zur neuesten deutschen Literatur: Gespräche, Werke, Porträts* (Oldenburg: Igel, 1999), 173–85. On Grünbein see Wolfgang Riedel, "Poetik der Präsenz: Idee der Dichtung bei Durs Grünbein," *Internationales Archiv für Sozialgeschichte der deutschen Literatur* 24/1 (1999): 82–105.

[24] For a lucid exploration of the links between the corporeal base of ecstatic states induced by music and the Orpheus myth see Peter Matussek, "Berauschende Geräusche: Trancetechniken im Medienwechsel," in *Rauschen: Seine Phänomenologie zwischen Sinn und Störung,* ed. Katja Stopka and Andreas Hiepko (Würzburg: Königshausen & Neumann, 2001), 225–40.

[25] Albert Meier, "Ironie ist Pflicht: Wie romantische Dichtung zu lesen ist," in *Text und Kritik,* vol. 143: *Aktualität der Romantik* (Munich: text & kritik, 1999), 12–21. See also Alexander von Bormann, "Wie aktuell ist die deutsche Romantik? Ein Umblick in der Forschung," *Euphorion* 78 (1984): 401–14.

[26] For summaries of this controversy see Rainer Moritz, "Nichts Halbherziges: 'Schlafes Bruder.' Das (Un-)Erklärliche eines Erfolges," in Moritz, ed., *Über "Schlafes Bruder,"* 11–29, esp. 18–22; also Steedts, *Schneiders "Schlafes Bruder,"* 10–17.

[27] See Thomas E. Schmidt, "Das Genie, das keines wurde," in Moritz, ed., *Über "Schlafes Bruder,"* 150–54.

[28] Schneider himself speaks of "Überzeichnung des Kitsches." Jan Malek, "Gesellenstück: Ein Interview mit Robert Schneider," *Buchkultur* (Wien) 18/6 (1992): 22.

[29] For recent discussions of the kitsch phenomenon that stress its important ambivalent affective potential see Wolfgang Braungart, "Kleine Apologie des Kitsches," *Sprache und Literatur* 28 (1997): 3–17; Jürgen Grimm, "Medienkitsch als Wertungs- und Rezeptionsphänomen: Zur Kritik des Echtheitsdiskurses," *Sprache im technischen Zeitalter* 39 (1998): 334–61; Bettina Bannasch, "Unsägliches oder Unsagbares? Zur Rede über Kitsch und Kunst," *Sprache und Literatur* 28 (1997): 40–53. Vol. 28 focuses especially on the clichés of kitsch and has numerous interesting articles.

[30] See Braungart, "Kleine Apologie," 9–10.

[31] On such "Doppelcodierung" as a typically postmodern feature see Charles Jencks, "Post-Modern und Spät-Modern," in *Falsche Dokumente: Postmoderne Texte aus den USA*, ed. Utz Riese (Leipzig: Reclam, 1993), 251–86; Uwe Wittstock, "Nachwort," in *Roman oder Leben: Postmoderne in der deutschen Literatur,* ed. Uwe Wittstock (Leipzig: Reclam, 1994), 315–40, esp. 328–29.

Contributors

STEFANIE BACH recently completed her doctoral thesis on the representation of Gypsy characters in German literature. She taught German at the University of Strathclyde as a DAAD-Lektorin for five years, and currently teaches German in adult education. She also coordinates a volunteer tutor project aimed at improving the integration of refugees. Her research interests include methodologies for teaching language through literature within a production-oriented context, and the interface of literature, music, and politics.

JÜRGEN BARKHOFF is Senior Lecturer in Germanic Studies at the University of Dublin, Trinity College, Fellow of Trinity College, and Director of the Centre for European Studies. His main areas of research are literature and anthropology in the Enlightenment, German Classicism and Romanticism, and man and nature in modern literature. He has published on Herder, Schiller, Goethe, music and Romanticism, mesmerism, Seghers, Grass, and contemporary Swiss literature.

LORRAINE BYRNE was awarded an IRCHSS Government of Ireland Post-Doctoral Fellowship in the Department of Germanic Studies, Trinity College Dublin in 2001, and was appointed a Post-Doctoral Fellow in the Department of Music, NUI Maynooth in 2003. She has published a piano reduction of the Schubert/Goethe Singspiel *Claudine von Bella Villa* (Dublin: Carysfort Press, 2002), and the book *Schubert's Goethe Settings* (Aldershot: Ashgate, 2003). She co-organized the international conference "Schubert and Goethe in Perspective and Performance," which took place at Trinity College Dublin in April 2003, and edited the conference proceedings, *Goethe and Schubert: Across the Divide* (Dublin: Carysfort Press, 2003). She is currently working on a critical translation of Goethe's letters to the composer Zelter.

DAVID HILL is Senior Lecturer in the Department of German Studies at the University of Birmingham and Director of the Centre for European Languages and Cultures. He has published widely on German literature of the late eighteenth century, particularly Goethe, Klinger, Lenz, Lessing, Wezel, and Wieland. He is editor of *Literature of the Sturm und Drang,* volume 6 of the Camden House History of German Literature, and is currently working on an edition of unpublished works by J. M. R. Lenz.

He has also written on music, and is working (with R. B. Meikle) on an edition of the Goethe/Reichardt Singspiel *Claudine von Bella Villa*.

JAMES HODKINSON has completed a doctoral thesis on the presentation of gender in the works of Novalis. He is a member of the *Internationale Novalis Gesellschaft*, and publishes on Romantic thought and literature. He has lectured in German at Liverpool and Cardiff universities, and is currently teaching in secondary education in the United Kingdom.

ANDREA HÜBENER is Lecturer in German Literature at the Seminar für deutsche Sprache und Literatur at the Technical University of Braunschweig, and is a contributing editor to the edition of the posthumous works of Wilhelm Heinse. Her doctoral dissertation on the reception of Hoffmann among the French Romantics is forthcoming with Winter in Heidelberg.

WERNER KEIL is Professor of Historical Musicology at the University of Paderborn and the Conservatory of Music in Detmold. He is founder-editor of the series *Diskordanzen*, of which the twelfth volume is his own: *Im Geisterreich des Unendlichen: Ein Streifzug durch die Musik des 19. Jahrhunderts* (Hildesheim: Olms, 2000). He has published widely on Romanticism. He is editor of the new critical commentary of Wilhelm Heinse, *Hildegard von Hohenthal: Musikalische Dialogen* (Hildesheim, Zurich, New York: Olms, 2002).

DAVID LARKIN holds B.Mus. and M.Litt. degrees from University College Dublin, the latter awarded for a dissertation entitled "Wagner and Liszt: Musical Symbiosis in Action?" He is currently pursuing doctoral studies at Christ's College, Cambridge, researching the influence of Wagner and Liszt on Strauss's development of the tone poem. He is a keen pianist.

RICHARD LITTLEJOHNS is Emeritus Professor of Modern Languages, Associate Lecturer in German, and Acting Head of the School of Modern Languages at the University of Leicester. He is the editor of volume 2 of the historical-critical edition of the collected works of Wackenroder (1991), and he has published on Tieck, Eichendorff, Novalis, August Wilhelm and Friedrich Schlegel, Görres, Goethe, Schiller, Wezel, Remarque, and Hildesheimer. In 1988 he was awarded the Oskar Seidlin prize by the Eichendorff Gesellschaft for his published research on Romanticism.

NATASHA LOGES lectures at the Guildhall School of Music and Drama and the Royal College of Music. She is coordinator of the Lyric Song Salon at the Royal Academy of Music, where she is completing her Ph.D. thesis on the poetry of Brahms's solo Lieder. She is also collaborating with Graham Johnson on an encyclopedia of Schubert's piano-accompanied vocal works. As a song accompanist, she has broadcast live for BBC Radio 3, and has performed in the United Kingdom and Asia.

JAMES PARSONS is Associate Professor of Music History at Southwest Missouri State University, USA. He has published on a variety of topics, including Lieder, Beethoven, and Schiller, and is editor of *The Cambridge Companion to the Lied* (forthcoming) to which he has contributed two articles, one on the eighteenth-century Lied, and one on the twentieth-century song.

JEANNE RIOU is Lecturer in German at University College Dublin. Her research interests are in cultural theory, literature of the Enlightenment, Romanticism and modernism, and the history of science. She has published essays on cultural criticism (Schiller and Nietzsche), Goethe, Grillparzer, images of technology in Weimar Berlin (Joseph Roth's feuilleton writing, forthcoming in 2004), and on the aesthetics of new technologies. Her monograph *Imagination in German Romanticism: Re-thinking the Self in its Environment* is to be published in 2004 by Peter Lang. She is a co-editor and contributor to the volume *Netzwerke: Kulturtechniken der Moderne* (Cologne, Vienna: Böhlau, 2004).

THOMAS STRÄSSLE is Lecturer in German Literature at the University of Zurich. He has published a monograph on Grimmelshausen's *Simplicissimus Teutsch,* and other articles on German Baroque literature, Romantic music aesthetics, adaptations of Socrates in German literature, and contemporary music. His current research is on the symbolism of salt in German literature.

Editors

SIOBHÁN DONOVAN is College Lecturer in the Department of German at University College Dublin. Her monograph *Der christliche Publizist und sein Glaubensphilosoph: Zur Freundschaftsbeziehung zwischen Matthias Claudius und Friedrich Heinrich Jacobi*, is to be published by Königshausen & Neumann in 2004. Current research and teaching interests include the history of ideas, German Romanticism and music, German opera, and opera as intermedial and transformational genre.

ROBIN ELLIOTT was College Lecturer in the Department of Music at University College Dublin from 1996 to 2002, with responsibility for courses in analysis, harmony, and nineteenth-century European music. He was appointed to the Jean A. Chalmers Chair in Canadian Music at the University of Toronto on 1 July 2002, and is a Senior Fellow of Massey College.

Index